TAROTORIAL®

EXPANDED GUIDEBOOK

*A Comprehensive Guide to Learning
the Rider Waite Smith Tarot System*

created by
PAMELA COE

Printed in the United States

Distributed by Raven and Rogue
900 Commerce Place #1022
Forsyth, IL 62535
United States

ravenandrogue.com

ISBN: 979-8-9876856-4-8

For Courtney, Gracie, and Annie

TABLE OF CONTENTS

INTRODUCTION

I've been studying Tarot since childhood. I grew up in a pagan household with an incredible Mom that opened the door to spiritual study. She fostered my curiosity and imagination for all things and encouraged me to learn about different types of spiritualism to formulate my own conclusions. When I became a stepparent, I wanted to create the same safe harbor for my stepdaughter to explore the world.

In June 2019, at 36, I suffered a stroke that left my dominant right hand temporarily incapacitated, and life suddenly came to a screeching halt. I had been working on a set of Tarot flashcards for my stepdaughter before my stroke and decided to make the project my primary focus during my recovery. At my physical therapist's suggestion, I worked the creation of the cards into my rehabilitation exercises.

Traditional educational methods often cater to the neurotypical, leaving out the neurodivergent—those with conditions like autism, dyslexia, and ADHD. This oversight extends to Tarot, where interpreting intricate symbolism and constantly referring to guides can deter newcomers. I aimed to simplify this.

Being someone with AuDHD and now navigating post-stroke challenges, I understood the unique struggles faced by the neurodivergent community. I've relied heavily on tools like flashcards for my aphasia and felt there was a niche for more accessible Tarot learning tools.

It took three months to finalize the first edition of the *Tarotorial® Tarot Training Deck*. Its completion revealed a wider impact beyond just my stepdaughter and me. The demand for the cards grew, inspiring me to convert the flashcards into a full Tarot deck. With my wife Courtney's unwavering support and her push to self-publish, what began as a personal project evolved into a shared journey.

This guidebook is rooted in the Rider Waite Smith Tarot system and designed to make Tarot more approachable. While it provides straightforward explanations of symbols, always remember that personal intuition plays a vital role in Tarot readings. And though this guide is tailored for the Tarotorial® deck, it's versatile enough for any Rider Waite Smith-style deck.

HISTORY OF TAROT

TAROT HAS BEEN AROUND FOR *CENTURIES*, MELDING
RELIGIOUS MOTIFS FROM MULTIPLE FAITHS AND
STIRRING *DEBATE* SINCE ITS INCEPTION

Most historians agree that the earliest recorded account of the Tarot originates in northern Italy in the late 14th century, with a bridge-like card game called tarocchi. Tarot derives from this word, whose root in Italian—taroch—translates to "foolishness." The term taroch was first used in the 15th century, when *Trionfi*, a 70-card game inspired by theatrical festivals common during the Italian Renaissance known as trionfo, was invented.

Many of these early versions were hand-painted and available only to the wealthy. The invention of the printing press made the medium more accessible, and the popularity of these card games spread across Europe. The decks included a series of suits. Many had four suits of pip cards with a repetitious symbol (i.e., spades, clubs, hearts, and diamonds) in ascending numerical assignments and four to six court cards. Some expanded to include a fifth suit, trumps, with a series of illustrated cards richly designed with symbolistic allegory.

Common symbolism in these early decks included Renaissance and Medieval Christian themes. But as the years progressed, iconography from other cultures and religions was imbued into the artwork. It's speculated that the cards were used for divination purposes early on. They contained imagery and rhetoric that eluded to fortune-telling and laid in patterns similar to Tarot spreads.

In 1507, the bulk of Tarot production centered in and around Marseilles, France. Later in 1748, after standardization with Roman numerals and French titles, a version of this French Tarot system was published called the *Tarot of Marseilles*. The system is still popular today and is the deck that inspired Arthur Edward Waite and Pamela Coleman Smith, creators of the *Rider Waite Smith* deck.

Using cards for divination has deep links to Roma esotericism. It was common for Romani women to take up cartomancy and fortune-telling as a sole means of income, as they were often barred from holding other types of employment due to oppressive racial stereotypes. It's believed that Romani cartomancers would also create their own Tarot decks in a pictorial style. What's unfortunate about learning the history of Tarot is that the sizable Romani influence is often left out. The Romani assuredly paved the way for Tarot to see mainstream interest as cartomancy spread across Europe.

We begin to see more evidence of the development of Tarot near the late seventeen hundreds. In 1770, Jean-Baptiste Alliette, best known by his moniker

Etteilla (his surname spelled backward), published *Etteilla, Or a Way to Entertain Yourself With a Deck of Cards*. His book was a how-to guide on using Tarot cards specifically for divination.

In 1781, French occultist Antoine Court de Gébelin circulated a series of essays linking the Tarot to the Hebrew alphabet and the Tree of Life. Both Etteilla and Court de Gébelin incorrectly reported that Tarot was created in Egypt by a group of seventeen Magi under the direction of Hermes Trismegistus, the author of *Hermetica*. There has been no supportive proof to substantiate those claims. However, occultists connected Tarot to Hermetic, Kabbalist, and astrological associations. Gébelin also claimed that Tarot cards were brought to Europe by Romani immigrants due to the incorrect belief that Romani people are of Egyptian descent.[1]

Éliphas Lévi, born Alphonse Louis Constant, was a French occultist who created several works that spoke of his interpretation of the Kabbalah and its connection to Tarot. There's no evidence of Lévi having studied with any Jewish scholars, but rather proof that he derived his interpretations from Cabala, a Christianized form of Qabalah. Lévi's works would become early influences of A.E. Waite and Aleister Crowley, who created the *Thoth Tarot* with Lady Frieda Harris, published in 1944.

Gébelin declared that the Major Arcana of the Tarot could be associated with the twenty-two Hebrew alphabet letters. Modern Tarot decks regularly draw from the spiritual depths of Kabbalah and Judaism. Yet, historians and Jewish scholars contend that these earliest occultists had a limited knowledge of Jewish mysticism, which can be attributed to an over-reliance on Cabala. While A.E. Waite endeavored to distinguish between various kinds of Qabalah, Gershom Scholem, an author and Jewish scholar, commented he "simply lacked the proper instruments needed for the task of really understanding Jewish Qabalah."[2]

During the 1880s, the Hermetic Order of the Golden Dawn was founded with the purpose of thoroughly exploring the occult sciences. Two of the most famous members of this order were A.E. Waite and Pamela Coleman Smith. They collaborated to create the initial *Rider Waite Smith Tarot* deck, which became one of the most successful commercially. Aleister Crowley, another Tarot deck creator, along with Waite and Smith, incorporated astrological symbols and associations into the cards, creating a strong connection between

---

[1] Michael Dummett, Ronald Decker, and Thierry Depaulis, *A Wicked Pack of Cards: Origins of the Occult Tarot*
[2] Wouter J. Hanegraaff, *Mysteries of Sex in the House of the Hidden Light: Arthur Edward Waite and the Qabalah*

Tarot and astrology. The aim was to capture a comprehensive view of the universe by linking the archetypal experiences reflected in the heavens and the cards. At the heart of this intertwining is the principle of correspondence, which pairs the elements, astrological signs, planets, and houses with specific Tarot cards, particularly within the Major Arcana. These associations add layers of meaning, offering a richer narrative during readings, especially for those understanding astrological nuances.

Tarot is a collective project formed by many global influences over the years, so it is vital to be aware of its cultural underpinnings and give them their due reverence. Various texts offer further insight into the dynamics around the medium and its invention, and I recommend you consult them as you deepen your studies.

Moving forward in this book, I'll spell out references to various systems that were incorporated into the *Rider Waite Smith Tarot* deck. We can pay tribute to Tarot's roots while educating ourselves about the parts and components that have been assimilated from other faiths. Judaism is a closed practice, demanding initiation or birth into the religion. Many traditional rules on Kabbalah were set in place to guarantee students had the necessary maturity and awareness to delve into the doctrine; these all directed towards the fact that an in-depth understanding of the Torah is essential. To truly grasp the ideas in the *Rider Waite Smith Tarot*, we should remain conscious of and give respect to the closed practices they reference.

TAROT + SYMBOLISM

THE TAROT CONTAINS DEEP ASTROLOGICAL AND
ELEMENTAL SYMBOLISM, WEAVING TOGETHER THESE
SYSTEMS OF ANCIENT WISDOM TO PROVIDE
LAYERED AND NUANCED READINGS

Arthur Edward Waite and Aleister Crowley designed Tarot decks that are among the most widely recognized and used today: the Rider Waite Smith and the Thoth Tarot, respectively. Their deep involvement in the Hermetic Order of the Golden Dawn shaped their choices to associate zodiac signs, elements, and planets with the Tarot cards. This esoteric organization played a significant role in the modern evolution of Tarot and their personal beliefs and mystical interpretations.

Waite and Crowley were members of the Hermetic Order of the Golden Dawn, which combined various esoteric systems, including Qabalah, astrology, and alchemy. Within this framework, the Tarot was seen not just as a tool for divination but as a map of the universe and the human soul. The Golden Dawn developed correspondences between the Major Arcana and the paths on the Qabalistic Tree of Life, which were associated with planets, elements, and zodiac signs.

While both drew from the same esoteric traditions, Waite and Crowley had different spiritual perspectives and interpretations. Waite's Tarot was deeply rooted in Christian mysticism, emphasizing inner transformation. Crowley's Thoth Tarot, on the other hand, was a product of his personal religion, Thelema, and highlighted the forces and energies at play in the universe.

While foundational Tarot decks, like the Tarot de Marseille, had elemental associations (particularly in the Minor Arcana), the detailed linkage of the Major Arcana cards with zodiac signs and planets was a more modern innovation. Both Waite and Crowley sought to update and reinterpret the Tarot for their era, adding layers of symbolism and meaning that they felt were missing or obscured in earlier decks.

It's worth noting that the Tarot decks crafted by Waite and Crowley reflected their personal spiritual journeys. Crowley's exploration of Eastern philosophies, magick, and Thelema profoundly influenced the Thoth Tarot. In contrast, Waite's Christian mysticism and more reserved approach to esotericism are evident in the imagery and symbolism of the Rider Waite Smith deck.

TAROT + QABALAH

OCCULTISTS LINKED QABALAH TO TAROT IN
THE 19TH AND 20TH CENTURIES

The term *Kabbalah* has multiple spellings—such as *Qabalah, Cabala,* and others—due to its linguistic origins and varied cultural adaptations. Stemming from the Hebrew word קבלה (*Qabbālāh*), which means "reception" or "to receive," its transliteration into Latin-based languages like English can produce various spellings. In the realm of the Western occult tradition, the spelling *Qabalah* is most commonly used. This variation distinguishes the Hermetic or esoteric interpretation of Kabbalah from its Jewish mystical origins (*Kabbalah*) and its Christian adaptations (*Cabala*). By using *Qabalah*, Western occultists signaled their unique take on these ancient teachings, incorporating them into a broader system of Hermeticism, alchemy, and ceremonial magick.

The combination of *Qabalah* and Tarot in Western esoteric traditions has given rise to a plethora of symbols, interpretations, and spiritual insights, despite Tarot not being an explicit part of traditional Qabalistic practices. The amalgamation of these two rich systems of symbols highlights humanity's never-ending pursuit of universal understanding and spiritual growth. Occultists aimed to unlock deeper levels of spiritual wisdom and found that *Qabalah*, with its profound mysticism, could expand the Tarot cards' esoteric meanings. By mapping the Tarot onto the Qabalistic Tree of Life, the cards could represent the emanations of the divine or stages of spiritual evolution.

The Renaissance and the 19th century witnessed significant cultural and spiritual exchanges in Europe, which led to a resurgence of interest in Hermeticism, alchemy, and other ancient wisdom traditions. *Qabalah*, reinterpreted in Christian and Hermetic contexts, became a significant part of this milieu. Prominent figures such as Éliphas Lévi, Arthur Edward Waite, and Aleister Crowley were instrumental in establishing and promoting these connections.

Incorporating Qabalistic elements into the Tarot became popular through institutions like the Hermetic Order of the Golden Dawn, with its influential members such as Arthur Edward Waite. The structured system of *Qabalah*, particularly the Sephirot and paths of the Tree of Life, allowed occultists to offer more in-depth and systematic Tarot readings, tapping into the layers of Qabalistic wisdom for meditation, divination, and spiritual growth.

The fusion of *Qabalah* and Tarot was part of a broader endeavor by occultists to bridge different esoteric systems, aiming for a profound understanding of the universe, humanity, and the divine. The combination provided a more intricate tapestry of symbols and meanings, enhancing the depth and applicability of Tarot readings. Thus, the synthesis of these rich systems of symbols underscores humanity's timeless quest for spiritual enlightenment.

The Ten Sephirot

According to Qabalah, the esoteric, hidden meaning of the Torah explains the relationship between our universe, the Divine, and infinity. The Tree of Life passes through four levels of existence on its way between heaven and earth. Exploring the Tree of Life can be a great introduction to various practices such as Golden Dawn and Thelema.

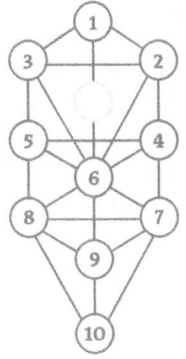

	SEPHIROT	CARD	MEANING
1	Kether (The Crown)	Aces	Infinite; between humanity and divinity
2	Chokmah (Wisdom)	Twos, Knights	Creation
3	Binah (Understanding)	Threes, Queens	Nurture
4	Chesed (Mercy)	Fours	Benevolence
5	Geburah (Severity)	Fives	Judgment
6	Tiphareth (Harmony)	Sixes, Kings	Meditation
7	Netzach (Triumph)	Sevens	Emotions
8	Hod (Glory)	Eights	Intellect
9	Yesod (Foundation)	Nines	Puts purified energy into the physical world
10	Malkuth (The Kingdom)	Tens	Stability in the physical world

The Four Worlds

In Qabalah, there are four worlds or planes of existence: *Atziluth* (Archetypal World), *Briah* (Creative World), *Yetzirah* (Formative World), and *Assiah* (Material World). Each of these worlds corresponds to a suit in the Minor Arcana of the Tarot: *Wands*, *Cups*, *Swords*, and *Pentacles*, respectively. When connected in order, the worlds create Jacob's Ladder.

י	ה	ו	ה
Yod	Heh	Waw	Heh
Wands	Swords	**Cups**	**Pentacles**
Fire	Air	Water	Earth
ATZILUTH	**BRIAH**	**YETZIRAH**	**ASSIAH**
The Divine	*Thought and Consciousness*	*Emotion and Relationships*	*Tangible World*

Jacob's Ladder

The connection between Tarot and Jacob's Ladder is rooted in integrating Qabalistic philosophy into Western esoteric traditions. Those who delve into the deeper esoteric meanings of the Tarot, particularly within the context of the *Hermetic Qabalah*, recognize Jacob's Ladder as an allegory for the ascent through various spiritual planes or spheres. Jacob's Ladder is a metaphor for spiritual evolution or the stairway to heaven.

The Qabalistic Tree of Life is a diagram comprising ten spheres, or Sephirot, interconnected by 22 paths, each corresponding to one of the 22 Major Arcana cards in the Tarot. This Tree of Life represents the descent of the divine into the material world and the potential ascent of the soul back to the divine source. It mirrors the ascent and descent of angels on Jacob's Ladder.

Just as Jacob's Ladder signifies a connection between the earthly and the divine realms, the Tarot, when interpreted through the lens of Qabalah, charts a journey of spiritual evolution. The Fool's Journey, which depicts the Fool's progress through the Major Arcana of the Tarot, is akin to a spiritual ascent, where one begins with innocence and ignorance and moves through various life lessons and spiritual insights, culminating in enlightenment or cosmic consciousness.

THE FOOL

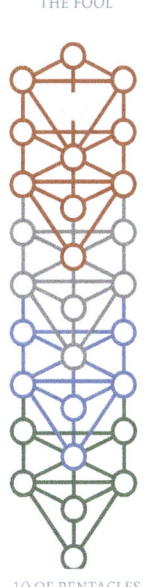

The central pillar of the Tree of Life is often compared to Jacob's Ladder because it represents a balanced path of ascent to the divine. This pillar consists of the Sephirot *Kether* (Crown), *Tiphareth* (Beauty), *Yesod* (Foundation), and *Malkuth* (Kingdom), which are regarded as stages of a spiritual journey, with the Tarot cards linked to the paths between them acting as guides or gateways.

Although the Tarot's origins are not directly related to the story of Jacob's Ladder, the integration of Qabalistic symbolism into the Tarot system by certain esoteric scholars and practitioners has interwoven the two in a rich tapestry of spiritual symbolism. For those who study the Tarot from a Qabalistic perspective, the allegory of Jacob's Ladder provides a profound narrative of spiritual ascent and the interrelatedness of the earthly and divine realms. Thus, the connection between Tarot and Jacob's Ladder is one of profound spiritual significance, representing the ascent of the human soul towards the divine.

10 OF PENTACLES

The 22 Paths

There are 22 paths that connect the Sephirot and complete the form of the Tree of Life. These paths are the origin of the major arcana. The energy of those cards is created by the flow of energy between their two connecting Sephirot. So, while they fully embody their own number, deeper meaning can be found if you look at them this way too.

For example: Strength is the path between *Chesed* (mercy) and *Geburah* (severity). With that in mind, it makes sense that Strength would represent gentle persuasion and understanding.

The paths also correspond to the 22 letters in the Hebrew alphabet, which is why those symbols appear on the cards in the Hermetic Tarot.

PATH	CONNECTING
11 - The Path of Aleph	Kether (Crown) and Chokhmah (Wisdom)
12 - The Path of Bet	Kether (Crown) and Binah (Understanding)
13 - The Path of Gimel	Kether (Crown) and Tiphareth (Beauty)
14 - The Path of Daleth	Chokmah (Wisdom) and Binah (Understanding)
15 - The Path of Heh	Chokmah (Wisdom) and Tiphareth (Beauty)
16 - The Path of Waw	Chokmah (Wisdom) and Chesed (Mercy)
17 - The Path of Zayin	Binah (Understanding) and Tiphareth (Beauty)
18 - The Path of Heth	Binah (Understanding) and Geburah (Severity)
19 - The Path of Tet	Geburah (Severity) and Chesed (Mercy)
20 - The Path of Yod	Chesed (Mercy) and Tipareth (Beauty)
21 - The Path of Kaph	Chesed (Mercy) and Netzach (Victory)
22 - The Path of Lamed	Geburah (Power) and Tiphareth (Beauty)
23 - The Path of Mem	Geburah (Severity) and Hod (Splendor)
24 - The Path of Nun	Tiphareth (Beauty) and Netzach (Victory)
25 - The Path of Samekh	Tiphareth (Beauty) and Yesod (Foundation)
26 - The Path of Ayin	Tiphareth (Beauty) and Hod (Splendor)
27 - The Path of Pe	Hod (Splendor) and Netzach (Victory)
28 - The Path of Tsadi	Netzach (Victory) and Yesod (Foundation)
29 - The Path of Qoph	Netzach (Victory) and Malkuth (Kingdom)
30 - The Path of Resh	Hod (Splendor) and Yesod (Foundation)
31 - The Path of Shin	Hod (Splendor) and Malkuth (Kingdom)

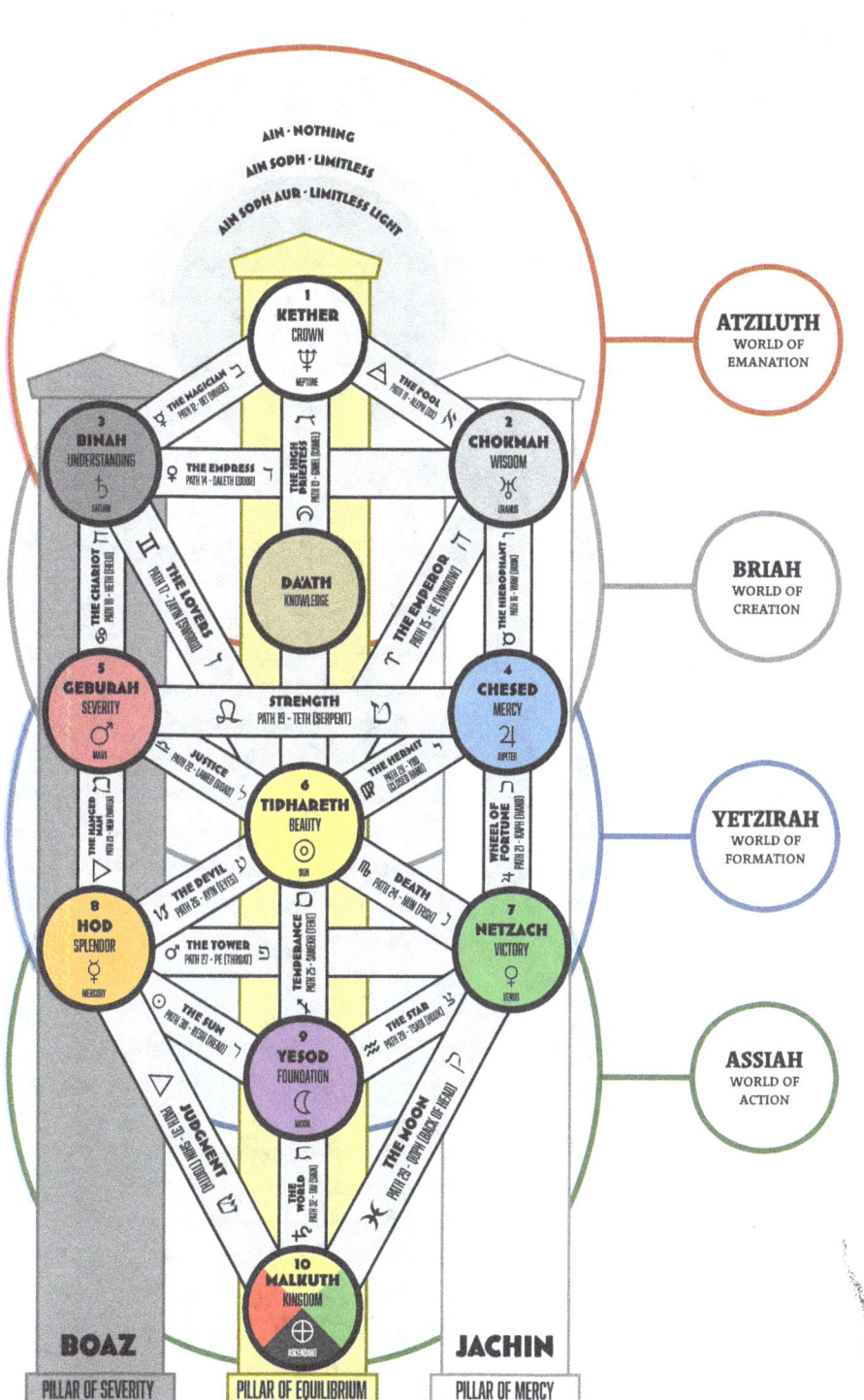

TAROT + NUMEROLOGY

EACH CARD HAS A NUMBER, AND THIS NUMBER
OFTEN PROVIDES DEEPER INSIGHT
INTO THE CARD'S MEANING

Numerology, the study of the mystical significance of numbers, has always been intertwined with the Tarot. Each card in a Tarot deck has a number, and this number often provides deeper insight into the card's meaning. Here's a breakdown of how numerology is incorporated into Tarot:

The Major Arcana
Cards 0 through 21 in the Major Arcana are numbered and each number has its own significance. For instance, the number 1 is usually associated with new beginnings, leadership, and potential, and this is reflected in The Magician (Card 1), who embodies manifestation, resourcefulness, and power.

The Minor Arcana
The numbered cards (Ace through 10) in each suit of the Minor Arcana also correspond with numerological meanings. The Aces (1s) typically signify beginnings or the pure essence of their suit. The 10s often indicate the culmination or completion of the suit's journey.

The Court Cards
Although most court cards don't have numbers, numerology can still be used in conjunction with their interpretation, especially when considering them in relation to the numbered cards of their suit. For instance, the Page can be associated with the energy of the 11, the Knight with 12, the Queen with 13, and the King with 14.

In numerology, numbers can be reduced to a single digit (except the master numbers). For instance, 15 can be reduced to 1+5 = 6. This technique can be used in Tarot to find deeper meanings. For example, the Tower card, numbered 16, can be reduced to 7 (1+6), linking its tumultuous energy to the introspective and challenging energy of the Chariot (Card 7).

#	MEANING
1 (Aces)	Beginnings, potential, initiative
2	Balance, partnerships, duality
3	Collaboration, growth, creativity
4	Structure, stability, foundation
5	Conflict, change, challenge
6	Harmony, cooperation, problem-solving
7	Reflection, assessment, internal challenge
8	Movement, action, change
9	Completion, preparation, introspection
10	Culmination, end of a cycle, renewal

Master Numbers
Some numbers, like 11, 22, and 33, are considered *Master Numbers* with unique significance. These can be associated with higher spiritual insight or energy. This association is more interpretive and not standard across all Tarot systems.

TAROT + COUNTS

COUNTING *ADDS ANOTHER LAYER OF ANALYSIS* AND
CAN BE ESPECIALLY HELPFUL IN SPREADS WHERE
CARDS ARE LAID OUT IN A SEQUENCE OR CIRCLE

You'll notice some *count* associations as you read this book. For those unfamiliar, counting in Tarot is used primarily in certain traditions or reading styles, most notably in the Golden Dawn system. This method involves determining card relationships and connections based on numerological sequences. Counting can provide additional insights into reading by revealing underlying themes or drawing attention to particular cards that significantly influence the situation.

The reading begins with a specific card, often the Significator or a card that stands out prominently in the spread. Each card in the deck has a numerical value. The Major Arcana are numbered 0 (The Fool) to 21 (The World), while the Minor Arcana use their face value (Ace as 1, Two as 2, etc., up to 10). Court cards have their own values: Page is 11, Knight is 12, Queen is 13, and King is 14.

Starting from the selected card, count through the cards in the spread based on the value of the starting card, usually in a particular direction (e.g., clockwise). The card you land on provides additional insights or emphasizes certain aspects of the reading.

Another method that complements counting is pairing. Once you have counted from the initial card, you can pair the cards on either side of the spread, working inwards. Each pair provides combined insights that deepen the reading's scope and add further layers of analysis.

In the Golden Dawn system, readers might also consider elemental dignities when using counting. This involves looking at the elemental associations of adjacent cards (i.e., their suit: Wands/Fire, Cups/Water, Swords/Air, Pentacles/Earth) to determine if they strengthen or weaken each other, which can adjust or refine the interpretation.

It's worth noting that not all Tarot readers use this method. Like many Tarot techniques, its effectiveness and relevance depend on the reader's intuition, training, and personal preference.

MAJOR ARCANA

THESE CARDS UNVEIL THE SOUL'S *KARMIC PURPOSE*;
THE SIGNIFICANT FORCES AND LESSONS THAT
INFLUENCE AND GUIDE US THROUGH LIFE

The Major Arcana is a set of twenty-two cards, spanning from 0, The Fool, to 21, The World. Rich in symbolism and ancient wisdom, the imagery of the Major Arcana draws from diverse philosophical, religious, and esoteric traditions, offering layers of meaning and insight.

A narrative often associated with the Major Arcana is "The Fool's Journey," an allegorical tale depicting an individual's life path from innocence to enlightenment. Starting with The Fool, symbolic of untapped potential and beginnings, the journey unfolds through subsequent cards, representing life's challenges, introspections, and revelations, culminating with The World, a symbol of realization.

The appearance of a Major Arcana card indicates that profound spiritual lessons, significant life events, or pivotal decisions are at play. Whereas the Minor Arcana might point to daily matters and transient influences, the Major Arcana zooms out, highlighting the broader narrative arc of one's life and the soul's evolution. Each card, from The Magician's manifestation power to the Death card's transformation theme, mirrors our deeper psyche and universal experiences.

The Major Arcana serves as the heart and soul of Tarot, capturing the essence of the human experience in its myriad forms. Through its archetypal imagery and profound symbolism, it offers guidance, reflection, and insight into our journey's spiritual and moral dimensions.

-0-
THE FOOL
M A J O R   A R C A N A

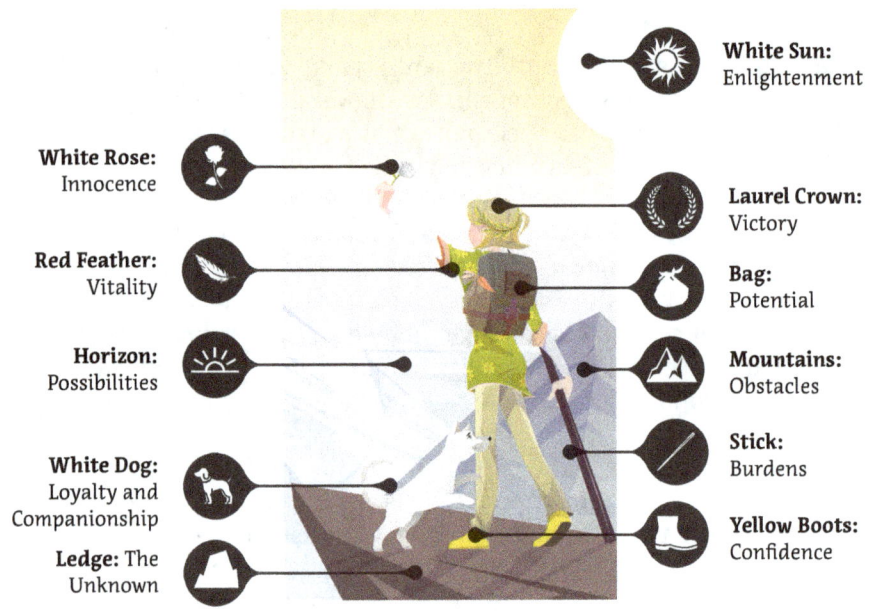

White Sun:
Enlightenment

White Rose:
Innocence

Laurel Crown:
Victory

Red Feather:
Vitality

Bag:
Potential

Horizon:
Possibilities

Mountains:
Obstacles

Stick:
Burdens

White Dog:
Loyalty and
Companionship

Ledge: The
Unknown

Yellow Boots:
Confidence

Yes/No Reading:

☑   ◯   ◯

Yes   No   Maybe

Names in Other Tarot Systems:
Golden Dawn: The Fool
Tarot of Marseilles: Le Mat
Thoth: The Fool

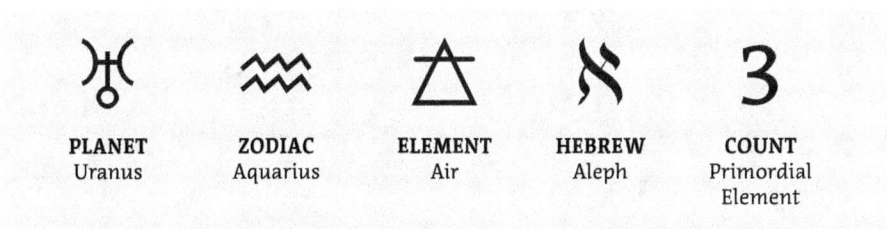

PLANET	ZODIAC	ELEMENT	HEBREW	COUNT
Uranus	Aquarius	Air	Aleph	Primordial Element

Upright: *Spontaneity, Potential, Optimism, Adventure, Unlimited Possibilities*
Representing the start of a journey, be it a physical or spiritual one, the upright Fool card is symbolic of new beginnings, innocent spontaneity, and taking a leap of faith into the unknown with trust. You may be entering a phase where you can experience the beauty of life, filled with hope and enthusiasm. The upright drawing of The Fool is a positive sign to encourage and inspire you to move forward with confidence.

When the upright Fool appears in a reading, it encourages embracing new opportunities with enthusiasm and trust, even if the path isn't clear. It's a time to take a leap of faith, trusting in the universe and intuition. Embracing change, staying open to the unexpected, and valuing innocence and spontaneity are essential messages of the card.

Reversed: *Recklessness, Hesitation, Poor Judgment, Avoiding Responsibilities*
When the Fool card is reversed, it often indicates a time of impulse, recklessness, or fear of moving forward or taking the next step. There may be a lack of foresight, and this reversal serves as a warning against impulsive decisions that could lead to challenges later on down the road.

The traditional depiction of the Fool card visually shows a young traveler at the edge of a cliff, with a small dog and a bag on a stick slung over their shoulder. In its reversed position, this image takes on a more ominous meaning, suggesting a fall or misstep due to lack of awareness or caution.

In readings, the reversed Fool may indicate second-guessing or doubt about a new venture or journey, leading to procrastination or inaction. It may signal a loss of spontaneity or faith in the universe, or a timely warning to re-evaluate one's current path and ensure proper preparation and understanding. Pause and reflect before stepping forward to avoid aimless wandering.

CHAKRA:
Crown

TIMING:
Now, or suddenly

NUMEROLOGY:
All

ARCANA RELATION:
All Major Arcana

DEITY:
Aeolus, Bacchus, Loki Nu,
Hoor-pa-Kraat, Zeus

ANIMAL:
Crocodile, Eagle, Man, Ox

CRYSTAL:
Agate, Aventurine, Chalcedony,
Green Quartz, Topaz,
Tourmaline

PLANT:
Aspen, Cedar, Columbine Flower,
Frankincense, Ginseng, Grapes,
Hawthorn, Laurel, Oak, Rose

MAGICKAL ITEM:
Dagger, Fan

ARCHANGEL:
Uriel

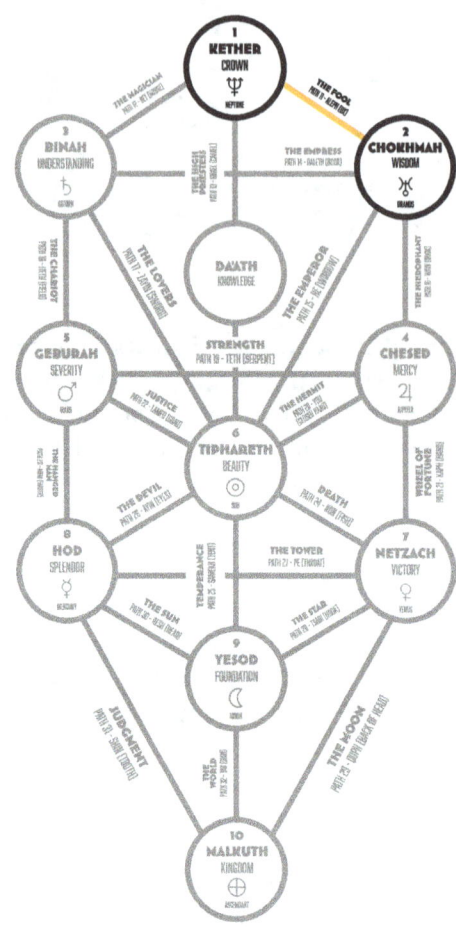

WHITE
Beginning,
Humility, Purity

YELLOW
Confidence, Joy,
Intellect, Optimism

RED
Desire, Passion,
Power, Vitality

GREEN
Balance, Fertility,
Growth, Harmony

The Fool often shows a youthful figure on a cliff's brink, ready to embark on an undefined journey. They hold a small bag, a symbol of the experiences and knowledge yet to be discovered, and a white rose, embodying innocence and purity. A playful dog at The Fool's feet can represent the distractions of the world or serve as a loyal guardian. The distant mountains behind hint at the challenges and teachings that lie in the past or await in the future.

This card embodies the spirit of new beginnings, impromptu actions, and courageous leaps into the unknown. It encourages embracing the journey with trust and hope, highlighting the themes of potential, exploration, and faith in the cosmic plan.

The Fool's Journey is a metaphor for the journey through life, using the 22 Major Arcana cards of the Tarot deck as symbolic stages of human experiences.

As the Fool embarks on their journey, they encounter various challenges and lessons and undergo a series of personal transformations. Each card symbolizes a specific stage or lesson in life, reflecting the ups, downs, joys, and sorrows of the human experience. The journey concludes with The World, where The Fool has achieved enlightenment and wholeness.

 ZODIAC: Aquarius (January 20 – February 18) is an Air sign ruled by Uranus. Aquarians are self-reliant, analytical, independent, clever, and optimistic.

 PLANET: Uranus is associated with extremes, breakthroughs, limitlessness, and outsiders. It's a planet of disruption, individuality, and change that emphasizes creative inspiration, mirroring The Fool's overall message.

 ELEMENT: Air represents logic, intellect, and communication. The intangible element is considered to be active, masculine energy. It is associated with Spring, the Suit of Wands, and the East cardinal direction.

 HERMETIC QABALAH Associated Hebrew Letter: Aleph, Ox (Primal Energy)

 TREE OF LIFE PATHWAY: 11th Path Between Kether (Crown) and Chokmah (Wisdom)

THE MAGICIAN

MAJOR ARCANA

Red Roses: Passion

Double Wand: Wisdom

Cup: Emotions

Pentacle: Intention

Table: Reality

Greenery: Abundance

Lemniscate: Unlimited Capacity

Ouroboros Belt: Reinvention

Sword: Intellect

Wand: Thoughts

White Lilies: Virtue

Yes/No Reading:

☑ Yes   ○ No   ○ Maybe

Names in Other Tarot Systems:

Golden Dawn: The Magician
Tarot of Marseilles: Le Bateleur
Thoth: The Magus

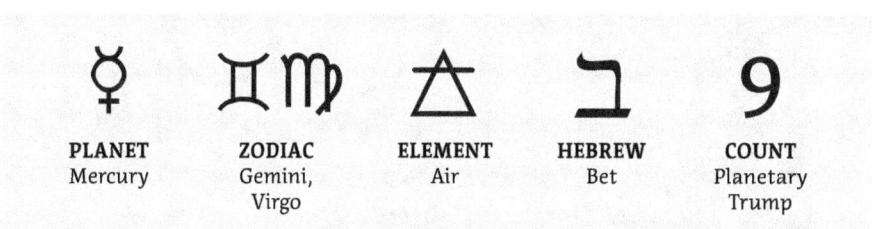

PLANET	ZODIAC	ELEMENT	HEBREW	COUNT
Mercury	Gemini, Virgo	Air	Bet	Planetary Trump

Upright: *Manifestation, Opportunities, Transformation, Willpower, Skill*
The Magician is pointing to the capability and resources at your disposal. The mind and the universe are reflections of one another. Remember that you are powerful enough to create your own reality and possess a full arsenal of tools to make your dreams come to life. Commit to your purpose.

If your current situation is out of control, The Magician reminds you that you have the tools to restore the balance. You can create, change, and destroy as long as you act. The Magician bestows the power of adaptability.

In readings regarding advice in a relationship, The Magician is very positive. They could tell you that you need to develop your communication skills with your partner(s) to ensure ultimate success. Or, this could be shaping an ideal partner.

Reversed: *Arrogance, Weakness, Missed Opportunities, Powerlessness*
When the Magician card is in reverse, it indicates the possibility of untapped power, manipulation, and dishonesty. This implies that the individual may have the means to reach their objectives but needs to be using them effectively. This may be caused by a lack of self-confidence, focus, or an incomplete understanding of their capabilities.

Furthermore, the reversed Magician warns of potential deceit and deception, whether by the querent or someone close to them. It suggests that not everything is as it seems, emphasizing the importance of being able to differentiate between the truth and falsehood. The card advises caution against using one's abilities for manipulative purposes or becoming the victim of someone else's manipulation. Thus, it urges the individual to reevaluate their motives and intentions, and gain a deeper understanding of their true potential.

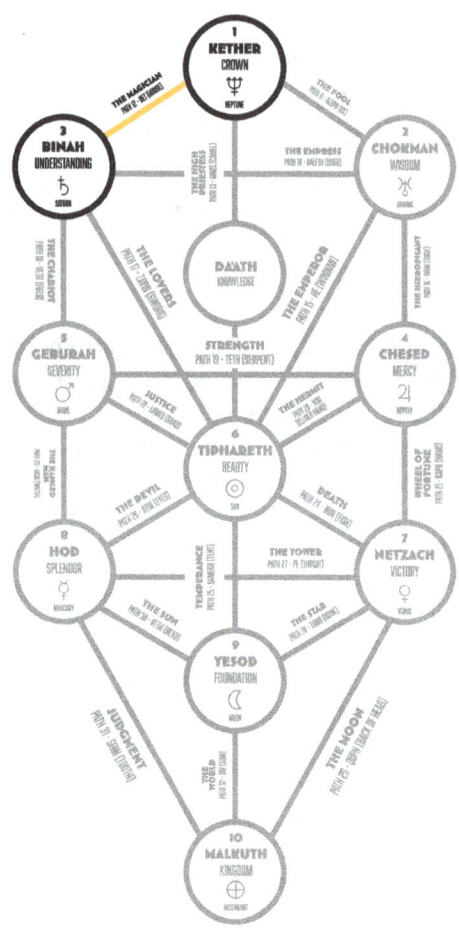

CHAKRA:
Throat, Solar Plexus

TIMING:
Quickly; or, you must take charge to make it happen

NUMEROLOGY:
1, 10, 19

ARCANA RELATION:
The Sun, Wheel of Fortune

DEITY:
Cynocephalus, Hermes, Loki, Mercury, Thoth

ANIMAL:
Ape, Ibis, Swallow

CRYSTAL:
Agate, Aquamarine, Citrine, Fire Opal, Garnet, Quartz, Sunstone, Tiger Eye

PLANT:
Astragulus, Carnation, Lime, Marjoram, Palm, Rosemary, Vanilla, Vervain

MAGICKAL ITEM:
Caduceus, Wand

ARCHANGEL:
Raphael and Raziel

WHITE
Beginning, Humility, Purity

YELLOW
Confidence, Joy, Intellect, Optimism

RED
Desire, Passion, Power, Vitality

GREEN
Balance, Fertility, Growth, Harmony

The four symbols on the table represent the four suits. The Magician can transmute intangible creativity and concepts into tangible results with each. One arm is stretched toward the heavens while the other points toward the Earth, signifying their role as a conduit between the divine realms and the physical world. This pose also references the magickal phrase, "As above, so below," meaning mind and matter are reflections of one another.

The Magician is all about manifestation, resourcefulness, and power. They signify the ability to harness and use the universe's energy to create and influence the physical world. This card indicates that you have the tools, resources, and knowledge to meet your goals and achieve your desires. When the Magician appears in a reading, it often suggests that it's an excellent time to begin a new project or start a new phase in your life, as the energies are suitable for manifestation.

At a deeper level, the Magician emphasizes the power of transformation and reminds us of their innate ability to shape their destiny. Drawing this card can mean a period where one's potential can be fully realized with focus, will, and intent. It serves as a reminder that you have the magic to create your desired life.

ZODIAC: Gemini (May 21 – June 20) is an Air sign ruled by Mercury. Geminis often feel as though they have two distinct sides to their personalities. Virgo (August 23rd – September 22nd) is an Earth sign ruled by Mercury. Virgos are selfless and dedicated, often putting others' needs above their own.

PLANET: Mercury is the smallest planet in our solar system and the closest to the Sun. Mercury, the messenger of the gods, represents communication and reasoning.

ELEMENT: Air represents logic, intellect, and communication. The intangible element is considered to be active, masculine energy. It is associated with Spring, the Suit of Wands, and the East cardinal direction.

HERMETIC QABALAH Associated Hebrew Letter: Bet, House (Temple)

TREE OF LIFE PATHWAY: 12th Path Between Kether (Crown) and Binah (Understanding)

-2-
THE HIGH PRIESTESS
M A J O R A R C A N A

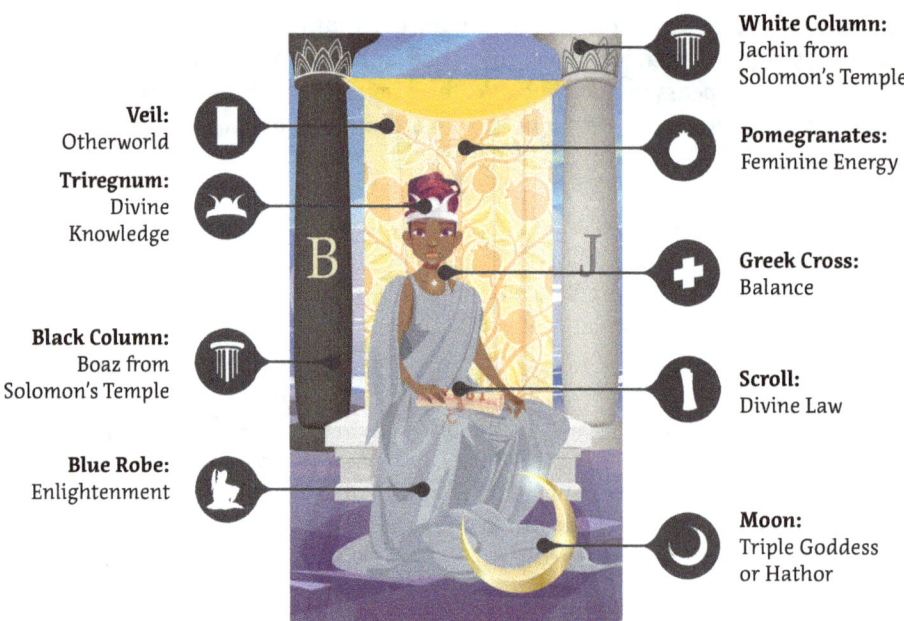

Veil:
Otherworld

Triregnum:
Divine
Knowledge

Black Column:
Boaz from
Solomon's Temple

Blue Robe:
Enlightenment

White Column:
Jachin from
Solomon's Temple

Pomegranates:
Feminine Energy

Greek Cross:
Balance

Scroll:
Divine Law

Moon:
Triple Goddess
or Hathor

Yes/No Reading:

○   ○   ☑
Yes   No   *Maybe*

Names in Other Tarot Systems:
Golden Dawn: The High Priestess
Tarot of Marseilles: La Papesse
Thoth: The Priestess

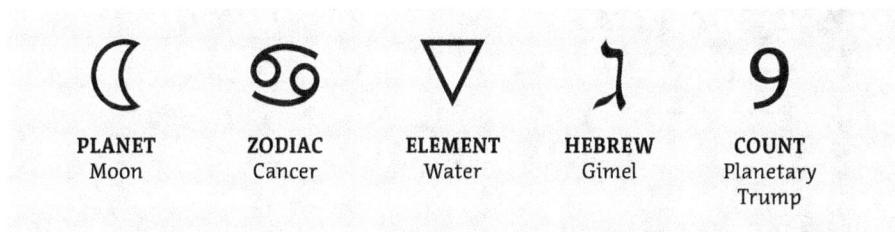

PLANET	ZODIAC	ELEMENT	HEBREW	COUNT
Moon	Cancer	Water	Gimel	Planetary Trump

Upright: *Divine, Dreams, Intuition, Psychic Power, Wisdom*
Trust your intuition. Take time to meditate, contemplate, and look within, for the answers lie inside you. You're on the brink of a phase of growth. Your situation may be clouded with hidden goals, but things will soon be revealed. Now is an excellent time for spiritual or creative development. Be sure to protect your work from others. Avoid unveiling projects or ideas before they're completed.

The High Priestess serves as a gatekeeper and may tell you to listen to the gatekeepers in your life. They're a maternal figure who is available to listen but will also safeguard your secrets. Protect your secrets, and do not explain yourself, your motives, or your intentions to anyone who cannot be trusted.

If you feel that you cannot dig within yourself for the answers you seek, lean on someone you can trust for their advice or help you develop your intuitive powers.

Reversed: *Lack of Self Confidence, Secrets, Silence, Withdrawal*
You might have to rely on yourself and tune into your instincts. In times of uncertainty, it's essential to trust your intuition and remain true to who you are. There could be silence or mystery stemming from friends, colleagues, or partners that must be addressed. Be mindful of hidden agendas. You or someone attached to your situation may be experiencing infertility, hormonal imbalance, menstrual issues, or body issues.

For those who work with psychic or intuitive energies, the reversed High Priestess can suggest blockages. It might be when spiritual insights are clouded or more challenging to come by. This could also imply overemphasizing logical or analytical thinking, excluding intuition or emotional understanding.

CHAKRA:
Third Eye, Sacral

TIMING:
Unknown, or in a moon cycle

NUMEROLOGY:
2, 11, 20

ARCANA RELATION:
Justice, Judgment

DEITY:
Artemis, Chomse, Diana,
Hathor, Hecate, Isis,
Persephone, Selene

ANIMAL:
Camel, Dog, Stork

CRYSTAL:
Aquamarine, Carnelian, Jet,
Kyanite, Labradorite, Lapis
Lazuli, Moonstone, Pearl,
Rose Quartz

PLANT:
Alder, Almond, Hazel,
Moonwort, Myrrh, Peony,
Pomegranate, Rowan Berries,
White Sandalwood,
Willow Bark

MAGICKAL ITEM:
Arrow, Crystal Ball,
Scrying Mirror

ARCHANGEL:
Gabriel and Hanael

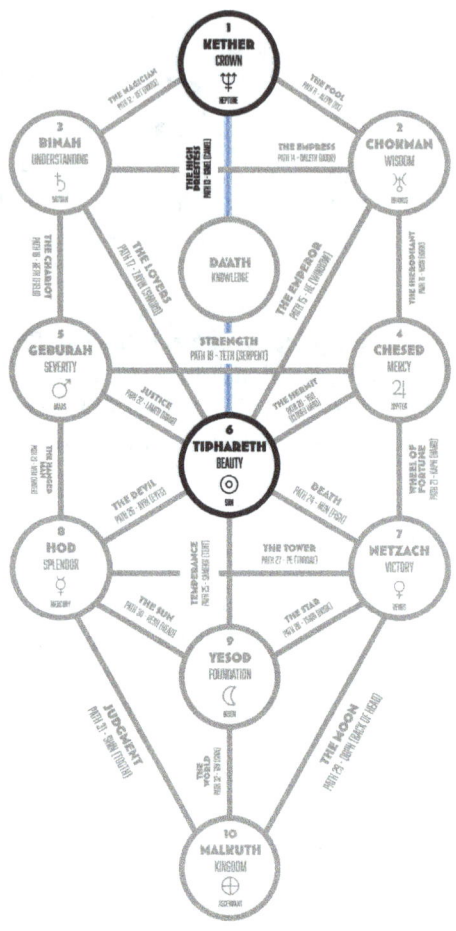

 WHITE
Beginning,
Humility, Purity

 YELLOW
Confidence, Joy,
Intellect, Optimism

 RED
Desire, Passion,
Power, Vitality

 BLUE
Stability, Loyalty,
Calm, Peace, Emotion

The High Priestess is typically depicted seated between two pillars, one black and one white, symbolizing duality. These pillars often carry the letters B and J, representing the pillars of Solomon's temple — Boaz and Jachin. The High Priestess embodies intuition, unconscious knowledge, and mysteries. When they appear in a reading, they often suggest that you rely more on your intuition and inner wisdom than on conscious, logical thinking. This card may also indicate that hidden influences are at play and that not everything is as it seems.

The High Priestess represents a deep understanding of the universe, a bridge between the seen and the unseen. They encourage introspection and self-reflection, urging one to look beyond the obvious and tap into the deeper realms of their psyche and the universe.

Drawing this card can also mean a time of waiting and patience. The answers one seeks might not be immediately apparent, and it's essential to trust the process, letting things unfold naturally. The High Priestess is a reminder of each individual's vast, untapped potential and wisdom, accessible through intuition, dreams, and meditation.

ZODIAC: Cancer (June 21 – July 22) is a Water sign ruled by the Moon. Cancers are highly empathetic, although they can be initially perceived as cold and distant. They're often caregivers and nurturing.

PLANET: The Moon is the ruler of Cancer and represents one's deepest emotional needs. It is associated with the mother and feminine energy. It rules rhythmic ebb and flow of activity and energy.

ELEMENT: Water rules emotions and is a symbol of healing, peace, dreams, and compassion. It is associated with Winter, the Suit of Cups, and the West cardinal direction.

HERMETIC QABALAH Associated Hebrew Letter: Gimel – Camel (Up, Unconscious)

TREE OF LIFE PATHWAY: 13th Path Between Kether (Crown) and Tiphareth (Beauty)

THE EMPRESS

MAJOR ARCANA

Scepter: Power

Cushioned Throne: Passion and Luxury

Heart-Shaped Shield: Venus, Feminine Energy

Wheat: Abundance and Fruitfulness

Diadem Crown: Flora and Fauna

Running Water: Life-Sustaining Force

White Gown: Purity

Fruit Pattern: Fertility

Yes/No Reading:

Yes   No   Maybe

Names in Other Tarot Systems:

Golden Dawn: The Empress
Tarot of Marseilles: L'Impératrice
Thoth: Empress

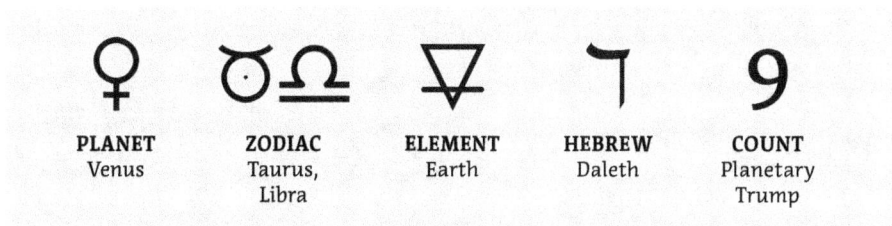

PLANET	ZODIAC	ELEMENT	HEBREW	COUNT
Venus	Taurus, Libra	Earth	Daleth	Planetary Trump

Upright: *Abundance, Nurture, Stability, Compassion, Creativity, Motherhood*
The Empress is a sensual and confident creature full of feminine, nurturing energy. They're a welcome sight in readings where questions regarding fertility, new projects, and finances are asked.

You may be experiencing new life in the form of romance, business, a new job, or a new project. Now is the time to accept creative impulses and bring your plans to fruition. The Empress could also be signaling a pregnancy, mainly if appearing in spreads alongside The Sun, The Ace of Cups, or the Page of Pentacles.

This card can suggest a period of comfort, luxury, or indulgence. It might be a call to treat oneself or to appreciate life's pleasures. There's a sense of balance and harmony associated with the Empress. Things align in your favor, and your life's a harmonious flow.

Reversed: *Domestic Troubles, Stagnation, Neglect, Lack of Confidence*
There may be financial or domestic issues plaguing you, causing immeasurable stress. There may also be a creative block or a needy person drawing too much of your energy. Just as the upright Empress represents nurturing, in reverse, they can indicate excessive care to the point of smothering or being overly protective.

In questions about pregnancy or conception, a reversed Empress might suggest challenges or frustrations. This could be literal, as in difficulties with physical image, or symbolic, such as projects and plans not coming to fruition as hoped.

As a card of abundance, its reversal can suggest financial difficulties or feelings of material lack. There may also be a lack of care or neglect towards oneself or others. It could indicate a time when one is feeling unloved or uncared for.

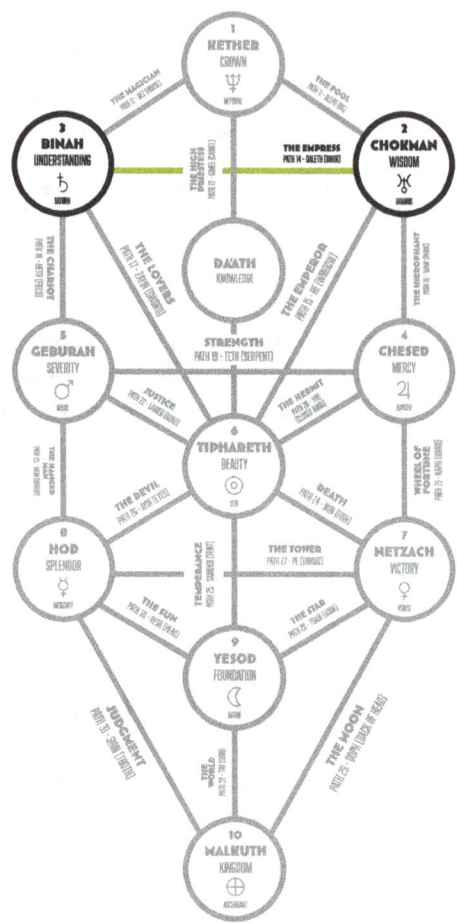

CHAKRA:
Throat, Heart, Sacral

TIMING:
According to conditions

NUMEROLOGY:
3, 12, 21

ARCANA RELATION:
The Hanged Man, The World

DEITY:
Aphrodite, Demeter, Hathor,
Isis, Persephone, Venus

ANIMAL:
Dove, Pelican, Sparrow, Sow

CRYSTAL:
Emerald, Peridot,
Pink Tourmaline,
aaRose Quartz, Turquoise

PLANT:
Apple, Clover, Corn, Cypress,
Dong Quai, Fig, Hazel, Myrtle,
Olive, Peach, Pomegranate,
Rose, Sunflower

MAGICKAL ITEM:
Cauldron

ARCHANGEL:
Anael and Chamuel

WHITE
Beginning,
Humility, Purity

YELLOW
Confidence, Joy,
Intellect, Optimism

RED
Desire, Passion,
Power, Vitality

GREEN
Balance, Fertility,
Growth, Harmony

The Empress is commonly depicted as sitting on a throne surrounded by a fertile landscape, symbolizing their deep connection with the Earth and the life it sustains. Their crown of twelve stars represents their rule over the zodiac and the passing of time. A.E. Waite likened The Empress to the Blessed Virgin Mary, describing them as a Refugium Peccatorum. This powerful force of nature embodies nurturing, fertility, and growth.

In the original artwork, The Empress is depicted as pregnant, sitting comfortably on a luxurious throne surrounded by a lush grain field. Their flowing white gown features pomegranate imagery, and they wear a crown with twelve stars. Holding a gold scepter in their right hand and resting their left on their knee, they stand upon a heart-shaped shield featuring the symbol of Venus.

The Empress card signifies a period of growth, abundance, and fertility. It also suggests that the querent is in a nurturing phase, whether of themselves or others. This card encourages embracing one's feminine side, savoring life's luxuries, and admiring the beauty surrounding us in all its forms.

ZODIAC: Taurus (April 20 – May 20) is an Earth sign, and Libra (September 23 – October 22) is an Air sign, both are ruled by Venus. The luxurious energy of Venus bonds with Taureans, while the relationship qualities of the planet align with Libras harmonious nature.

PLANET: Venus primarily governs love, harmony, and affection in relationships. It rules over our sentiments, what we value in romantic partnerships, and how we express affection.

ELEMENT: Earth represents death and rebirth. It is the realm of abundance, prosperity, and wealth. It is associated with Autumn, the Suit of Pentacles, and the North cardinal direction.

HERMETIC QABALAH Associated Hebrew Letter: Daleth – Door (Pathway, Nourishment)

TREE OF LIFE PATHWAY: 14th Path Between Chokmah (Wisdom) and Binah (Understanding)

4

THE EMPEROR

M A J O R   A R C A N A

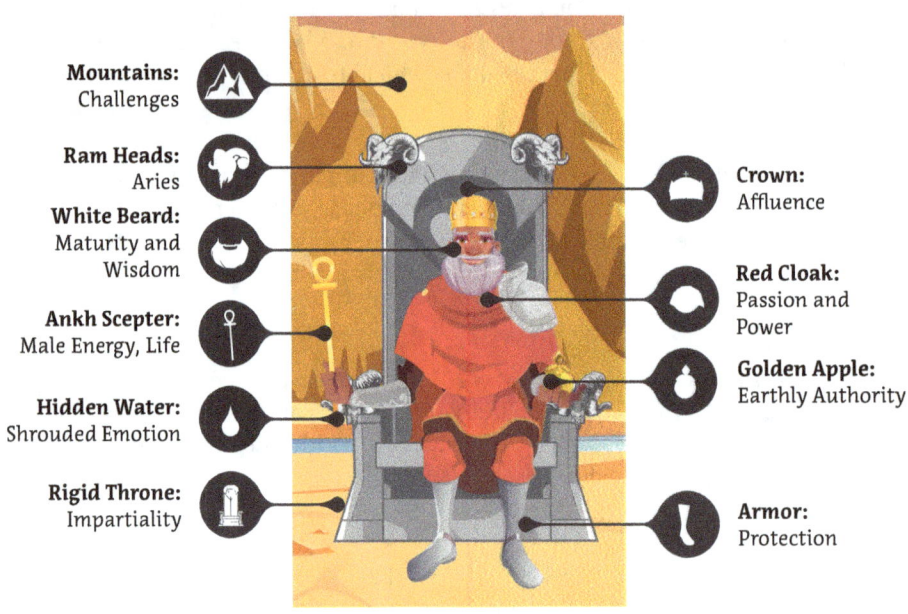

Mountains:
Challenges

Ram Heads:
Aries

White Beard:
Maturity and
Wisdom

Ankh Scepter:
Male Energy, Life

Hidden Water:
Shrouded Emotion

Rigid Throne:
Impartiality

Crown:
Affluence

Red Cloak:
Passion and
Power

Golden Apple:
Earthly Authority

Armor:
Protection

Yes/No Reading:

✓ ○ ○
Yes *No* *Maybe*

Names in Other Tarot Systems:
Golden Dawn: The Emperor
Tarot of Marseilles: L'Empereur
Thoth: The Emperor

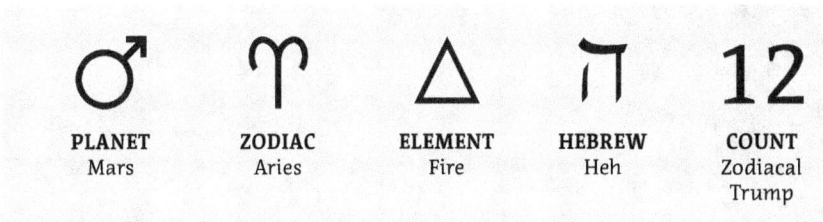

PLANET	**ZODIAC**	**ELEMENT**	**HEBREW**	**COUNT**
Mars	Aries	Fire	Heh	Zodiacal Trump

Upright: *Leadership, Structure, Law and Order, Stability, Discipline*

The Emperor stands for structure, order, and leadership. Drawing this card might indicate that someone is providing guidance or setting clear boundaries in your life, or it may suggest it's time for you to take on this role yourself. Embracing the Emperor's energy involves taking charge, being disciplined, and upholding traditions or structures that have proven effective.

The Emperor is a strategist. They think logically, value structure, and might advise careful planning over impulse. You may receive valuable advice or guidance from someone in a position of authority or experience. This could be a mentor, a boss, or a parental figure. The Emperor values traditions and conventions. The card might suggest that you adhere to established methods or that there's wisdom in the tried and true. An Emperor-driven solution often relies on logic, practicality, and facts. It might be a time to set emotions aside and reason about a situation.

Reversed: *Manipulation, Overbearing, Control, Tyrannical, Rigidity, Cruelty*

The reversed Emperor can indicate someone in a position of authority who is misusing or abusing their power. It may point to dominance, control, or even tyranny. The card can indicate a leader who isn't stepping up, lacking confidence, or failing to make necessary decisions. This could also represent an inability to control one's life or circumstances. Just as The Emperor stands for power and leadership, its reversal can indicate a fall from grace or being overthrown from a position of authority.

While the upright Emperor champions structure and order, its reversal can denote excessive rigidity, leading to stagnation. It may be a sign that existing systems or rules are too constricting. The reversed Emperor can also suggest a desire to break free from established conventions, traditions, or structures. It might be a call to challenge the status quo.

CHAKRA:
Solar Plexus, Root

TIMING:
March 21 – April 19

NUMEROLOGY:
4, 13

ARCANA RELATION:
Death

DEITY:
Zeus, Men Thu

ANIMAL:
Ram, Owl

CRYSTAL:
Bloodstone, Carnelian,
Fire Agate, Garnet,
Hematite, Red Jasper,
Ruby, Sapphire

PLANT:
Atractylodes, Geranium, Ginger,
Laurel, Mugwort, Oak, Olive,
Tiger Lily

MAGICKAL ITEM:
Burin, Horns, Staff

ARCHANGEL:
Anael and Chamuel

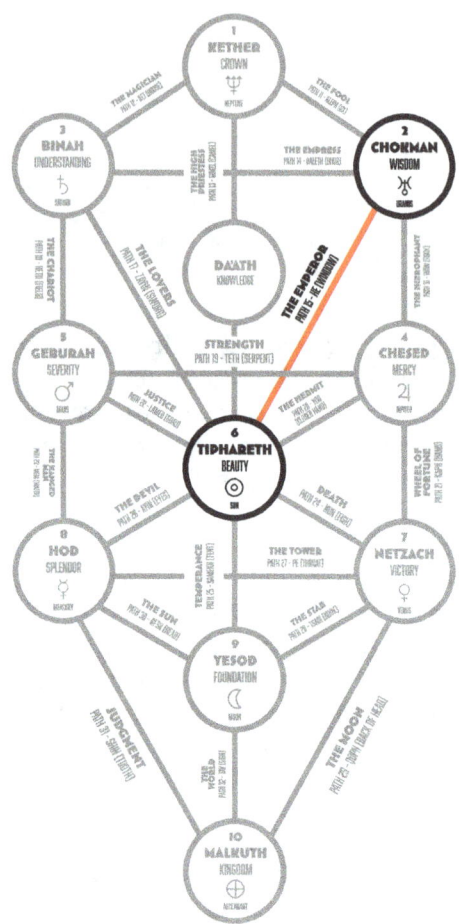

BLACK
Dignity, Force,
Stability, Protection

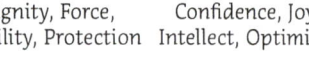

YELLOW
Confidence, Joy,
Intellect, Optimism

RED
Desire, Passion,
Power, Vitality

ORANGE
Energy, Vitality,
Stimulation

Seated confidently on a stone throne, the Emperor often displays symbols of power and leadership, such as the ankh or a globe. Beneath their red robes lies armor, alluding to their role as a protector and a leader in battles. Representing the father figure of the Tarot, the Emperor embodies the ideals of structure, order, and leadership.

This card signifies the need for a strong foundation, security, and stability. The Emperor represents a protective force or the necessity to become one. It embodies the values of discipline, control, and regulation. It emphasizes the importance of establishing rules, enforcing boundaries, and ensuring order.

The Emperor is an assertive and dominant figure. Drawing this card suggests that it may be time to stand one's ground or confront situations where someone may be exerting too much power. It is a reminder of the value of experience and established norms.

♈ **ZODIAC:** Aries (March 21 – April 19) is a Fire sign ruled by Mars. This sign embodies a determined, impulsive, and resolute energy.

♂ **PLANET:** Mars primarily governs energy, drive, and ambition. Mars is about starting new things, taking the initiative, and pioneering efforts. It's also associated with with sexual attraction and raw physical energy.

△ **ELEMENT:** Fire represents energy, creativity, and power. It is the realm of love, courage, and action. It is associated with Summer, the Suit of Wands, and the South cardinal direction.

ה **HERMETIC QABALAH** Associated Hebrew Letter: Heh – Window (Vision, Reasoning)

TREE OF LIFE PATHWAY: 15th Path Between Chokmah (Wisdom) and Tipheret (Beauty)

5

THE HIEROPHANT

M A J O R   A R C A N A

Columns:
Spiritual
Enlightenment

Mitre:
Spiritual Authority

Blessing Gesture:
As Above So Below

Two Monks:
Community

Papal Cross:
Shepherd

Red Cloak:
Passion and
Power

Keys: Spiritual
Mysteries

Yes/No Reading:

Yes   No   Maybe

Names in Other Tarot Systems:
Golden Dawn: The Hierophant
Tarot of Marseilles: Le Pape
Thoth: Hierophant

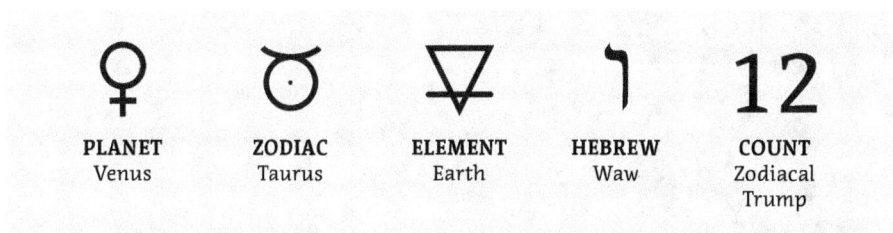

PLANET	ZODIAC	ELEMENT	HEBREW	COUNT
Venus	Taurus	Earth	Waw	Zodiacal Trump

Upright: *Religion, Ethics, Tradition, Beliefs, Conformity*
When the Hierophant appears upright, it's a nudge to embrace and rely on spiritual and societal customs. For those just beginning their journey, it's wise to turn to honorable institutions and mentors for guidance. For the seasoned, taking on the role of a teacher can be equally enlightening, as there's much to learn from one's students. This upright card emphasizes the importance of tapping into one's cultural or religious roots for deeper understanding, further enriching The Fool's journey.

You are encouraged to act with integrity and honesty, sticking to your principles and established moral codes. The presence of the Hierophant can indicate that you'll either seek a mentor or be in the position of mentoring someone else, guiding them through established practices or beliefs. The card can hint at the importance of community or group involvement. It might be a time to engage more deeply with your religious, spiritual, or even social community.

Reversed: *Rebellion, Rejection of Values, Non-Conformity, Ignorance*
You might be feeling restricted or confined by established traditions and norms. Break free from conventions that no longer serve you. You might be feeling rebellious, challenging the status quo, or rejecting societal or religious structures that are outdated or restrictive. Develop your own beliefs or moral code rather than mindlessly following what has been laid down by society or a religious institution.

In some instances, the reversed Hierophant can indicate a mentor or institution that is misleading or not acting in one's best interest. It might suggest you feel out of step with your community or society due to your beliefs or actions. You might feel judged or misunderstood by those around you. Instead of structured or formal education, the card might point you toward more alternative, unconventional methods of learning or spiritual exploration.

CHAKRA:
Throat

TIMING:
April 20 – May 20

NUMEROLOGY:
5, 14

ARCANA RELATION:
Temperance

DEITY:
Ameshet, Apis, Asar, Hymen

ANIMAL:
Ram, Owl, Bull

CRYSTAL:
Carnelian, Diamond, Emerald,
Jade, Lapis Lazuli, Sapphire,
Septarian, Topaz

PLANT:
Lavender, Lemon, Mallow, Sage,
Sugar Cane, Sweet Pea, Violet

MAGICKAL ITEM:
Altar, Key, Nail, Shepherd's
Crook, Throne

ARCHANGEL:
Anael and Chamuel

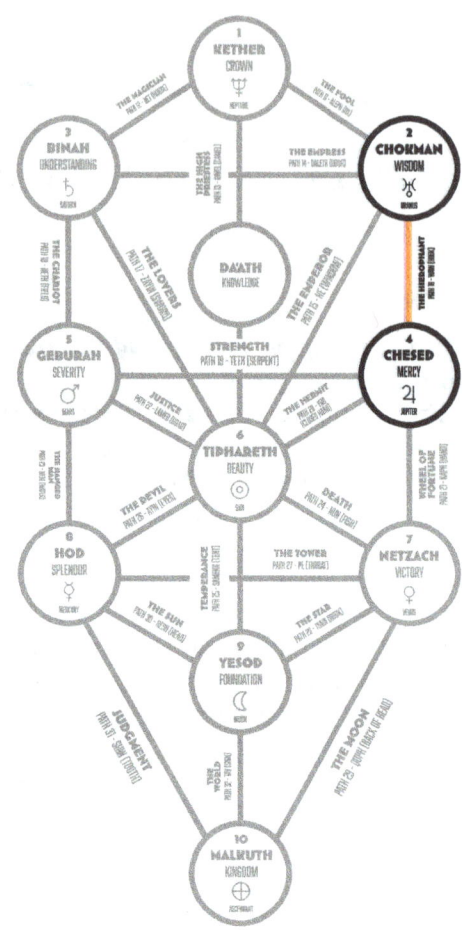

BROWN
Solidity, Grounding,
Strength

GREY
Stability,
Neutrality, Reserve

RED
Desire, Passion,
Power, Vitality

BLUE
Stability, Loyalty,
Calm, Peace, Emotion

The Hierophant is also sometimes referred to as the High Priest or Pope. Traditionally, they are depicted as a religious figure seated between two pillars symbolizing law and liberty or obedience and disobedience. They wear a crown with three tiers, representing the three realms they rule over the conscious, subconscious, and superconscious. In their left hand, they wield a scepter ending in a tri-fold Papal cross, and with the right-hand forms a significant ecclesiastical gesture, representing the balance between visible and hidden teachings.

The intersecting keys lie in the foreground, and two clerical aides bow. While many recognize the Hierophant as the Pope, this label merely narrows the broader role they signify. They embody the overt authority of formal religion, juxtaposed against the High Priestess, who represents the inner, esoteric power. Over time, interpretations of this card have been muddled. Some correctly see the Hierophant as a symbol of conventional religious teachings and the outer journey toward understanding. Others have mistakenly cast the Hierophant as the guardian of secret doctrines.

ZODIAC: Taurus (April 20 – May 20) is an Earth sign ruled by Venus. This sign embodies those that are grounded, practical, and stable.

PLANET: Venus primarily governs love, harmony, and affection in relationships. It rules over our sentiments, what we value in romantic partnerships, and how we express affection.

ELEMENT: Earth represents death and rebirth. It is the realm of abundance, prosperity, and wealth. It is associated with Autumn, the Suit of Pentacles, and the North cardinal direction.

HERMETIC QABALAH Associated Hebrew Letter: Waw – Hook, Nail (Connections, Secure)

TREE OF LIFE PATHWAY: 16th Path Between Chokmah (Wisdom) and Chesed (Mercy)

6

THE LOVERS

MAJOR ARCANA

Angel:
Healing

Fruit Tree:
Material World

Snake:
Temptation

Mountains:
Challenges

Burning Tree:
Enlightenment

Lovers:
Polarities

Yes/No Reading:

✓ ○ ○
Yes *No* *Maybe*

Names in Other Tarot Systems:
Golden Dawn: The Lovers
Tarot of Marseilles: L'Amoureux
Thoth: The Lovers

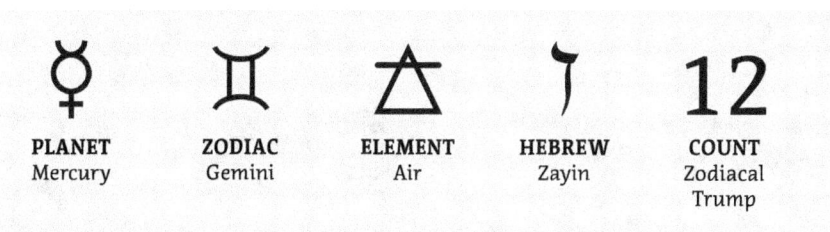

PLANET	ZODIAC	ELEMENT	HEBREW	COUNT
Mercury	Gemini	Air	Zayin	Zodiacal Trump

Upright: *Connection, Partnership, Commitment, Love, Trust, Marriage*
The Lovers card, in its upright form, stands as a testament to the bonds formed between two entities. Whether these ties are romantic, platonic, or spiritual, there's a deep connection and understanding between the involved parties. This card can signify the blossoming of a romantic relationship or the strengthening an existing bond. Beyond romance, it may indicate a choice with the heart, emphasizing the importance of personal values and integrity.

There is a harmony between the conscious and subconscious mind. Your decisions at this time are likely aligned with your higher self and personal truths. It can also imply that, in a situation, partnership or collaboration will bring about the best outcome. The Lovers can also signal a crossroads in one's life, where choices rooted in personal beliefs and values come into play. It urges you to make decisions with both the heart and mind, maintaining an equilibrium between emotion and logic.

Reversed: *Unwise Plans, Conflict, Infidelity, Separation, Imbalance*
Reversed, The Lovers card indicates potential strife, misalignment, or a lack of harmony in relationships or decisions. It could be a sign of a relationship facing challenges, miscommunication, or the possibility of a breakup. The bond that once felt so strong may now be tested, urging you to reflect upon the foundation of your relationship.

A reversed Lovers card can also point to internal conflict, especially regarding personal choices and values. You might be facing a decision that challenges your moral beliefs or causes inner turmoil. It's a reminder to realign with your core values, even when faced with tough choices.

You might feel out of sync with your inner self, leading to choices that may not be in your best interest. It prompts introspection, asking you to reassess the decisions you're making and the relationships you're nurturing.

CHAKRA:
Heart

TIMING:
May 21 – June 20

NUMEROLOGY:
6, 15

ARCANA RELATION:
The Devil

DEITY:
Apollo, Castor and Pollux,
Heru-Ra-Ha, Hymen,
Merti, Rehkt

ANIMAL:
Magpie, Parrot, Penguin, Zebra

CRYSTAL:
Alexandrite, Aventurine,
Emerald, Iceland Spar, Jade,
Malachite, Pink Tourmaline,
Rose Quartz, Ruby

PLANT:
Apple, Dragon's Blood,
Hawthorn, Lavender,
Meadowsweet, Orchids, Parsley,
Rose, Rush, Violet

MAGICKAL ITEM:
Sword, Tripod

ARCHANGEL:
Zadkiel, Raphael

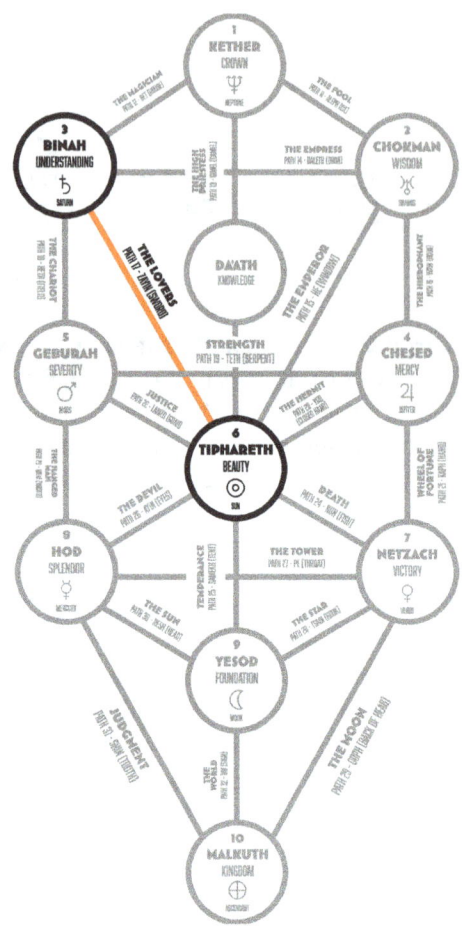

WHITE
Beginning, Humility,
Purity

YELLOW
Confidence, Joy,
Intellect, Optimism

PINK
Affection, Friendship,
Companionship

GREEN
Balance, Fertility,
Growth, Harmony

The depiction on the Lovers card usually portrays two individuals, often identified as Adam and Eve, basking in the warm glow of sunlight. This card symbolizes the essence of duality, representing the fusion of the masculine and feminine, the interplay between the conscious and unconscious mind, and the balance between the tangible and spiritual worlds. It encourages reflection on the harmonious union of such contrasting elements.

A guardian angel, commonly recognized as Archangel Raphael, hovers above the couple with his expansive wings, creating a protective aura around them and granting them blessings and guardianship. The background features a mountain, which represents both challenges and the peaks of desire. Next to one of the figures stands a fruit-bearing tree, which is a symbol of material desires and temptations. In contrast, a tree ablaze with fiery leaves or flames represents spiritual awakening and fervor, encompassing life's dualities.

While The Lovers card is often associated with deep romantic connections, it goes beyond that scope. It resonates with strong bonds, whether they be platonic, familial, or related to one's life pursuits. Similar to the story of Adam and Eve, the card intertwines a narrative of ethics and core beliefs. It may draw attention to moments of decision-making, where moral values are weighed against tempting allure.

ZODIAC: Gemini (May 21 – June 20) is an Air sign ruled by Mercury. The dual nature of Gemini embodies a mix of yin and yang, and Geminis often feel as though they have two distinct sides.

PLANET: Mercury is the smallest planet in our solar system and the closest to the Sun. Mercury, the messenger of the gods, represents communication and reasoning.

ELEMENT: Air represents logic, intellect, and communication. The intangible element is considered to be active, masculine energy. It is associated with Spring, the Suit of Wands, and the East cardinal direction.

HERMETIC QABALAH Associated Hebrew Letter: Zayin – Sword (Discernment, Cut Off)

TREE OF LIFE PATHWAY: 17th Path Between Binah (Understanding) and Tiphareth (Beauty)

THE CHARIOT

M A J O R   A R C A N A

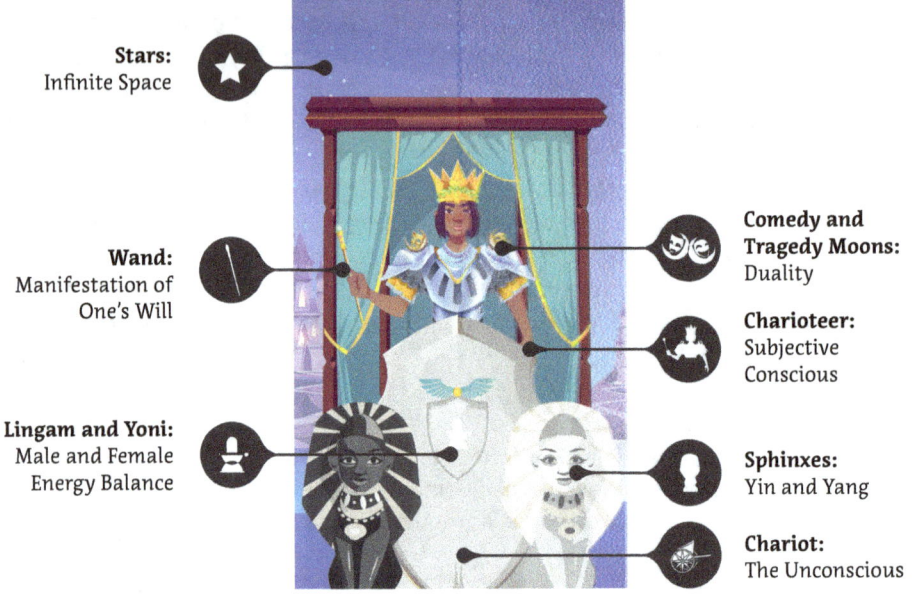

Stars:
Infinite Space

Wand:
Manifestation of
One's Will

Lingam and Yoni:
Male and Female
Energy Balance

**Comedy and
Tragedy Moons:**
Duality

Charioteer:
Subjective
Conscious

Sphinxes:
Yin and Yang

Chariot:
The Unconscious

Yes/No Reading:

Yes   No   Maybe

Names in Other Tarot Systems:
Golden Dawn: The Chariot
Tarot of Marseilles: Le Chariot
Thoth: The Chariot

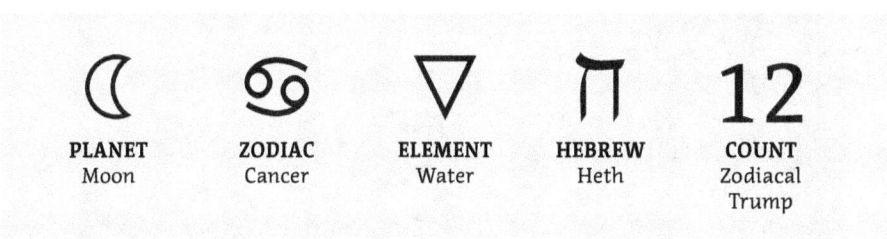

(	♋	∇	ת	**12**
PLANET	**ZODIAC**	**ELEMENT**	**HEBREW**	**COUNT**
Moon	Cancer	Water	Heth	Zodiacal Trump

Upright: *Ambition, Confidence, Determination, Victory, Journey, Success*
The Chariot card stands as a beacon of triumph, success, and navigating challenges with unwavering confidence and control. It underscores the power of self-restraint, assertiveness, and steering one's path with intent and zeal.

At its heart, the card delves into mastering inner turmoil, bringing together contrasting elements of one's being (depicted by the two sphinxes or horses), and propelling forward in sync with one's aspirations and higher consciousness. It represents dominion over one's surroundings, both within and without.

The Chariot implies that you hold the reins of your journey, and with steadfast purpose and resolve, you can overcome impending obstacles. It denotes a phase where your mental tenacity and sheer will can mold your desired outcomes.

Reversed: *Stagnation, Travel Issues, Aggression, Self-Doubt, Lack of Control*
When the Chariot card emerges inverted in a Tarot spread, it often indicates a feeling of being overwhelmed, directionless, or at the mercy of conflicting energies. The balance and dominance observed in its upright position have become unsteady, leading the individual to perceive their actions as fragmented or misdirected.

One may sense an unsettling chaos, questioning how to reclaim their balance and purpose. Doubts about one's own capabilities could surface, causing hesitation in taking decisive steps forward or maintaining a chosen path.

The creatures depicted on the card, be it sphinxes or horses, mirror inner tensions or self-conflicts. Additionally, this card can hint at a misguided journey, perhaps steered by unclear intentions or external pressures.

CHAKRA:
Solar Plexus

TIMING:
June 21 – July 22

NUMEROLOGY:
7, 16

ARCANA RELATION:
The Tower

DEITY:
Apollo, Khephra

ANIMAL:
Crab, Sphinx, Turtle, Whale

CRYSTAL:
Amber, Chalcedony, Citrine,
Flourite, Moonstone, Pearl,
Pyrite, Ruby

PLANT:
Cyperus, Iris, Lotus, Olive,
St. John's Wort, Watercress

MAGICKAL ITEM:
Cup, Sea Salt

ARCHANGEL:
Gabriel

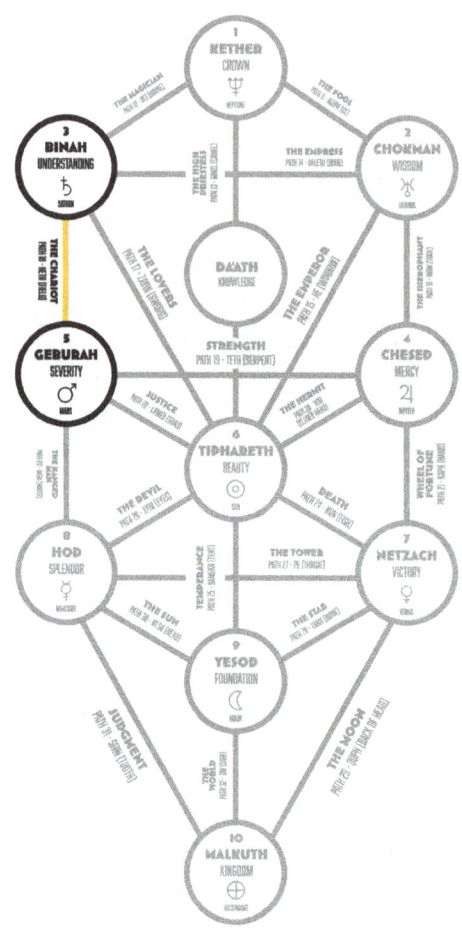

WHITE
Beginning, Humility,
Purity

YELLOW
Confidence, Joy,
Intellect, Optimism

RED
Desire, Passion,
Power, Vitality

ORANGE
Energy, Vitality,
Stimulation

Perched prominently in a chariot, the charioteer embodies an individual's sense of self or ego, exuding confidence while holding the reins and exerting control. Their journey is multidimensional, rooted in both the physical and spiritual realms. This poised figure represents taking control of one's own destiny, adorned in armor as a symbol of readiness, discipline, and a protective aura, demonstrating their ability to confront and overcome any forthcoming challenges. The chariot is an emblem of willpower and physicality, embodying a seamless combination of the spiritual and material worlds, hinting at achievements on various fronts.

The sphinx creatures, often depicted in contrasting shades of black and white, highlight the concept of duality and opposing energies. The charioteer's ability to guide these entities reveals a deeper understanding and mastery of both their light and shadow aspects, or their conscious and unconscious desires.

The distant urban landscape underscores social norms, structures, and collective expectations. As the charioteer traverses this terrain, it signifies either a deviation from societal norms or the forging of an individual path.

ZODIAC: Cancer (June 21 – July 22) is a Water sign ruled by the Moon. Cancerians are known for their emotional depth, intuition, and sensitivity.

PLANET: The Moon is often associated with feminine energy and the divine feminine, and represents introspection, the endless cycles of death and rebirth, and otherworldly experiences.

ELEMENT: Water rules emotions and is a symbol of healing, peace, dreams, and compassion. It is associated with Winter, the Suit of Cups, and the West cardinal direction.

HERMETIC QABALAH Associated Hebrew Letter: Heth – Field, Fence (Separate, Enclose)

TREE OF LIFE PATHWAY: 18th Path Between Binah (Understanding) and Geburah (Severity)

- 8 -
STRENGTH
MAJOR ARCANA

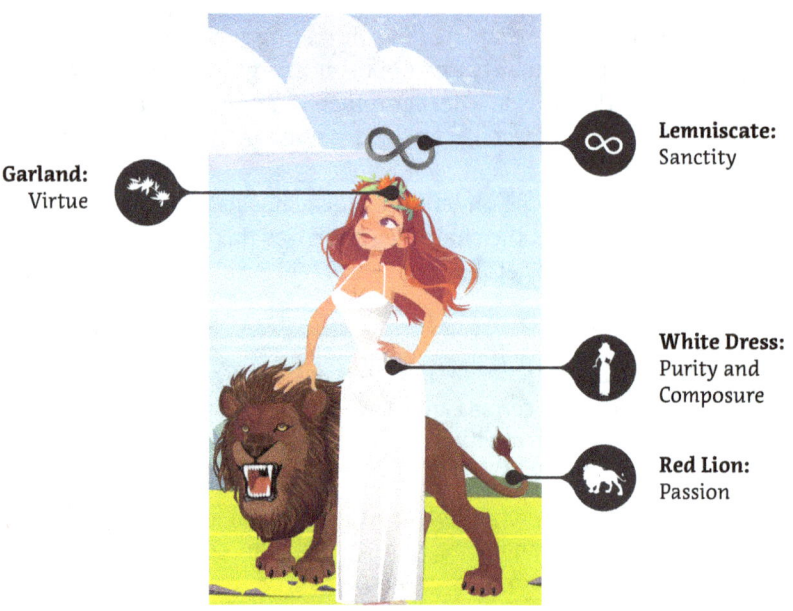

Garland:
Virtue

Lemniscate:
Sanctity

White Dress:
Purity and
Composure

Red Lion:
Passion

Yes/No Reading:

☑   ◯   ◯

Yes   *No*   *Maybe*

Names in Other Tarot Systems:
Golden Dawn: Strength
Tarot of Marseilles: La Force
Thoth: Lust

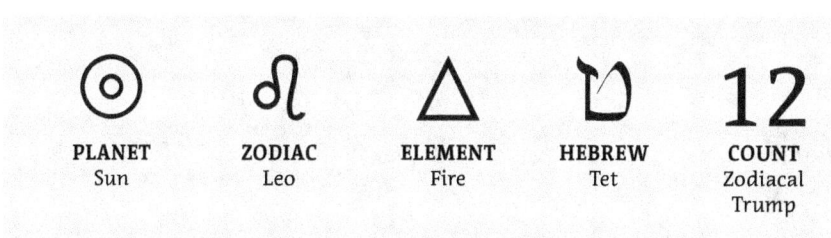

PLANET	ZODIAC	ELEMENT	HEBREW	COUNT
Sun	Leo	Fire	Tet	Zodiacal Trump

Upright: *Courage, Confidence, Virility, Focus, Compassion, Valor*
In the upright position, the Strength card reveals mastery over one's raw emotions and urges, suggesting they've been directed constructively. This card places emphasis on the virtues of patience, discipline, and maintaining a balanced spirit, suggesting that true might isn't about physical prowess, but about emotional and spiritual tenacity. The Strength card also champions compassion and gentleness, prompting one to handle situations with calm rather than react impulsively or aggressively. It serves as a testament that genuine power stems from understanding and balance, not force or domination.

In matters of the heart, it indicates a relationship grounded in mutual respect and genuine connection. If health concerns are present, this card signifies a robust inner spirit and the capacity to recover and heal. Professionally, it hints at dedication and unwavering commitment to one's goals. At its core, the Strength card symbolizes the inner fortitude and courage required to navigate life's challenges with grace.

Reversed: *Stubbornness, Weakness, Aggression, Insecurity, Indulgence*
A reversed Strength card highlights a potential inner struggle or wavering self-discipline. This might manifest as being consumed by personal insecurities, uncertainties, or apprehensions. Such a position suggests unchecked emotions or instincts, which can spur hasty or impulsive choices. You might find yourself battling intense emotions such as anger or frustration, or perhaps suppressing these emotions, risking future internal chaos or unexpected emotional eruptions.

In relational contexts, this reversed card might hint at power imbalances or a dynamic where one individual feels overshadowed or undervalued by the other. When considering health, it could emphasize neglected vulnerabilities or areas of weakness. Professionally, it might indicate hesitancy in decision-making or feeling overwhelmed by occupational hurdles.

CHAKRA:
Heart

TIMING:
July 23 – August 22

NUMEROLOGY:
8, 17

ARCANA RELATION:
The Star

DEITY:
Demeter, Sekhet,
Ra-Hoor-Khuit

ANIMAL:
Cat, Lion, Serpent, Tiger

CRYSTAL:
Cats Eye, Chrysolite, Golden
Topaz, Red Sunstone, Rose
Quartz, Ruby, Tiger's Eye,
Topaz, Tree Jasper

PLANT:
Angelica, Basil, Cayenne,
Comfrey, Fennel, Sunflower,
Tarragon, Thyme

MAGICKAL ITEM:
Rose Petals, Wand

ARCHANGEL:
Raziel, Michael

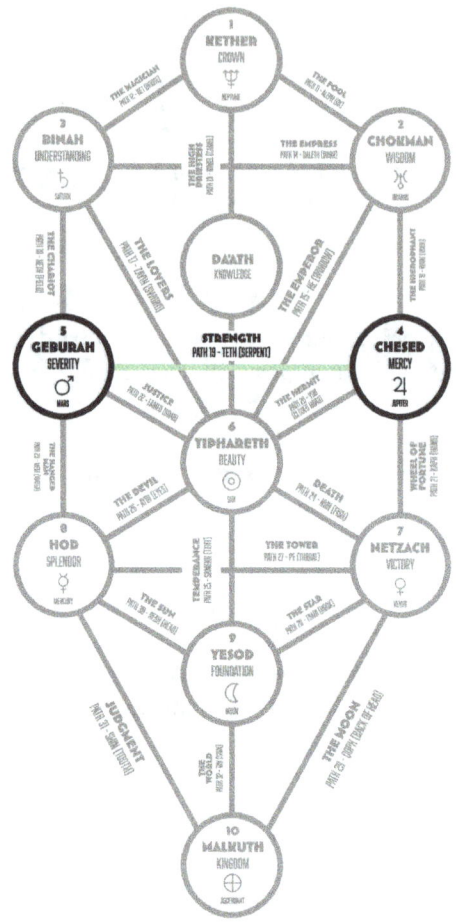

GREY
Stability, Neutrality,
Reserve

YELLOW
Confidence, Joy,
Intellect, Optimism

PURPLE
Spirituality, Wisdom,
Peace, Idealism

RED
Desire, Passion,
Power, Vitality

The Strength card commonly depicts a gentle figure grasping the mouth of a lion, either riding it or standing beside it. This lion serves as a representation of untamed passions, raw instincts, and intense desires.

The figure's head is adorned with an infinity symbol, which symbolizes boundless strength, empowerment, and the timeless nature of existence. They are often crowned with a lemniscate or garlanded with flowers, both of which represent spiritual purity and the unending cycle of life.

In the background, imposing mountains are frequently featured as a reminder of life's challenges, tests, and obstacles. They highlight that genuine strength arises from confronting and surmounting these adversities. Overhead, a radiant golden light envelops the figure and the lion, implying a spiritual awakening, profound insight, and divine protection that encircles those who act with genuine courage and moral conviction.

ZODIAC: Leo (July 23 – August 22) is a Fire sign ruled by the Sun. Leos are known for their self-assurance and innate ability to take the center stage in most situations.

PLANET: The Sun represents the divine light and energy that animates and sustains life. It's a symbol of clarity, illumination, and enlightenment, driving away darkness and negativity.

ELEMENT: Fire represents energy, creativity, and power. It is the realm of love, courage, and action. It is associated with Summer, the Suit of Wands, and the South cardinal direction.

HERMETIC QABALAH Associated Hebrew Letter: Tet – Serpent, Twist (Surround)

TREE OF LIFE PATHWAY: 19th Path Between Geburah (Severity) and Chesed (Mercy)

-9-
THE HERMIT
M A J O R   A R C A N A

**Seal of
Solomon Star:**
Wisdom

Staff:
Grounding

Lantern:
Guidance

Yes/No Reading:

○   ○   ☑

Yes   No   *Maybe*

Names in Other Tarot Systems:
Golden Dawn: The Hermit
Tarot of Marseilles: L'Ermite
Thoth: The Hermit

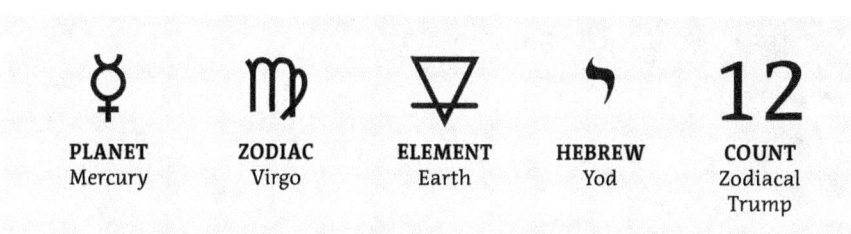

PLANET	ZODIAC	ELEMENT	HEBREW	COUNT
Mercury	Virgo	Earth	Yod	Zodiacal Trump

Upright: *Wisdom, Isolation, Introspection, Patience, Self-Reflection*
Delving into the depths of one's soul, the Hermit card suggests a period of introspection and the quest for profound truths. You're encouraged to set external counsel aside and trust the guidance from within.

Choosing to embrace solitude, not out of loneliness but for genuine self-reflection, can yield transformative insights. A period of meditation or thoughtful contemplation can be especially illuminating, offering clarity and direction.

While this introspective phase might be temporary, it provides an essential opportunity to realign, reevaluate, and move forward with a rejuvenated sense of purpose. Guided by the Hermit's lantern, you're on a path to unveil hidden truths and deeper understanding.

Reversed: *Withdrawal, Exile, Rejection, Paranoia, Loss of Self, Fear*
Reversed, the Hermit might point to feelings of involuntary isolation, loneliness, or exclusion. This can imply not heeding one's intuition or inner voice, potentially leading to choices that aren't in alignment with one's true purpose. There's a potential danger of becoming overly isolated, causing stagnation instead of personal growth. This can stem from an extended period of introspection without taking decisive actions or perhaps from apprehensions about facing external realities. Yet, there's a silver lining. The reversed Hermit might also symbolize the conclusion of a phase of solitude or introspection, hinting at a readiness to step back into society, armed with newfound wisdom and insights.

It's also worth considering that this card, when reversed, could signify a misguided quest—possibly seeking clarity from the wrong sources or over-relying on outside opinions, rather than trusting one's own innate wisdom.

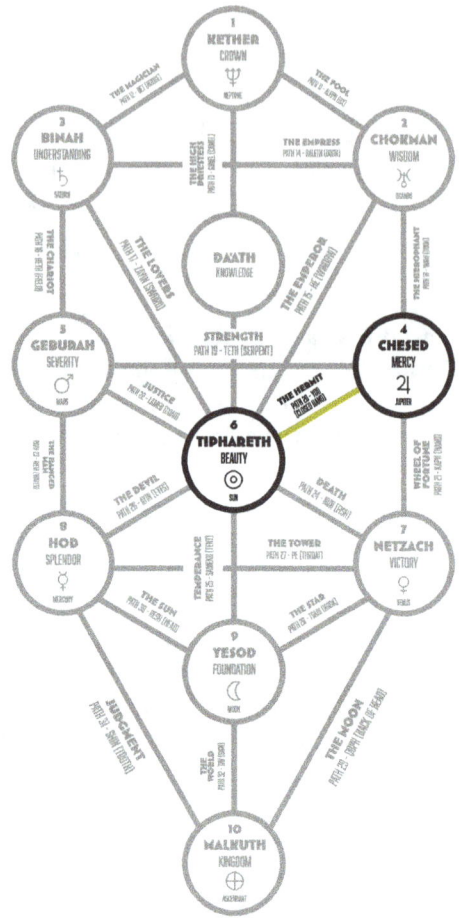

CHAKRA:
Third Eye

TIMING:
August 23 – September 22

NUMEROLOGY:
9, 18

ARCANA RELATION:
The Moon

DEITY:
Adonis, Attis, Ceres, Isis, Vesta

ANIMAL:
Anchorite, Rhinoceros,
Solitary Animals

CRYSTAL:
Amethyst, Ametrine, Aragonite,
Bloodstone, Carnelian, Citrine,
Dumortierite, Gaspeite,
Peridot, Sodalite

PLANT:
Angelica, Aspen, Chamomile,
Licorice, Lily, Mistletoe,
Narcissus, Sage, Snowdrop

MAGICKAL ITEM:
Bread, Flail, Lamp,
Owl Feathers, Wand

ARCHANGEL:
Metatron, Raphael

GREY
Stability, Neutrality,
Reserve

GREEN
Balance, Fertility,
Growth, Harmony

PURPLE
Spirituality, Wisdom,
Peace, Idealism

INDIGO
Emotion, Fluidity,
Expressiveness

The card's central image features a mature, thoughtful figure symbolizing profound wisdom, introspection, and inner clarity. This individual is often depicted atop a mountain, emphasizing their intentional retreat from external distractions and their journey inward.

In one hand, the figure holds a lantern with a single beam of light. The lantern contains the six-pointed Seal of Solomon, a symbol of the Hermit's unique understanding and insight.

In the other hand, the figure grasps a staff, which represents their steadfastness and conviction. This staff reflects the Hermit's unwavering commitment to their beliefs and wisdom.

Clad in a subtle gray cloak, this figure embodies discretion and subtlety. The Hermit's devotion to solitary reflection and meditation is underscored by their choice of dress and manner.

♍ **ZODIAC:** Virgo (August 23 – September 22) is an Earth sign ruled by Mercury. Virgos are selfless and dedicated, often putting others' needs above their own.

☿ **PLANET:** Mercury is the smallest planet in our solar system and the closest to the Sun. Mercury, the messenger of the gods, represents communication and reasoning.

🜃 **ELEMENT:** Earth represents death and rebirth. It is the realm of abundance, prosperity, and wealth. It is associated with Autumn, the Suit of Pentacles, and the North cardinal direction.

٦ **HERMETIC QABALAH** Associated Hebrew Letter: Yod – Closed Hand (Deed, Work)

TREE OF LIFE PATHWAY: 20th Path Between Chesed (Mercy) and Tipareth (Beauty)

10

WHEEL OF FORTUNE

MAJOR ARCANA

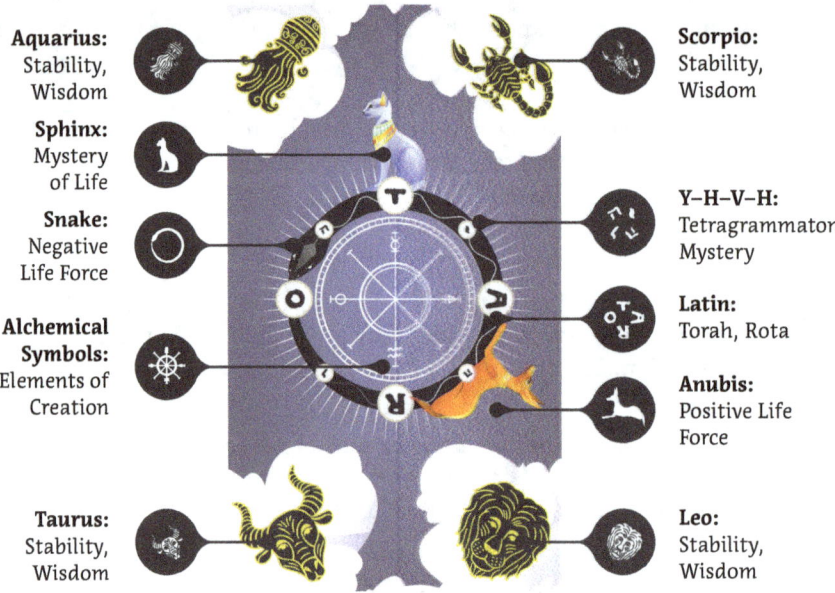

Aquarius:
Stability,
Wisdom

Sphinx:
Mystery
of Life

Snake:
Negative
Life Force

**Alchemical
Symbols:**
Elements of
Creation

Taurus:
Stability,
Wisdom

Scorpio:
Stability,
Wisdom

Y–H–V–H:
Tetragrammaton,
Mystery

Latin:
Torah, Rota

Anubis:
Positive Life
Force

Leo:
Stability,
Wisdom

Yes/No Reading:

☑ ◯ ◯
Yes   No   Maybe

Names in Other Tarot Systems:
Golden Dawn: Wheel of Fortune
Tarot of Marseilles: La Roue de Fortun
Thoth: Fortune

2$\!\!\!\mid$	△	כ	9
PLANET	**ZODIAC**	**ELEMENT**	**HEBREW**	**COUNT**
Jupiter		Fire	Kaph	Planetary Trump

Upright: *Luck, Destiny, Opportunity, Fate, Turning Point, Win, Cycles*
The upright Wheel of Fortune represents the cyclical nature of life and the interconnectedness of events. It serves as a reminder that life is a constant ebb and flow of ups and downs, with everything coming full circle in due time. When this card appears, it often signifies that a turning point is near and that destiny, luck, or the universe's energies will play a significant role in the outcome.

The appearance of the upright Wheel of Fortune in a reading indicates that change is inevitable, whether one is currently experiencing a high or facing challenges. It advises going with the flow and embracing the cycles while trusting in the universe's timing. Recognizing patterns in one's life is important, taking control where possible, but also surrendering to the greater forces at play. By doing so, fortuitous outcomes may occur.

Reversed: *Bad Luck, Misfortune, Fear of Change, Disappointment, Perseverance*
When the Wheel of Fortune appears reversed, it indicates disruptions in the natural flow of life and unexpected shifts that may not always align with one's desires. This can result in setbacks, delays, or unwanted changes. However, it is essential to recognize that this is just a temporary phase and the wheel will eventually turn again.

Additionally, the reversed Wheel of Fortune may suggest feeling stuck in a cycle or pattern, resulting in stagnant energy due to resistance to change or an inability to adapt. It is a reminder to reevaluate one's approach and become more proactive or even change direction.

Moreover, the reversed card serves as a warning against complacency and taking things for granted, emphasizing the importance of staying grounded and being prepared for potential challenges. The Wheel of Fortune highlights the fact that change is the only constant in life, whether it feels prosperous or challenging.

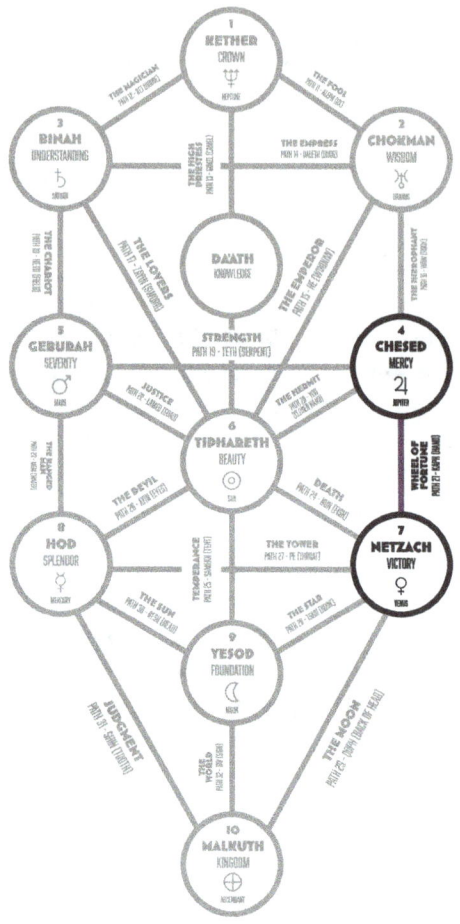

CHAKRA:
Throat

TIMING:
Any time and without notice

NUMEROLOGY:
1, 10, 19

ARCANA RELATION:
The Magician,
The Sun

DEITY:
Amoun-Ra, Fortuna,
Tyche, Zeus

ANIMAL:
Eagle, Praying Mantis

CRYSTAL:
Amethyst, Aquamarine,
Aventurine, Blue Lace Agate,
Lapis Lazuli, Opal, Sapphire,
Sugilite, Topaz

PLANT:
Arnica, Ash, Caraway, Cedar,
Chervil, Clover, Coca, Daisy, Fig,
Heather, Hyssop, Ivy, Jasmine,
Oak, Pine, Poplar, Poppy,
Slippery Elm

MAGICKAL ITEM:
Index Finger, Scepter

ARCHANGEL:
N/A

GREY
Stability, Neutrality,
Reserve

BLUE
Stability, Loyalty,
Calm, Peace, Emotion

PURPLE
Spirituality, Wisdom,
Peace, Idealism

INDIGO
Emotion, Fluidity,
Expressiveness

The Wheel of Fortune is a potent card in the Tarot deck, symbolizing cycles, destiny, and pivotal changes. As its name suggests, the card signifies the ever-turning wheel of life, representing the ups and downs, successes and failures, and the various turns of fortune one can encounter. It reminds us of the cyclical nature of life and the inevitability of change, urging acceptance of our position on the wheel, whether at a high or low point.

Visually, the card usually features a large, rotating wheel, often with the letters T, A, R, and O inscribed upon it or the symbols for alchemical elements. Around or within the wheel, different creatures or figures are typically depicted, each associated with different zodiac signs or representing different aspects of life. These figures might include a sphinx, an eagle, a lion, and a bull. The presence of these beings reminds the viewer of the broader universe's cosmic influence and the interconnectedness of various elements in one's life.

The Wheel of Fortune symbolizes the ebb and flow of circumstances, indicating that events are set in motion and change is inevitable, regardless of our expectations. Although the card can suggest luck or a positive turn of events, its primary message is the impermanence of all things and the natural rhythm of life's ever-changing circumstances.

PLANET: Jupiter is the planet of higher learning and philosophy. It signifies expansion, growth, and abundance. When Jupiter's influence is felt, things tend to magnify.

ELEMENT: Fire represents energy, creativity, and power. It is the realm of love, courage, and action. It is associated with Summer, the Suit of Wands, and the South cardinal direction.

HERMETIC QABALAH Associated Hebrew Letter: Kaph – Open Hand (Cover, Grasp)

TREE OF LIFE PATHWAY: 21st Path Between Chesed (Mercy) and Netzach (Victory)

11

JUSTICE

MAJOR ARCANA

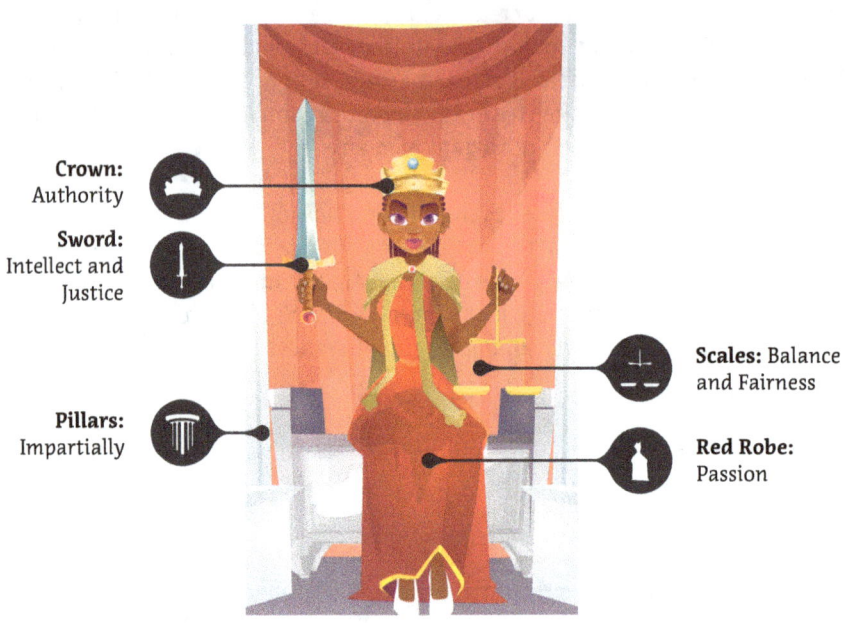

Crown: Authority

Sword: Intellect and Justice

Pillars: Impartially

Scales: Balance and Fairness

Red Robe: Passion

Yes/No Reading:

○ Yes   ○ No   ☑ *Maybe*

Names in Other Tarot Systems:
Golden Dawn: Justice
Tarot of Marseilles: Justice
Thoth: Adjustment

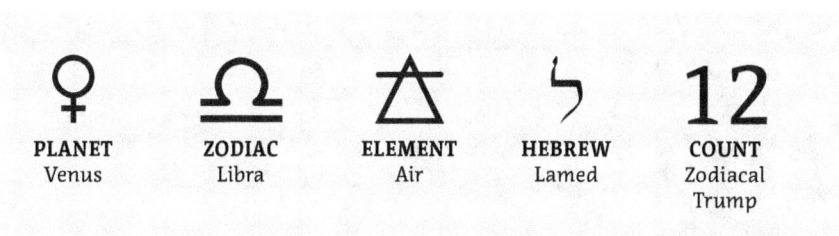

PLANET	ZODIAC	ELEMENT	HEBREW	COUNT
Venus	Libra	Air	Lamed	Zodiacal Trump

Upright: *Integrity, Truth, Fairness, Balance, Accountability, Law, Reality*
When the Justice card appears in a Tarot reading, it represents principles of honesty, balance, and the consequences of one's actions. The card suggests that decisions must be made with a thorough understanding of their repercussions and that actions have outcomes.

The Justice card often indicates that a legal dispute will end in the querent's favor or that a significant decision must be made after weighing all potential consequences. It encourages integrity and treating others with fairness. On a personal level, the Justice card implies that one is considering all aspects of a situation and emphasizes using both intuition and logic to guide decisions.

Above all, the card emphasizes the principle of fairness and the law of karma: one's actions will eventually have consequences.

Reversed: *Lack of Responsibility, Dishonesty, Corruption, Retaliation, Lies*
If the Justice card appears in reverse during a reading, it could indicate that an unjust decision, prejudice, or bias is affecting you or someone close to you.

Additionally, it could suggest that either you or someone else is attempting to evade responsibility or avoid facing the consequences of their actions. Should you find yourself involved in a legal matter, the reversed Justice card could indicate delays, setbacks, or an unfavorable verdict.

It is important to consider any internal or external imbalances that may be influencing your decision-making, as this card may signify that you are relying too heavily on emotion rather than logic. Reflect on whether your actions and decisions align with your values and if you are being truthful with yourself and others.

CHAKRA:
Heart

TIMING:
September 23 — October 22

NUMEROLOGY:
2, 11

ARCANA RELATION:
The High Priestess

DEITY:
Eid, Ma, Nemesis,
Themis, Vulcan

ANIMAL:
Elephant, Spider

CRYSTAL:
Ametrine, Aventurine, Cat's Eye,
Chrysolite, Chrysoprase, Coral,
Emerald, Green Tourmaline,
Jade, Jet, Peridot, Petrified
Wood, Tiger's Eye

PLANT:
Aloe, Garlic, Honeysuckle,
Plantain, Tobacco

MAGICKAL ITEM:
Copper Cauldron, Dove Feathers,
Geranium Essential Oil, Mirror

ARCHANGEL:
Anael, Jophiel

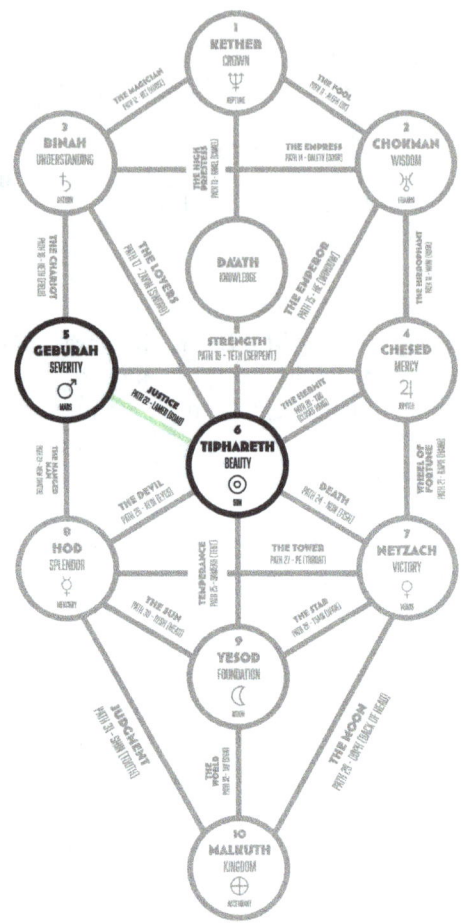

BLUE
Stability, Loyalty, Calm,
Peace, Emotion

GREEN
Balance, Fertility,
Growth, Harmony

The Justice card showcases a dignified figure, typically depicted as an individual, sitting gracefully on a throne. They represent the ideals of truth and impartiality, holding perfectly balanced scales in one hand to symbolize fairness and the importance of equilibrium in judgment. Their other hand clutches a double-edged sword pointing upwards, a representation of objective decision-making and an acknowledgment of the dual outcomes that can arise from any ruling.

This embodiment of Justice often adorns a crown adorned with a distinctive square, signifying the clarity and rationality required in rendering fair judgments. Clad in flowing robes of deep red or royal purple, they exude an unwavering passion for truth and command a regal presence.

The background features two grey pillars, reminiscent of those on the High Priestess card, which highlight the interplay between intuition and logic that is necessary for harmony and balance.

♎ **ZODIAC:** Libra (September 23 – October 22) is an Air sign ruled by Venus. Libras often strive for harmony and balance in their lives.

♀ **PLANET:** Venus primarily governs love, harmony, and affection in relationships. It rules over our sentiments, what we value in romantic partnerships, and how we express affection.

△ **ELEMENT:** Air represents logic, intellect, and communication. The intangible element is considered to be active, masculine energy. It is associated with Spring, the Suit of Wands, and the East cardinal direction.

ל **HERMETIC QABALAH** Associated Hebrew Letter: Lamed – Goad, Staff (Prod, Tongue)

TREE OF LIFE PATHWAY: 22nd Path Between Geburah (Power) and Tiphareth (Beauty)

12

THE HANGED MAN

M A J O R   A R C A N A

Bound Foot:
Balance Between
the Physical
and Spiritual

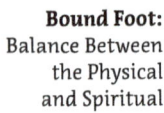

Position:
Unifying the
Spiritual and
Material Worlds

Halo:
Holiness

Yes/No Reading:

Yes ○   No ○   Maybe ☑

Yes *No* *Maybe*

Names in Other Tarot Systems:

Golden Dawn: The Hanged Man
Tarot of Marseilles: Le Pandu
Thoth: The Hanged Man

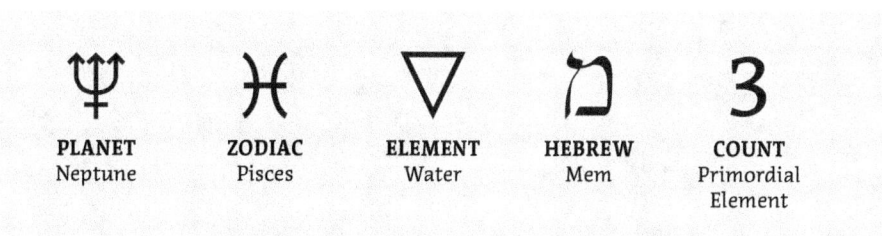

PLANET	ZODIAC	ELEMENT	HEBREW	COUNT
Neptune	Pisces	Water	Mem	Primordial Element

Upright: *Perspective, Sacrifice, Surrender, Metamorphosis, Suspension*
The Hanged Man indicates that you may be in a situation where nothing seems to be moving, and it's a time to pause, reflect, and gain clarity. Rather than pushing forward, it is an opportune moment to pause and reflect, gaining clarity and assessing your current position. During this voluntary non-action period, you may find it helpful to let go of old patterns and beliefs that no longer serve you. Surrendering to the natural flow of life, even if it feels counterintuitive, can offer fresh insights and new perspectives.

Emulating the Hanged Man, you may consider making a temporary sacrifice or giving up certain comforts in exchange for greater understanding or long-term rewards. Although it may feel like stagnation or delay, remember that this pause can be beneficial. Allow things to unfold naturally instead of forcing decisions or actions, and you may be surprised at the positive outcomes that follow.

Reversed: *Burnout, Ego, Resistant to Change, Stalling, Apathy, Confusion*
When the Hanged Man is reversed, it can signify a reluctance to accept necessary changes or sacrifices. This resistance may stem from a fear of letting go of old habits and patterns, despite recognizing their potential for transformation. There may be a tendency to avoid introspection or reject alternate perspectives, due to discomfort with facing the truth about oneself. If you've been waiting for a particular event or outcome, the reversed Hanged Man can suggest mounting frustration over delays or unfulfilled expectations.

However, instead of taking a passive approach, the reversed Hanged Man urges taking proactive steps. Overthinking or excessive analysis can impede progress. Additionally, it may indicate that current actions or decisions don't align with personal beliefs and values, prompting a reassessment of choices to better reflect one's true self.

CHAKRA:
Crown

TIMING:
Undetermined

NUMEROLOGY:
3, 12

ARCANA RELATION:
The Empress

DEITY:
Attis, Artemis, Buddha, Ishtar,
Jesus, Persophone, Odin, Osiris

ANIMAL:
Eagle, Scorpion, Snake

CRYSTAL:
Aquamarine, Aquamarine,
Beryl, Lepidolite, Moss Agate,
Tiger's Eye

PLANT:
Ash, Grape, Ivy, Kelp, Lotus,
Marigold, Valerian, Water Plants

MAGICKAL ITEM:
Conch, Cross of Suffering,
Crystal Ball, Cup, Trident, Wine

ARCHANGEL:
N/A

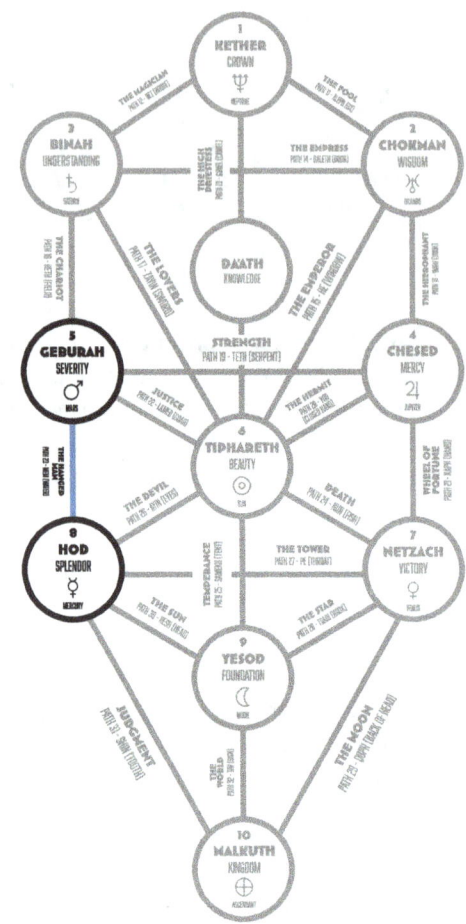

WHITE
Beginning, Humility,
Purity

SEA GREEN
Renewal,
Fluidity

INDIGO
Emotion, Fluidity,
Expressiveness

At the core of the Hanged Man card lies a captivating feature: a person who is suspended upside-down in a precarious position, yet still appears tranquil, often encompassed by a halo or radiant light signifying enlightenment or a newfound perspective. This suspended figure represents sacrifice, particularly the act of sacrificing oneself for a higher purpose or to attain greater comprehension.

One of the person's legs is securely fastened to a crossbeam, while the other is bent at a right angle, creating a shape that evokes the number 4. This pose embodies introspection and deep reflection. Depending on the deck, the Hanged Man's arms may be positioned behind their back or forming a triangular shape with their head, underscoring the themes of sacrifice and spiritual perception.

The backdrop of the card differs depending on the deck, with some featuring a plain background indicating solitude, while others depict foliage that implies growth and transformation through self-sacrifice.

♓ **ZODIAC:** Pisces (February 19 – March 20) is a Water sign ruled by Neptune. Pisceans are known for their emotional depth and keen intuition.

♆ **PLANET:** Neptune governs the realm of dreams, fantasies, and illusions. It blurs the lines between reality and the ethereal, making it hard to distinguish between what's tangible and what's imagined.

▽ **ELEMENT:** Water rules emotions and is a symbol of healing, peace, dreams, and compassion. It is associated with Winter, the Suit of Cups, and the West cardinal direction.

מ **HERMETIC QABALAH** Associated Hebrew Letter: Mem – Water (Overpower, Reversal)

TREE OF LIFE PATHWAY: 23rd Path Between Geburah (Severity) and Hod (Splendor)

- 13 -
DEATH
M A J O R A R C A N A

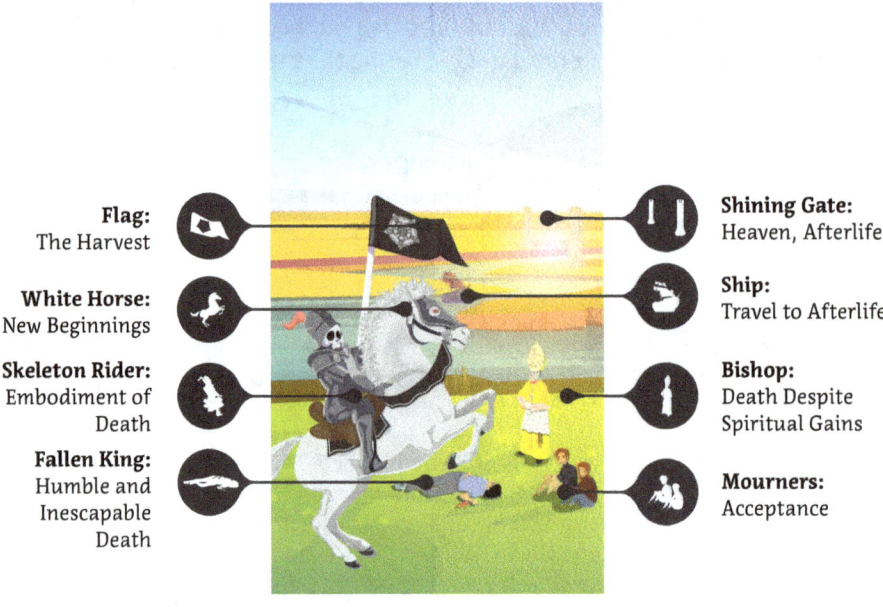

Flag:
The Harvest

White Horse:
New Beginnings

Skeleton Rider:
Embodiment of
Death

Fallen King:
Humble and
Inescapable
Death

Shining Gate:
Heaven, Afterlife

Ship:
Travel to Afterlife

Bishop:
Death Despite
Spiritual Gains

Mourners:
Acceptance

Yes/No Reading:

○   ☑   ○

Yes   *No*   *Maybe*

Names in Other Tarot Systems:
Golden Dawn: Death
Tarot of Marseilles: La Mort
Thoth: Death

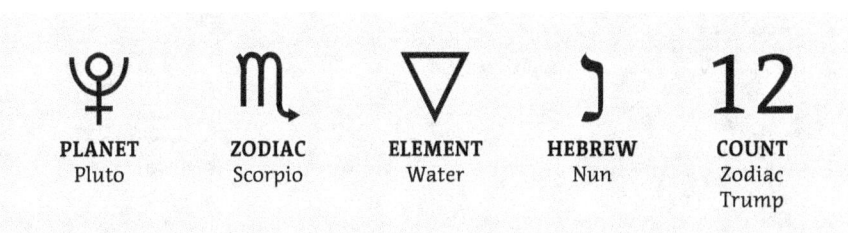

♇	♏	▽	כ	12
PLANET	**ZODIAC**	**ELEMENT**	**HEBREW**	**COUNT**
Pluto	Scorpio	Water	Nun	Zodiac Trump

Upright: *Change, Metamorphosis, Endings, New Beginnings, Transformation*
The upright Death card in the Tarot heralds a period of transformation, shifting circumstances, and the closure of a specific chapter in one's journey. This card underscores life's ever-changing rhythm.

When this card emerges in a reading, it suggests an impending transformational shift in your life. This could mark the conclusion of a relationship, the end of a known life phase, or a significant change in your worldviews. While the concept of "death" can evoke apprehension, in this context, it represents renewal and a chance to start anew.

Life, like the seasons, is cyclical and change is a crucial component of personal growth and evolution. The Death card implies a need to release obsolete beliefs, patterns, or relationships. This process opens up space for fresh perspectives, new experiences, and personal growth.

Reversed: *Resistance, Blocked, Depression, Illness, Fear of Change, Stagnation*
When the Death card appears reversed, it implies an aversion to change and a reluctance to let go of past beliefs and situations. There may be a fear of the unknown that prompts one to hold onto what's familiar, even if it no longer serves a purpose.

The card's position suggests a necessary transformation, yet one may feel stuck or uncertain about what steps to take. Despite outward appearances, inner growth and self-reflection may be occurring. Sometimes, this reversed card indicates a delay in an inevitable shift or conclusion.

Although this pause offers an opportunity for introspection, it's crucial not to prolong it unnecessarily. It's essential to remember that change is inevitable and that embracing it is necessary for growth.

CHAKRA:
Sacral

TIMING:
Within a month,
or Oct 23 – Nov 21

NUMEROLOGY:
4, 13

ARCANA RELATION:
The Emperor

DEITY:
Apep, Apollo, Ares, Khephra,
Mars, Thanatos, Typhon

ANIMAL:
Beetle, Crayfish, Lobster,
Scorpion, Shark, Wolf

CRYSTAL:
Amber, Black Tourmaline,
Bloodstone, Garnet, Jet,
Lodestone, Obsidian, Opal,
Ruby, Snakestone, Tiger's Eye

PLANT:
Aspen, Blackberry, Bramble,
Cactus, Elder Flowers, Myrtle,
Nettle, Periwinkle, Yew

MAGICKAL ITEM:
The Pain of the Obligation

ARCHANGEL:
Azrael, Jeremiel

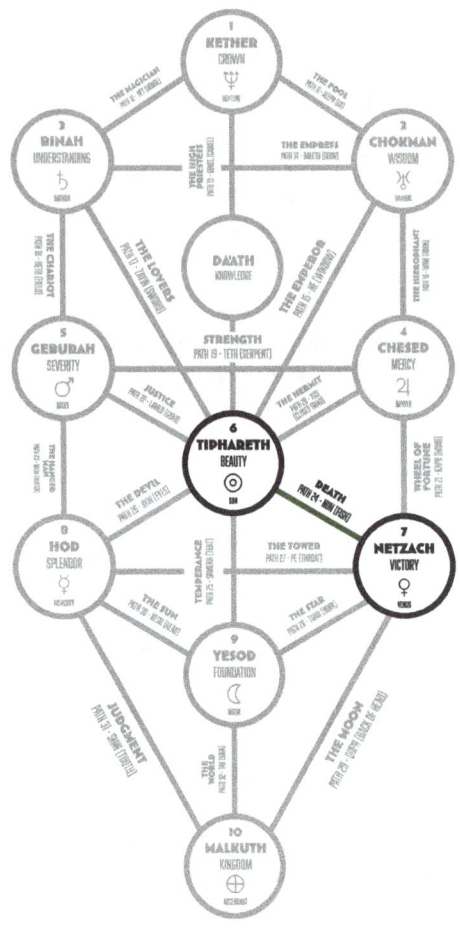

RED
Desire, Passion,
Power, Vitality

BLACK
Dignity, Force,
Stability, Protection

PURPLE
Spirituality, Wisdom,
Peace, Idealism

BROWN
Endurance, Solidity,
Grounding, Strength

The Death card in the Tarot deck is an iconic but commonly misconstrued card. Despite its eerie reputation, it rarely represents actual death. Rather, it symbolizes profound transformations, endings, and new beginnings.

Visually, the Death card displays a skeletal figure riding on a horse and advancing forward. The skeleton, stripped of all superficial layers, embodies the most basic and inevitable aspect of human existence: mortality. The horse, usually white, signifies purity and the unstoppable flow of time and life. In some versions, the rider carries a black flag adorned with a white, five-petaled rose, representing beauty, purification, and immortality.

Surrounding the skeletal figure, other characters of various social statuses are often depicted, emphasizing the universality of death. In the background, the card may display a rising sun, a ship sailing on water, or two towers, signifying the cyclicality of life and the promise of continuity after every ending. The Death card conveys not fear but rather acceptance, transformation, and the natural rhythms of life and death.

♏ **ZODIAC:** Scorpio (October 23 – November 21) is a Water sign ruled by Pluto. Scorpios are known for their intensity and depth.

♇ **PLANET:** Pluto is named after the Roman god of the underworld. Its characteristics and influences are associated with deep transformation, rebirth, and the unseen depths of the psyche.

▽ **ELEMENT:** Water rules emotions and is a symbol of healing, peace, dreams, and compassion. It is associated with Winter, the Suit of Cups, and the West cardinal direction.

ℶ **HERMETIC QABALAH** Associated Hebrew Letter: Nun – Fruit, Fish (Sprouting, Activity, Life)

✺ **TREE OF LIFE PATHWAY:** 24th Path Between Tiphareth (Beauty) and Netzach (Victory)

14

TEMPERANCE

MAJOR ARCANA

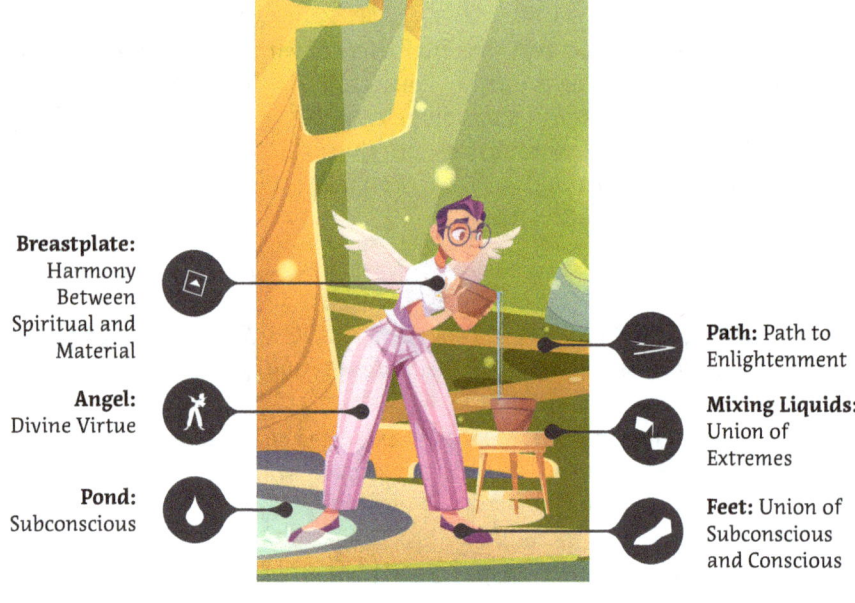

Breastplate: Harmony Between Spiritual and Material

Angel: Divine Virtue

Pond: Subconscious

Path: Path to Enlightenment

Mixing Liquids: Union of Extremes

Feet: Union of Subconscious and Conscious

Yes/No Reading:

Yes ☑   No ○   Maybe ○

Names in Other Tarot Systems:

Golden Dawn: Temperance
Tarot of Marseilles: Tempérance
Thoth: Art

♃	♐	△	ס	12
PLANET	**ZODIAC**	**ELEMENT**	**HEBREW**	**COUNT**
Jupiter	Sagittarius	Fire	Samekh	Zodiac Trump

Upright: *Peace, Calm, Moderation, Patience, Alchemy, Balance, Tranquility*
When the Temperance card appears upright, it suggests a period where balance is achieved or necessary in your life. It indicates that you are learning or need to blend different elements in your life harmoniously. This card often points to the importance of compromise and finding the middle ground in disagreements or conflicts. The card also speaks to the virtue of patience, hinting that through measured steps and moderation, you can achieve your goals. It may also reflect a current state of inner peace and serenity, regardless of any external tumult.

Temperance encourages self-control and restraint, steering away from extremes. It can indicate the successful merging of opposites in your life, like work and play or logic and emotion. In relationships, the card can mean harmonious partnerships and the balance of giving and taking. In terms of health, it can point to healing and the restoration of balance in the body and mind.

Reversed: *Extremes, Recklessness, Disruption, Chaos, Excess, Lack of Balance*
The reversed Temperance card suggests that you may be struggling to find middle ground or harmony in certain aspects of your life. Whether it's within relationships, work, or personal habits, there's a tendency toward extremes rather than finding a balanced approach. It can also indicate a possible resistance to change or an unwillingness to adapt, which can further hinder the process of finding balance. In some instances, the card might suggest that you are juggling too many things at once, leading to stress or overwhelm.

In relationships, reversed Temperance might hint at conflicts arising from a lack of compromise or understanding. Both parties might be stubborn, unwilling to bend or see the other's viewpoint. From a health perspective, this card can warn against overindulgence, whether it's in food, drink, or other habits, suggesting that moderation is key to well-being.

CHAKRA:
Crown, Third Eye, Heart

TIMING:
November 22 — December 21

NUMEROLOGY:
5, 14

ARCANA RELATION:
The Hierophant

DEITY:
Iris, Maat, Trivia

ANIMAL:
Dog, Centaur, Hippogriff, Horse

CRYSTAL:
Amethyst, Diamond, Golden
Topaz, Jacinth, Sapphire

PLANT:
Agrimony, Echinacea, Foxglove,
Kunzite, Rush, Valerian

MAGICKAL ITEM:
Arrow, Book of Shadows

ARCHANGEL:
Raguel, Sachiel

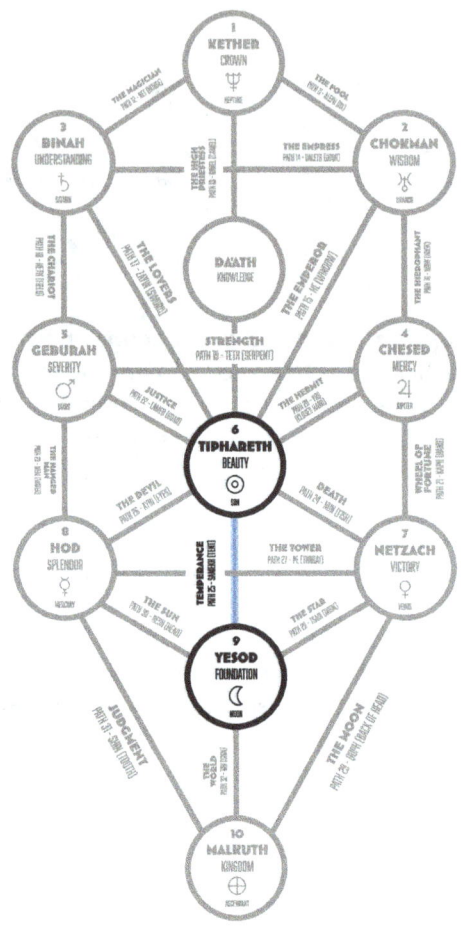

RED
Desire, Passion,
Power, Vitality

INDIGO
Emotion, Fluidity,
Expressiveness

PURPLE
Spirituality, Wisdom,
Peace, Idealism

GOLD
Inner Strength,
Understanding

The Temperance card emphasizes the significance of balance and harmony in life. It prompts the seeker to embrace moderation, steer clear of extremes, and strive for equilibrium in all endeavors. Central to this card is an androgynous angel, poised with one foot on land and the other in water, capturing the essence of balance between the tangible and intangible realms. This angel is often portrayed transferring fluid from one vessel to another, a symbolic gesture of energy equilibrium and the blending of opposites.

In the backdrop, a pathway stretches towards a distant mountain crowned by a radiant sun or emblem, an allegory for the long quest towards enlightenment or spiritual fulfillment. The wings of the angel allude to divine communications and celestial realms. In some artistic renditions, a triangle graces the angel's brow, embodying the spirit and divine connectivity.

ZODIAC: Sagittarius (November 22 – December 21) is a Fire sign ruled by Jupiter. Sagittarians are often seen as the optimists of the zodiac, always looking at the brighter side of life.

PLANET: Jupiter is the planet of higher learning and philosophy. It signifies expansion, growth, and abundance. When Jupiter's influence is felt, things tend to magnify.

ELEMENT: Fire represents energy, creativity, and power. It is the realm of love, courage, and action. It is associated with Summer, the Suit of Wands, and the South cardinal direction.

HERMETIC QABALAH Associated Hebrew Letter: Samekh – Tent, Prop (Support, Doctrine)

TREE OF LIFE PATHWAY: 25th Path Between Tiphareth (Beauty) and Yesod (Foundation)

15

THE DEVIL

MAJOR ARCANA

Priestly Blessing Hand Gesture: Benevolence

Inverted Pentacle: Dark Occultism

Human Poses: Subservience

Chains: Choice in Imprisonment

Black Box: The Unknown

Tails: Lust and Drunkenness

Yes/No Reading:

○   ✓   ○
Yes   *No*   *Maybe*

Names in Other Tarot Systems:
Golden Dawn: The Devil
Tarot of Marseilles: Le Diable
Thoth: The Devil

♄	♑	▽	ע	12
PLANET	**ZODIAC**	**ELEMENT**	**HEBREW**	**COUNT**
Saturn	Capricorn	Earth	Ayin	Zodiac Trump

Upright: *Addiction, Limitations, Obsession, Secrecy, Envy, Temptation, Fear*
The upright Devil card is a powerful symbol of temptation and the allure of material wealth, serving as a reminder of the seductive nature of all physical and emotional desires. Overindulging in habits, substances, or relationships can lead to bondage, and not just in the physical sense. Emotional dependencies and behaviors can also hold you back from personal growth.

The Devil card delves into the realm of the shadow self, bringing to light the aspects of one's psyche that is often suppressed. These can be dark desires, repressed emotions, or deep-seated fears that you struggle to confront. Acknowledging these parts of yourself is the first step towards healing.

Moreover, the Devil card warns against placing emphasis on material pleasures and instant gratification at the expense of spiritual growth and deeper connections. It prompts one to reflect on their priorities and consider whether they're sacrificing long-term fulfillment for short-term gains. It reminds to find a more balanced and holistic approach to life and avoid being blinded by materialism.

Reversed: *Independence, Release, Recovery, Restoring Control, Revelation*
The reversed Devil symbolizes liberation from restrictions and boundaries. What were once seemingly unbreakable chains now appear feeble, marking a newfound sense of freedom from past dependencies, unhealthy relationships, and self-imposed limitations. This position signifies a time of self-liberation and empowerment, as individuals come to terms with the restraints they've been held back by and actively strive to free themselves.

After confronting one's darker side and the allure of temptations, there comes a phase of enlightenment where individuals acknowledge the power of their own decisions. By taking the time to reflect and confront their fears, cravings, and harmful habits, they emerge with a better understanding of their true selves, prepared to make healthier choices in the future.

CHAKRA:
Root

TIMING:
December 22 – January 19

NUMEROLOGY:
6, 15

ARCANA RELATION:
The Lovers

DEITY:
Lilith, Bacchus, Baphomet,
Dionysus, Lucifer,
Mephistopheles, Pan,
The Morrigan, Satan

ANIMAL:
Ass, Goat, Oyster

CRYSTAL:
Apache Tears, Black Diamond,
Black Garnet, Black Onyx,
Hematite, Jet, Malachite,
Obsidian, Tektite,
Tourmaline, Turquoise

PLANT:
Carnation, Fig, Indian Hemp,
Lobelia, Marijuana, Mugwort,
Orris Root, Rosemary,
Thistle, Yohimba

MAGICKAL ITEM:
Patchouli

ARCHANGEL:
Azrael, Cassiel

GREY
Stability, Neutrality,
Reserve

INDIGO
Emotion, Fluidity,
Expressiveness

BLACK
Dignity, Force,
Stability, Protection

RED
Desire, Passion,
Power, Vitality

The Devil card is an impactful and evocative image, inciting strong emotional responses. This card often portrays a towering, horned devil sitting on a throne, observing two chained individuals, usually a man and a woman. This imposing creature represents temptation, materialism, bondage, and the darker aspects of humanity that lead to excess and addiction.

The figures chained at the card's base symbolize the consequences of surrendering to temptations or allowing primal instincts to govern one's actions. Their chains indicate their self-imposed captivity, signifying the feelings of entrapment, addiction, or unhealthy attachments one may face. However, a closer examination reveals that the chains are loose, indicating that one can escape such bondage with sufficient self-awareness and determination.

The card's overall dark palette, with its deep blacks, browns, and fiery reds, creates a sense of foreboding. The torch held by the Devil, often pointing downward, suggests the illumination of the underworld and the inversion of spiritual enlightenment. The barren, fiery background, void of any life or vegetation, speaks to the destructive nature of unchecked passions and the potential desolation that can result from being consumed by materialism and base desires.

ZODIAC: Capricorn (December 22 – January 19) is an Earth sign ruled by Saturn. Capricorns are known for their grounded, pragmatic approach, and are often focused on tangible outcomes.

PLANET: Saturn is often referred to as the "taskmaster" of the planets. It brings structure, discipline, and the boundaries that are necessary for both personal and societal functioning.

ELEMENT: Earth represents death and rebirth. It is the realm of abundance, prosperity, and wealth. It is associated with Autumn, the Suit of Pentacles, and the North cardinal direction.

HERMETIC QABALAH Associated Hebrew Letter: Ayin – Eyes (Experience, Knowledge)

TREE OF LIFE PATHWAY: 26th Path Between Tiphareth (Beauty) and Hod (Splendor)

16

THE TOWER

MAJOR ARCANA

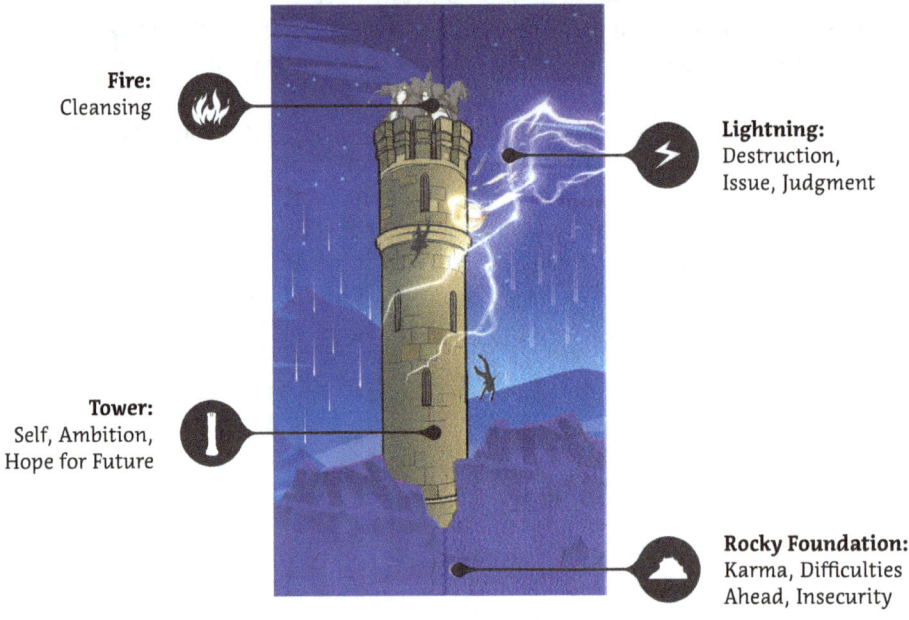

Fire:
Cleansing

Lightning:
Destruction,
Issue, Judgment

Tower:
Self, Ambition,
Hope for Future

Rocky Foundation:
Karma, Difficulties
Ahead, Insecurity

Yes/No Reading:

Yes *No* Maybe

Names in Other Tarot Systems:

Golden Dawn: The Tower
Tarot of Marseilles: La Maison Dieu
Thoth: The Tower

PLANET	ZODIAC	ELEMENT	HEBREW	COUNT
Mars		Fire	Pe	Planetary Trump

Upright: *Ruin, Trauma, Sudden Changes, Disgrace, Catastrophe, Destruction*
You may be undergoing a significant and unexpected change or disruption in your life, which can be disorienting and unsettling, particularly if you believed that everything was stable and secure. The Tower card serves as a reminder that sometimes shaky foundations need to collapse to make room for stronger structures, beliefs, or situations. The lightning bolt striking the tower represents a moment of clarity or epiphany, revealing truths that may have been hidden from view. It's a wake-up call.

Despite the apparent chaos and destruction, the Tower also brings some opportunities. Like a building that has been demolished to make way for new construction, situations that are dismantled in our lives often create space for fresh opportunities and growth that are more aligned with our true selves. Although the initial impact can be daunting or surprising, the long-term effects often lead to positive growth. The key is to find the strength and resilience to rebuild from the ruins.

Reversed: *Rebuilding Foundations, Illness, Fear of Suffering, Avoiding Disaster*
When the Tower card is reversed, the disruption and chaos that it usually signifies may not be as severe or might be contained within oneself. There's a feeling of unease or anxiety about potential upheaval, and you might be trying to avoid the inevitable.

In contrast to the upright Tower, which is typically associated with external circumstances, the inverted Tower signifies internal transformation and change. You may be grappling with profound realizations or facing deep-seated personal fears. Although it can be unsettling, this process presents an opportunity for personal growth and development.

In this position, the card is a prompt to confront and accept the necessary changes, rather than trying to resist or delay them.

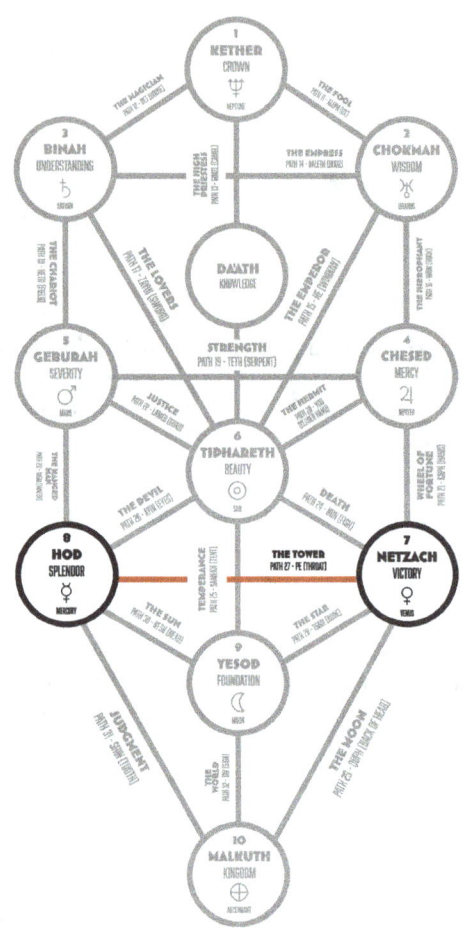

CHAKRA:
Solar Plexus, Root

TIMING:
Unexpectedly

NUMEROLOGY:
7, 16

ARCANA RELATION:
The Chariot

DEITY:
Athene, Ares, Horus

ANIMAL:
Bear, Boar, Horse, Wolf

CRYSTAL:
Bloodstone, Chrysocolla,
Garnet, Hematite, Lodestone,
Magnetite, Ruby

PLANT:
Heather Honeysuckle, Garlic,
Tobacco, Rue, Wormwood,
Yarrow

MAGICKAL ITEM:
Sword

ARCHANGEL:
Camael

GREY
Stability, Neutrality,
Reserve

EMERALD
Renewal, Balance,
Foundations

BLACK
Dignity, Force,
Stability, Protection

RED
Desire, Passion,
Power, Vitality

The Tower presents a striking scene of dramatic upheaval. Central to its imagery is a lofty tower, standing high on a craggy mountain's peak, symbolizing ambitions or constructs that once felt invincible and untouchable. Without warning, a bolt of lightning fiercely strikes the tower, causing windows to erupt in flames and indicating a divine or unexpected intervention. This sudden force leads to chaos as figures, once secure within the tower's walls, now find themselves in free fall, a powerful representation of unforeseen changes and disruptions.

The tower's foundation, assumed to be the strongest part, seems to be collapsing or fracturing, creating a vivid image of outdated beliefs, ideologies, or life situations built on weak ground. This chaos occurs under a brooding sky, heavy with dark clouds, emphasizing unexpected challenges and the need to confront and rebuild.

This tumultuous atmosphere highlights the profound disruption and transformation that the card represents, indicating that sometimes, we need a stark shake-up to progress and grow.

PLANET: Mars primarily governs energy, drive, and ambition. Mars is about starting new things, taking the initiative, and pioneering efforts. It's also associated with with sexual attraction and raw physical energy.

ELEMENT: Fire represents energy, creativity, and power. It is the realm of love, courage, and action. It is associated with Summer, the Suit of Wands, and the South cardinal direction.

HERMETIC QABALAH Associated Hebrew Letter: Pe – Throat, Mouth (Speak, Word)

TREE OF LIFE PATHWAY: 27th Path Between Hod (Splendor) and Netzach (Victory)

- 17 -
THE STAR
MAJOR ARCANA

8-Pointed Star: Purity

7 Stars: Direction, 7 Chakras

Water Vessels: Conscious and Subconscious

Nude Person: Freedom, Peace

Falling Water: Cycle of Life, Hope, Renewal

Yes/No Reading:

☑   ◯   ◯
Yes   *No*   *Maybe*

Names in Other Tarot Systems:
Golden Dawn: The Star
Tarot of Marseilles: Le Toile (L'Étoile)
Thoth: The Star

			ץ	12
PLANET	**ZODIAC**	**ELEMENT**	**HEBREW**	**COUNT**
Uranus	Aquarius	Air	Tsadi	Zodiac Trump

Upright: *Good Health, Inspiration, Renewal, Faith, Serenity, Opportunity, Hope*
When this card appears upright in a reading, it is regarded as a positive sign, indicating an upcoming period of healing and tranquility. It promises that despite past darkness, a new dawn is on the horizon, bringing inspiration, optimism, and rejuvenation. This is a time to have faith in the universe and anticipate the goodness that lies ahead.

During this phase, one may experience deep intuition and inner clarity, where their spiritual guidance and inner voice can guide them to the right path. Just like the figure pouring water, this card suggests a harmonious giving and receiving, a flow of emotional and spiritual sustenance. The act of pouring water also symbolizes generosity, indicating a time when you may be called to give selflessly or receive kindness from others.

Reversed: *Despair, Hopelessness, Disappointment, Illness, Disconnection*
You could be going through a phase where things are not going according to plan and there is a struggle to have faith in a higher power or the universe. This can cause uncertainty or feelings of spiritual isolation, as previously solid spiritual beliefs might now be in flux. The reversed Star suggests that this innate wisdom is being ignored or mistrusted, potentially leading you away from your intended path.

In addition, there might be an excessive focus on personal challenges, hindering your ability to see the bigger picture or the external resources that could be available to you. This pessimistic outlook could become a self-fulfilling prophecy if negative anticipations are continually harbored and acted upon. The reversed Star can impede the rejuvenation and smooth transitions represented by the upright Star, indicating obstacles in overcoming past wounds or adversities.

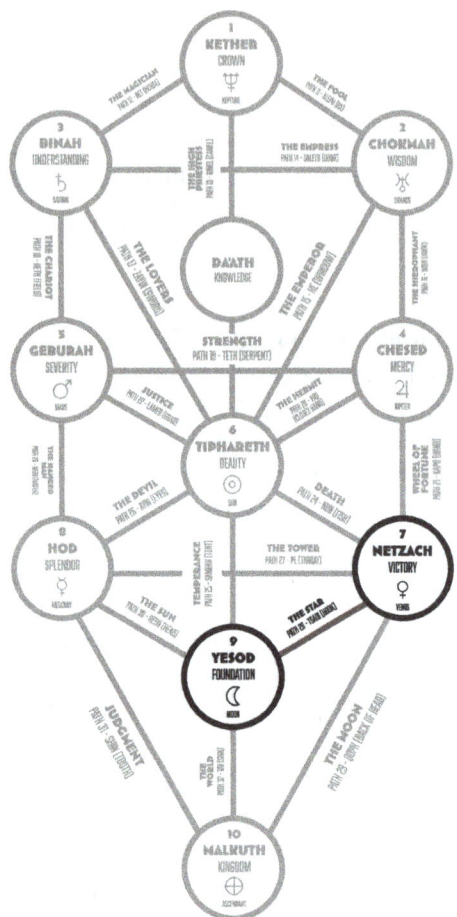

CHAKRA:
Crown

TIMING:
January 20 – February 18

NUMEROLOGY:
8, 17

ARCANA RELATION:
Strength

DEITY:
Aeolus, Ahephi,
Ganymede, Juno

ANIMAL:
Eagle, Man

CRYSTAL:
Azurite, Chalcedony, Moldavite,
Quartz, Sodalite, Sugulite,
Tektite, Turquoise

PLANT:
Bluebell, Coconut, Daisy, Olive,
Rose, Silver Fir, Skullcap

MAGICKAL ITEM:
Aspergillus, Censer

ARCHANGEL:
Cassiel, Uriel

BLUE
Stability, Loyalty,
Calm, Peace, Emotion

VIOLET
Wisdom,
Spirituality

LIGHT BLUE
Reliability, Trust,
Security

The Star card features a bare figure kneeling gracefully by a peaceful water body, with one foot touching the water to symbolize intuition and the psyche, and the other grounded on solid land to represent reality and the physical world. The figure holds two containers from which water flows seamlessly into the land and water below, depicting the harmonious relationship between dreams and tangible existence, and exemplifying healing, rejuvenation, and life's perpetual rhythm.

Above the figure is an expanse of sky adorned with numerous stars, with one eight-pointed star shining brilliantly in the center, surrounded by seven more modest stars that may allude to the seven Chakras or the seven celestial bodies in astrology. These steadfast stars represent hope, aspirations, and guidance from the heavens.

Although other elements like birds and trees may appear in the background, the starry sky remains the card's primary focus, evoking a serene atmosphere and inspiring feelings of renewal, tranquility, and limitless potential.

ZODIAC: Aquarius (January 20 – February 18) is an Earth sign ruled by Saturn. Capricorns are known for their grounded, pragmatic approach, and are often focused on tangible outcomes.

PLANET: Uranus is associated with sudden change, rebellion, and revolution. Uranus symbolizes the concept of enlightenment, where a flash of insight disrupts previously held beliefs.

ELEMENT: Air represents logic, intellect, and communication. The intangible element is considered to be active, masculine energy. It is associated with Spring, the Suit of Wands, and the East cardinal direction.

HERMETIC QABALAH Associated Hebrew Letter: Tsadi – Hook (Honesty, Harvest)

TREE OF LIFE PATHWAY: 28th Path Between Netzach (Victory) and Yesod (Foundation)

THE MOON

M A J O R   A R C A N A

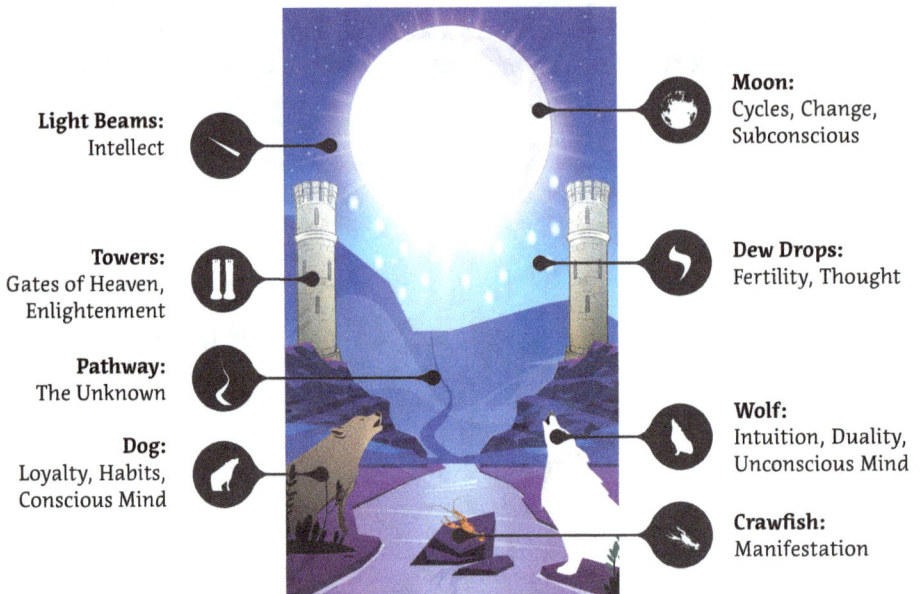

Light Beams:
Intellect

Towers:
Gates of Heaven,
Enlightenment

Pathway:
The Unknown

Dog:
Loyalty, Habits,
Conscious Mind

Moon:
Cycles, Change,
Subconscious

Dew Drops:
Fertility, Thought

Wolf:
Intuition, Duality,
Unconscious Mind

Crawfish:
Manifestation

Yes/No Reading:

○   ☑   ○

Yes   *No*   *Maybe*

Names in Other Tarot Systems:
Golden Dawn: The Moon
Tarot of Marseilles: La Lune
Thoth: The Moon

		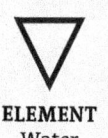		12
PLANET	**ZODIAC**	**ELEMENT**	**HEBREW**	**COUNT**
Neptune	Pisces	Water	Qoph	Zodiac Trump

Upright: *Illusion, Secrets, Unconscious, Risk, Intuition, Caution, Confusion*
The Moon stands tall as a beacon of intuition, dreams, and the subconscious. With the pale moon at the forefront, it illuminates an otherworldly scene that hints at a hidden reality beneath the surface. This card encourages individuals to trust their inner wisdom, especially when faced with uncertainty and ambiguity. Despite the absence of the sun's clarity, the moon's gentle glow reminds us that we possess an internal compass to guide us.

Below the moon lies a tranquil pool that reflects its light, representing the depths of our subconscious mind. A crayfish emerges from these waters, representing the surfacing of primal emotions and instincts that we often ignore. Acknowledging these hidden aspects of our psyche can offer invaluable insights into our true selves.

While we may encounter unforeseen challenges and illusions, The Moon card reminds us that tuning into our emotional and intuitive faculties can help us navigate these complexities with heightened awareness and discernment.

Reversed: *Misinterpretation, Uncertainty, Fear, Repressed Emotion, Mysteries*
This typically heralds a period of enlightenment, signifying a departure from confusion, delusions, or misunderstandings. It indicates that the fog of uncertainty is lifting, revealing clearer insights and truths. The shadows and misconceptions that clouded judgment during the Moon's upright position are beginning to fade, making way for enhanced comprehension and illumination.

Yet, this card in its reversed form can also point to a reluctance to trust one's intuition or a failure to address internal fears and doubts. It might highlight a pattern of disregarding intuitive insights, dreams, or emotional realities. Such evasion could stem from an unwillingness to confront harsh truths or from profound insecurities that undermine self-belief. It could suggest that there is a tendency to overlook or suppress psychic messages, dreams, or emotional truths.

CHAKRA:
Third Eye

TIMING:
February 19 – March 20

NUMEROLOGY:
9, 18

ARCANA RELATION:
The Hermit

DEITY:
Artemis, Chandra, Chang Xi,
Diana, Hecate, Hermes, Igaluk,
Khephra, Lona, Luna, Mayari,
Máni, Neptune, Poseidon,
Selene, Tsukuyomi, iNyanga

ANIMAL:
Crayfish, Dog, Dolphin, Jackal,
Rabbit

CRYSTAL:
Ammonite, Labradorite,
Moonstone, Pearl, Selenite

PLANT:
Cinquefoil, Eucalyptus, Lemon
Balm, Lotus, Mangrove,
Mugwort, Opium, Poppy,
Rose, Sandalwood, Unicellular
Organisms, Willow Bark

MAGICKAL ITEM:
Ambergris, Mirror, Twilight

ARCHANGEL:
Sachiel, Sandalphon

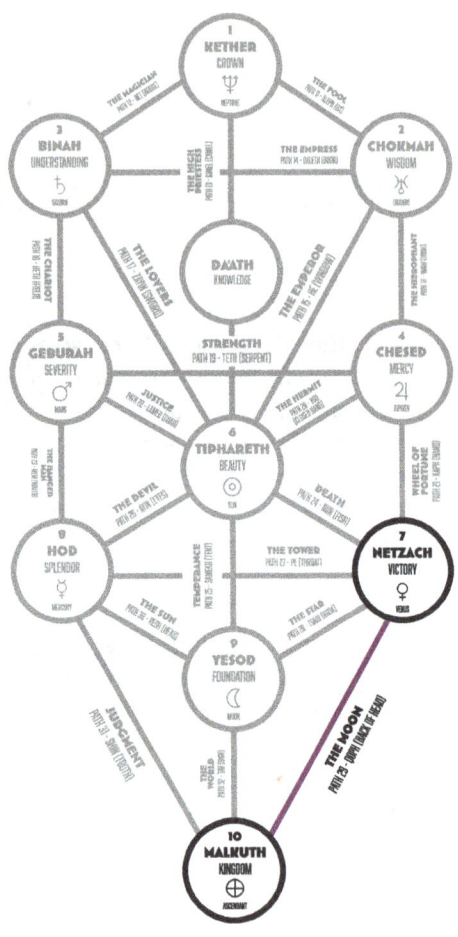

CRIMSON
Courage, Vigor,
Love, Affection

VIOLET-RED
Sensitivity,
Spirituality

LIGHT BLUE
Reliability, Trust,
Security

PURPLE
Spirituality, Wisdom,
Peace, Idealism

The Moon evokes a world of mystery, illusion, and the subconscious. Dominating the card is a large, pale moon, often featuring a face, casting a silvery, dim light over the scene below. This celestial body symbolizes emotions, instincts, and the ever-shifting realm of dreams and intuition.

Nestled below is a serene body of water, either a tranquil pond or a flowing stream, reflecting the moon's glow. A crayfish or lobster emerges from this water, representing primal instincts and emotions surfacing from the depths of our unconscious. On either side of a serpentine path departing from the water, two canines raise their voices in a howl. They serve as symbols of our untamed nature, primal fears, and the raw, instinctual side of humanity, which often reacts to the intangible pull of the moon.

The path, representing life's journey, winds towards the horizon, leading the viewer's eyes towards two distant towers and a range of mountains. These towers stand as gateways or barriers between known and unknown realms, while the mountains signify challenges or higher understanding. This card, with its dreamlike landscape, calls on us to delve deep into the realms of our psyche, confront illusions, and trust our intuition amidst life's uncertainties.

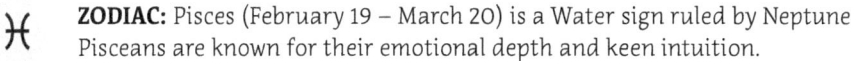 **ZODIAC:** Pisces (February 19 – March 20) is a Water sign ruled by Neptune. Pisceans are known for their emotional depth and keen intuition.

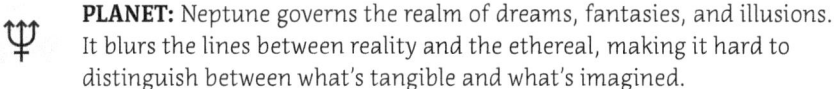 **PLANET:** Neptune governs the realm of dreams, fantasies, and illusions. It blurs the lines between reality and the ethereal, making it hard to distinguish between what's tangible and what's imagined.

ELEMENT: Water rules emotions and is a symbol of healing, peace, dreams, and compassion. It is associated with Winter, the Suit of Cups, and the West cardinal direction.

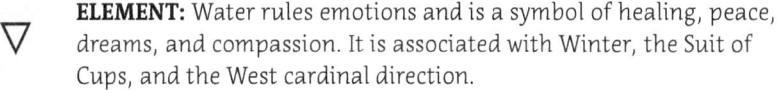 **HERMETIC QABALAH** Associated Hebrew Letter: Qoph – Back of Head (Hidden, Behind)

 **TREE OF LIFE PATHWAY:** 29th Path Between Netzach (Victory) and Malkuth (Kingdom)

- 19 -
THE SUN
MAJOR ARCANA

Sun: Consciousness

Red Flag: Passion, Strength

Child: Purity, Innocence, Enlightenment

Horse: Freedom, Life

Flowers: Vitality, Life, Joy

Yes/No Reading:

☑ ⭘ ⭘
Yes *No* *Maybe*

Names in Other Tarot Systems:
Golden Dawn: The Sun
Tarot of Marseilles: Le Soleil
Thoth: The Sun

PLANET	ZODIAC	ELEMENT	HEBREW	COUNT
Sun		Fire	Resh	Planetary Trump

Upright: *Joy, Authenticity, Success, Enlightenment, Marriage, Vitality*
With The Sun card appearing in an upright position, it is said that a period of abundance and success is on the horizon. After working towards your goals, this is a time for celebration and recognizing your achievements in various aspects of your life. This period will bring with it positive outcomes and an overall sense of fulfillment.

The brightness of The Sun shines on all, bringing clarity and truth to light. It dispels any doubts, confusion, or misunderstandings that you may have been experiencing, providing a fresh perspective that is free of any misconceptions. You'll gain insight and a clear understanding of your surroundings.

The Sun is the source of life and energy for our planet, and as such, The Sun card represents a surge of vitality and enthusiasm in your life. You will feel full of life, motivation, and energy, and your well-being will be overwhelming. This is a time when you are ready to tackle any challenges with a positive spirit.

Reversed: *Lack of Clarity, Sadness, Depression, Negativity, Mania*
When The Sun is in reverse, it may not radiate the same level of positive energy as it does in its upright position. Nonetheless, The Sun is inherently optimistic, so its reversal isn't entirely negative. There may be some minor hurdles or setbacks in your plans. Although the desired outcomes may be postponed, it's only temporary. The Sun's energy is still at play, albeit in a muted form, reminding you to persevere and not lose heart. You may not see a situation for what it is, possibly due to preconceived notions or being overly optimistic without considering the facts.

When The Sun card is reversed, its vibrant energy and confidence may wane. You may experience moments of self-doubt, feel out of sync with your surroundings, or have a dip in your overall mood. It could also signify a time when you're not recognizing or celebrating your achievements as much as you should.

CHAKRA:
Solar Plexus

TIMING:
Daytime or Summer

NUMEROLOGY:
1, 10, 19

ARCANA RELATION:
Wheel of Fortune,
The Magician

DEITY:
Alectrona, Amaterasu, Amun,
Anyanwu, Apollo, Bast, Hathor,
Helios, Icarus, Inti, Lucifer, Ra,
Sekhmet, Sopdu, Étaín

ANIMAL:
Leopard, Lion, Sparrowhawk

CRYSTAL:
Amber, Citrine, Crysolith, Pyrite,
Sunstone, Tiger's Eye, Yellow
Calcite

PLANT:
Angelica, Geranium, Heliotrope,
Laurel, Marigold, Nuts,
Sunflower

MAGICKAL ITEM:
Fire

ARCHANGEL:
Michael

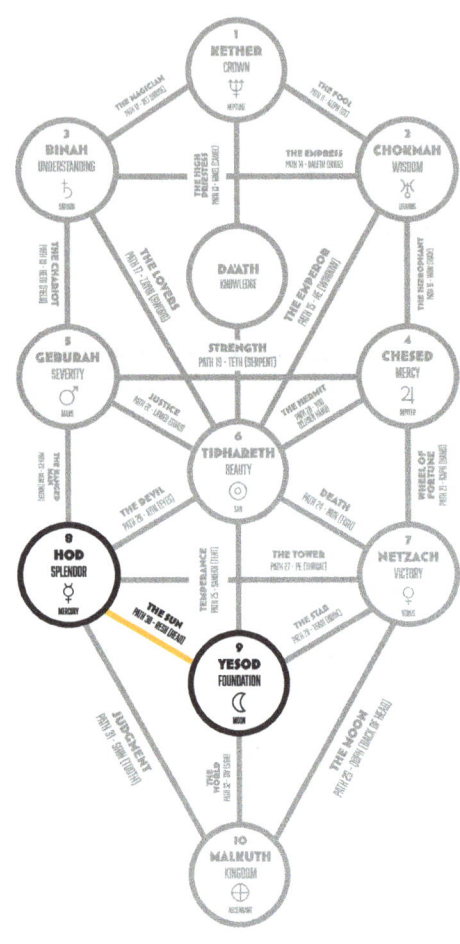

 YELLOW
Confidence, Joy,
Intellect, Optimism

 ORANGE
Energy, Vitality,
Stimulation

 AMBER
Warmth, Brilliance,
Optimism

 GOLD
Divinity, Generosity,
Compassion

The Sun card is centered around a luminous and expansive sun, which is often portrayed with a human visage. This brilliant sun exudes a constant and intense light, radiating beams in all directions. It's the embodiment of transparency, veracity, and the elimination of obscurity or ambiguity. Its omnipresence in the sky is indicative of universal truth and enlightenment.

A pristine and clear blue sky serves as the background to the sun, unencumbered by clouds. This clear sky signifies the absence of confusion, uncertainty, or impediments. Under the sun's bright and clarifying rays, everything is visible, promoting lucidity and candor.

A jubilant child often graces the foreground, mounted on a white horse in many depictions. The child may appear unadorned, symbolizing innocence, purity, and unrestrained liberty. This youthful figure epitomizes joy, simplicity, and an unburdened disposition. The white horse represents fortitude, beauty, and an advancing vitality. The card's illustrations sometimes incorporate sunflowers or other blooming flora, which orient themselves towards the sun. These blossoms epitomize development, vitality, and plenitude. They can also embody the human soul's rapport with a divine source.

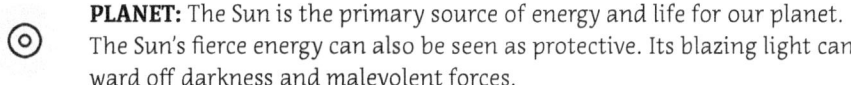 **PLANET:** The Sun is the primary source of energy and life for our planet. The Sun's fierce energy can also be seen as protective. Its blazing light can ward off darkness and malevolent forces.

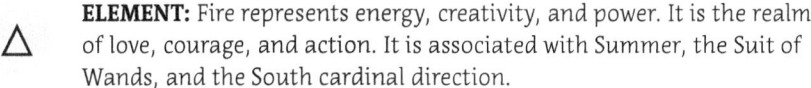 **ELEMENT:** Fire represents energy, creativity, and power. It is the realm of love, courage, and action. It is associated with Summer, the Suit of Wands, and the South cardinal direction.

 **HERMETIC QABALAH** Associated Hebrew Letter: Resh – Face (Redemption, Highest)

TREE OF LIFE PATHWAY: 30th Path Between Hod (Splendor) and Yesod (Foundation)

JUDGMENT

M A J O R   A R C A N A

Angel:
Wisdom,
Confidence

Trumpet:
Authority

Mountains:
End of Journey

Crowd:
Community,
Embracing Truth

Yes/No Reading:

Yes   No   Maybe

Names in Other Tarot Systems:
Golden Dawn: Judgment
Tarot of Marseilles: Le Jugement
Thoth: Æon

PLANET	ZODIAC	ELEMENT	HEBREW	COUNT
Pluto		Fire	Shin	Primordial Element

Upright: *Redemption, Rebirth, Awakening, Epiphany, Transition, Decisions*
The upright Judgment card signals a momentous occasion of inner awakening and self-realization. It is a time of rebirth, often following introspection and evaluation, encouraging you to release past regrets and embrace a new beginning. Pay attention to your heart's desires and your conscience's clarity as they offer insight.

Moreover, Judgment calls for self-examination and reflection. It invites you to take a moment to consider your past actions and decisions and understand their consequences. By acknowledging and learning from your past, you can make peace with it, offering forgiveness to both yourself and others where necessary. This card may also urge you to reconcile with something from your past, granting closure and allowing for personal growth.

The trumpet's sound on the card represents a higher calling or purpose, beckoning you towards your destiny. Judgment urges you to heed this inner call, whether it's a passion project, a spiritual journey, or a significant life change. Align with your authentic self and pursue what truly matters to you. Embrace this transformative moment, as it may shape the next chapter of your life.

Reversed: *Lacking Logic, Denial, Hasty Decisions, Criticism, Stunted Growth*
You may be facing unresolved issues, internal conflict, or an inability to come to terms with the past. This may lead to an avoidance of making essential decisions or resisting personal transformation. Past actions, regrets, self-doubt, and guilt may cloud your judgment and hinder progress, making it difficult to move forward.

The reversed Judgment card also points to fear of being judged by others, leading to self-imposed isolation or reluctance to confront societal scrutiny. Avoiding responsibility or deflecting issues perpetuates negative behavior cycles and stunts growth. Moreover, the reversed card may signify missed opportunities or ignoring a higher calling. To reconnect with your life's purpose, you must re-evaluate personal values, confront shadows, and be open to transformative powers.

CHAKRA:
Crown

TIMING:
None

NUMEROLOGY:
2, 20

ARCANA RELATION:
The High Priestess

DEITY:
Elohim, Hades, Horus,
Kabeshunt, Mau, Pluto,
Thoum-aesh-Neith,
Vulcan, Yahshuah

ANIMAL:
Lion, Sphinx

CRYSTAL:
Azurite, Black Diamond,
Fire Opal, Flourite, Hematite,
Kyanite, Labradorite, Malachite,
Meteorite, Moldavite,
Snowflake Obsidian

PLANT:
Goldenseal, Hibiscus, Marigold,
Red Poppy, Violet

MAGICKAL ITEM:
Pyramid of Fire, Wand,
Winged Egg

ARCHANGEL:
Gabriel, Michael

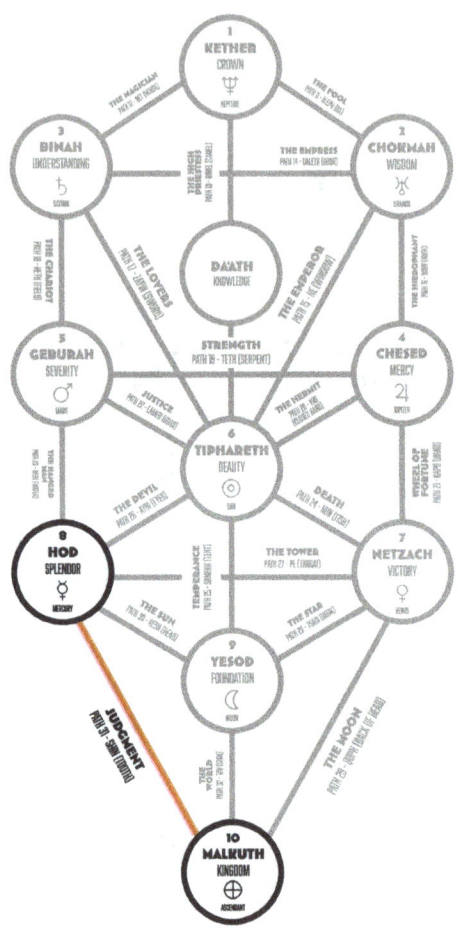

PURPLE
Spirituality, Wisdom,
Peace, Idealism

ORANGE
Energy, Vitality,
Stimulation

WHITE
Beginning, Humility,
Purity

GOLD
Divinity, Generosity,
Compassion

At the top of the card, an imposing angel—recognized as the Archangel Gabriel—dominates the space, boasting expansive wings and holding a trumpet aloft. Often attached to the trumpet is a flag adorned with a cross. Archangel Gabriel's trumpet signifies a higher calling, urging one to answer the divine or embrace a new path. The card can indicate a sense of redemption, or a fresh start after a period of upheaval.

Below the angel, a group of individuals rise from coffins that appear to be floating on water. Arms outstretched, they gaze in reverence towards the angel, embodying a sense of rebirth and awakening to a new purpose in life. In the far distance, the card depicts imposing mountains, sometimes covered in snow or with a bluish tint. The mountains, although they represent challenges, also signify transformation, suggesting that the journey ahead leads to higher enlightenment.

The primary theme of the Judgment card centers on resurrection, rebirth, and an inner calling. Those emerging from the coffins symbolize newfound purpose and direction, indicative of reflection, evaluation, and self-judgment.

 PLANET: Pluto is named after the Roman god of the underworld. Its characteristics and influences are associated with deep transformation, rebirth, and the unseen depths of the psyche.

 ELEMENT: Fire represents energy, creativity, and power. It is the realm of love, courage, and action. It is associated with Summer, the Suit of Wands, and the South cardinal direction.

 HERMETIC QABALAH Associated Hebrew Letter: Shin – Tooth (Consume, Destroy)

 TREE OF LIFE PATHWAY: 31st Path Between Hod (Splendor) and Malkuth (Kingdom)

- 21 -
THE WORLD
MAJOR ARCANA

Aquarius:
Guidance

Red Ribbon:
Cycle Completion

Scorpio:
Vision

Wreath:
Victory,
Cycles of Life

Wands:
Spiritual
Wisdom

Taurus:
Power

Leo:
Bravery

Yes/No Reading:

☑ Yes ○ No ○ Maybe

Names in Other Tarot Systems:
Golden Dawn: The World
Tarot of Marseilles: Le Monde
Thoth: The Universe

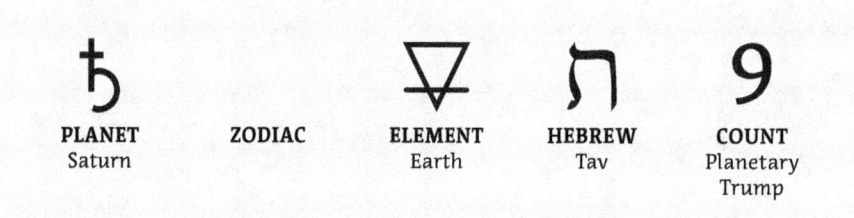

♄	▽	ת	9
PLANET	**ZODIAC**	**ELEMENT**	**HEBREW**	**COUNT**
Saturn		Earth	Tav	Planetary Trump

Upright: *Completion, Harmony, Filfillment, Accomplishment, Possibilities*
Drawing The World card in an upright position symbolizes completion, achievement, and celebration, marking the end of a journey that could be personal, emotional, or spiritual. This card represents gaining the knowledge and experiences needed to move forward with a sense of understanding and fulfillment.

The World also represents unity and wholeness, signifying a balance between the spiritual and physical realms. This card indicates enlightenment and everything falling into place, leaving a feeling of accomplishment and satisfaction from the efforts, struggles, and perseverance taken.

It is a celebratory card that not only marks the end of a chapter but also signifies exciting new beginnings. By embracing the energy of The World card, one recognizes their accomplishments, understands their worth, and prepares to embark on a new journey with the wisdom of past experiences.

Reversed: *Delayed Success, Failed Plans, Stagnation, Emptiness*
A reversal may indicate a lack of fulfillment, unfulfilled potential, or delayed progress towards one's goals. It may point towards self-imposed or external limitations hindering progress, such as emotional or mental obstacles. It urges the reader to re-examine their path, identify unresolved issues, and tackle them to move forward. The reversed World card may also suggest a feeling of stagnation, where one feels stuck in a particular stage of life, unable to progress further.

However, there is also a positive interpretation of the reversed card. It may signify that the end goal is within reach, with only a few final adjustments needed for completion. This card reminds us not to rush the process but to take time to ensure every detail is in place and every lesson understood before moving forward. Patience, introspection, and perseverance are encouraged, emphasizing that every journey may have setbacks, but with determination, the desired destination can ultimately be reached.

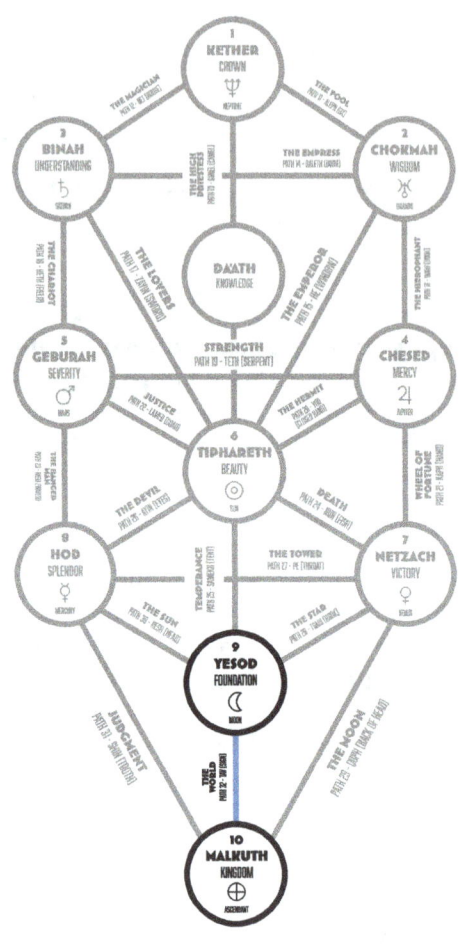

CHAKRA:
Root

TIMING:
Winter, or Slow and Delayed

NUMEROLOGY:
3, 21

ARCANA RELATION:
The Empress

DEITY:
Ahapshi, Ameshet, Asar,
Astraea, Athene, Bacchus, Ceres,
Demeter, Gaia, Iacchus, Kronos,
Mako, Nephthys, Sebek

ANIMAL:
Bull, Crocodile

CRYSTAL:
Black Pearl, Jet, Kunzite,
Lapis Lazuli, Larimar, Onyx,
Rhyolite, Unakite

PLANT:
Bay Laurel, Comfrey,
Cypress, Hellebore, Ivy,
Nightshade, Rose, Yew

MAGICKAL ITEM:
Salt

ARCHANGEL:
Cassiel, Uriel

BROWN
Solidity, Grounding,
Strength

GREY
Stability, Neutrality,
Reserve

BLACK
Dignity, Force,
Stability, Protection

The World is a powerful and profound symbol of ultimate fulfillment, completion, and jubilation. Centrally located on the card is a mesmerizing and dancing figure, typically depicted as an individual who embodies the essence of accomplishment and wholeness, celebrating the victorious end of a long and arduous journey or cycle. Their dance exudes sheer joy and gratitude, symbolizing the harmonious balance with the universe that they have achieved. The oval wreath that surrounds them is a poignant representation of the unceasing cycle of life and seasons, signifying that every ending is merely the precursor to a new beginning.

Located at the four corners of the card, surrounding the central figure, are typically four guardian figures representing the fixed signs of the zodiac: the angel or human (Aquarius), the eagle (Scorpio), the bull (Taurus), and the lion (Leo). These figures embody the interconnectedness of all things and symbolize the balance between spiritual and earthly matters. Their presence on the World card emphasizes the attainment of mastery over diverse realms and unifies the purpose and spirit of all who behold it.

The ultimate theme of the World card is that of unity, wholeness, and achievement. It is an acknowledgment of a significant milestone achieved, a dream realized, or a goal attained. It is the culmination of the journey that the Fool started at the beginning of the Tarot deck and serves as a profound understanding of life's lessons and a recognition of personal growth and development. This card inspires us to celebrate our achievements, no matter how small or significant they may be, and to eagerly look forward to new adventures, secure in the knowledge that with every ending comes the possibility of a new beginning.

PLANET: Saturn is often referred to as the "taskmaster" of the planets. It brings structure, discipline, and the boundaries that are necessary for both personal and societal functioning.

ELEMENT: Earth represents death and rebirth. It is the realm of abundance, prosperity, and wealth. It is associated with Autumn, the Suit of Pentacles, and the North cardinal direction.

HERMETIC QABALAH Associated Hebrew Letter: Tav – Sign, Cross (Covenant, Seal, Truth)

TREE OF LIFE PATHWAY: 32nd Path Between Yesod (Foundation) and Malkuth (Kingdom)

MINOR ARCANA

THESE CARDS REPRESENT OUR *DAY-TO-DAY*;
THE COMPONENTS OF OUR DAILY EXISTENCE AS WE
PARTICIPATE IN ROUTINE TASKS

The Minor Arcana offer detailed insights into our daily experiences, feelings, and events. These cards delve into the more mundane aspects of life, providing a nuanced understanding of the querent's situation. While the Major Arcana deals with overarching life themes and spiritual lessons, the Minor Arcana gives practical advice and highlights areas of focus.

The Minor Arcana was designed to be a counterpart to the Major Arcana, which deals with larger, overarching life themes and archetypal energies. While the Major Arcana addresses universal life stages and experiences, the Minor Arcana zooms in on day-to-day events. Its creation was inspired by the desire to have a set of cards that could offer insights into the more mundane or specific aspects of life, making the Tarot a comprehensive tool for divination and introspection.

The cards within these suits depict various stages or facets of their respective realms, allowing the reader to gain insight into specific circumstances and dynamics at play. In a Tarot reading, the presence and interplay of Minor Arcana cards provide a comprehensive narrative that addresses both profound and practical aspects. They pinpoint challenges, potential solutions, and the energies surrounding the querent, adding depth and richness to the reading.

SUITS OF THE
MINOR ARCANA

In the Rider Waite Smith system, there are fifty-six total cards in the Minor Arcana, divided into four suits with fourteen cards each. Those suits are **Wands, Swords, Cups, and Pentacles**.

Wands are a symbol of inspiration, spirituality, determination, strength, intuition, creativity, and ambition. They represent our dreams, passions, and motivations and how we express them. The suit has its origins in traditional playing cards' "batons" or "clubs" suits, which were used to depict the peasantry's connection to agriculture and the earth. Over time, the wands evolved to represent spiritual growth and enterprise.

Cups deal with emotions, relationships, connections, and intuition. This suit delves deeply into the realm of feelings, love, connections, and emotional well-being. The "hearts" suit in regular playing cards originally denoted the clergy and reflected their emotional and spiritual orientation. In Tarot, it came to represent the realm of emotions and interpersonal relationships.

Swords are associated with action, change, force, power, oppression, ambition, conflict, and strife. Originally representing the nobility, who had ties to the military, swords evolved from the "spades" suit in traditional playing cards. In Tarot, it came to symbolize mental processes and challenges.

Pentacles represent the material aspects of life, such as work, business, trade, property, money, and other possessions. They emphasize the physical outcomes of one's efforts and touch on themes of security, physical health, and tangibility. The "diamonds" suit in regular card decks originally represented the merchant class and their wealth and property. In Tarot, pentacles evolved to represent the material realm and physical outcomes.

The Suit of Wands

The Suit of Wands is closely associated with a variety of positive attributes, including inspiration, spirituality, determination, strength, intuition, creativity, ambition, and expansion. These cards are closely connected with the element of Fire and capture the raw energy and driving force of the human spirit. When exploring the Suit of Wands, individuals will delve deep into their own passions, motivations, and personal goals, tapping into the inner flame that propels them forward.

Visually, Wands cards typically feature wooden staffs that are either budding or blossoming, symbolizing growth and potential. These staffs act as a bridge between the earth and the divine, allowing individuals to anchor their ideas into tangible reality. During a reading, Wands may indicate new beginnings, ventures, and paths of self-discovery, though they can also signal challenges that require determination and enthusiasm to overcome.

The numbered cards within the Suit of Wands represent various stages of a journey, starting with the initial inspiration of the Ace and culminating in the accomplishment of the Ten. The court cards—Page, Knight, Queen, and King—represent different personas or aspects of the fiery, spirited energy that characterizes the Suit of Wands. Depending on the reading, these figures may symbolize personalities or specific energies. Overall, the Suit of Wands speaks to the power of life force, spirit, and the drive to pursue one's passions.

Element: Fire

Suit Traits: Leadership, self-growth, entrepreneurship

Direction: South

Zodiac Signs: Aries, Leo, Sagittarius

Season: Summer

Other Names: Batons, Staves, Rods, Scepters, Clubs

Chakra: Solar Plexus (Manipura)

Qabbalistic World: Atziluth, the Archetypal World

Jungian Function: Intuition

The Suit of Swords

The Suit of Swords is a powerful representation of the element of Air, closely tied to the realms of intellect, thought, and action. This suit delves deep into the complexities of the mind, exploring its ability to reason, communicate, and make decisions. As a symbol of conflict and challenge, the Swords are emblematic of the power of discernment, highlighting the double-edged nature of the mind, capable of both illuminating truth and creating chaos.

The visual imagery of the Swords often portrays sharp blades, and the cards can be stark or even unsettling, reflecting the potential for pain, betrayal, or adversity. These symbols may represent clarity and precision, but they also signify the potential for harm. When interpreted in readings, the Swords may point to difficulties arising from miscommunication, overthinking, or disagreements. They encourage clear thought and may indicate a time for decision-making or confronting difficult truths.

Throughout the numbered cards (Ace through Ten) in the Suit of Swords, we witness an intellectual journey from the raw power of the Ace to the overwhelming force of the Ten. The court cards—Page, Knight, Queen, and King—represent different personas or facets of the cerebral energy of Swords. These characters may symbolize individuals or specific energies within a reading. The Swords invite introspection, encouraging us to harness the power of our minds constructively while being aware of its potential pitfalls.

Element: Air

Suit Traits: Quick resolutions, academics, law, ideas

Direction: West

Zodiac Signs: Gemini, Libra, Aquarius

Season: Spring

Other Names: Spades

Chakra: Heart (Anahata)

Qabbalistic World: Yetzirah, the Formative World

Jungian Function: Thinking

The Suit of Cups

The Suit of Cups embodies the element of Water and intertwines deeply with emotions, relationships, feelings, and the intricacies of the human heart. This particular suit illuminates the realms of love, intuition, compassion, and emotional fulfillment. With great insight, the Cups enlighten us about our connections with others and how we interact with the world on an emotional level. They are symbolic of our dreams, hopes, fears, and the varied feelings that life presents.

The Cups feature chalices or goblets filled with water or other liquids. This representation highlights the fluid and ever-changing nature of emotions. The imagery in this suit is dreamy, romantic, and melancholic at times, reflecting the many emotional states one experiences. The Cups predominantly address relationships, love, emotional choices, and the depths of the human psyche.

Within the Suit of Cups, the numbered cards from Ace to Ten illustrate an emotional journey from intuitive connection to emotional culmination. The court cards—Page, Knight, Queen, and King—represent various personas of the watery, emotional energy of Cups. They can be indicative of specific people in one's life or represent particular emotional states or developments. Overall, the Suit of Cups encourages introspection and emotional awareness, urging us to embrace the entire spectrum of human emotions and nurture our heart's desires and connections.

Element: Water

Suit Traits: Subconscious, imagination, relationships

Direction: East

Zodiac Signs: Cancer, Scorpio, Pisces

Season: Winter

Other Names: Chalices, Grails, Goblets, Cauldrons, Hearts, Vessels

Chakra: Sacral (Svadhisthana)

Qabbalistic World: Briah, the Creative World

Jungian Function: Feeling

The Suit of Pentacles

The Suit of Pentacles has a profound association with the element of Earth and delves into the realm of materiality, physicality, and the tangible world. This suit is a reflection of all that concerns wealth, work, business, property, health, and the daily aspects of life. The Pentacles within this suit represent the physical outcomes of one's endeavors, signifying both financial prosperity and scarcity. This suit stresses the importance of staying grounded, having stability, and the fruits of labor and persistence.

The cards within the Pentacles suit feature visuals of gold coins, sometimes referred to as disks or pentacles, set against luxurious gardens, thriving landscapes, and trade and craftsmanship scenes. This imagery highlights the strong link between effort, value, and reward. The luscious scenes embody the harvest of hard work, the prosperity that results from diligence, and the sense of satisfaction derived from a job well done.

The numbered cards within the Pentacles Suit, from Ace to Ten, present a journey of financial and material undertakings, starting from the raw potential of Ace and culminating in the riches and security of Ten. The court cards, namely Page, Knight, Queen, and King, portray diverse personalities or stages within the sphere of finance and material well-being. These characters can represent people in one's life or different aspects of an individual's approach to the physical world. When coming across the Pentacles Suit in a Tarot reading, it presents an opportunity to scrutinize and assess one's relationship with the material world, financial objectives, and physical health. This Suit encourages us to recognize the worth of tangible things and appreciate the mundane aspects of our lives.

Element: Earth

Suit Traits: Foundation, ambition, stubbornness

Direction: North

Zodiac Signs: Taurus, Virgo, Capricorn

Season: Autumn

Other Names: Disks, Coins, Deniers, Stones, Diamonds

Chakra: Root (Muladhara)

Qabbalistic World: Assiah, the World of Action

Jungian Function: Sensation

Numbered Cards

The inclusion of numbers serves as a fundamental component that contributes to the structure and significance of its interpretation. Among the suits are cards ranging from Ace (1) to 10. With the amalgamation of numbers and the essence of each suit, each card assumes a unique significance by tapping into the principles of numerology and the symbolism that each number holds.

1: (Aces), change, opportunity, potential

2: Balance, duality, union, partnership

3: Creativity, growth, development, groups

4: Structure, manifestation, foundation, stability

5: Difficulty, conflict, struggle, instability

6: Cooperation, harmony, realignment

7: Reflection, knowledge, overcoming struggles

8: Advancement, success, shifts, achievement

9: Fulfillment, transition, materialization

10: Completion, culmination, rest, end of a cycle

Court Cards

The Court cards are the four cards at the end of each suit: Pages, Knights, Queens, and Kings. *Page* cards typically reference adolescence and inexperience. These influences are usually spontaneous and full of adventure. Knight cards are all about action and focus on the journey. *Knights* can be impulsive in their behavior. Queen cards show maturity and gentle energy. *Queen* cards are often nurturing and offer subtle and relaxed encouragement or advice. *King* cards show control and knowledge. These cards represent dominant energy.

ACE OF WANDS

M I N O R   A R C A N A

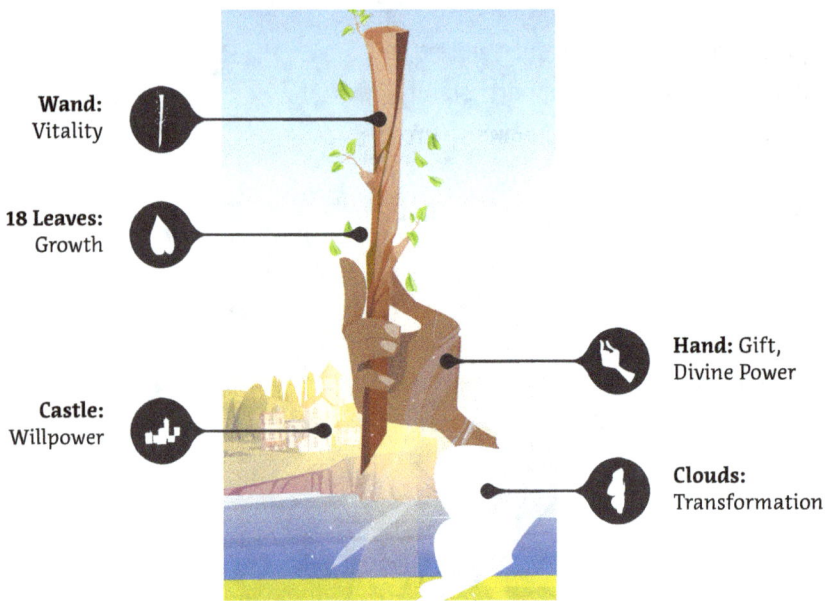

Wand:
Vitality

18 Leaves:
Growth

Castle:
Willpower

Hand: Gift,
Divine Power

Clouds:
Transformation

Yes/No Reading:

Yes   No   Maybe

Names in Other Tarot Systems:

Golden Dawn: The Radix of the Powers of Fire
Tarot of Marseilles: Ace of Clubs
Thoth: The Root of the Powers of Fire

♈ ♌ ♐	△	1, 10	5, 11
PLANET	**ELEMENT**	**NUMEROLOGY**	**COUNT**
ZODIAC Aries, Leo, Sagittarius	Fire		

Upright: *Creation, Potential, Willpower, Desire, Inspiration, Enterprise*
An upright Ace of Wands is a powerful indicator of fresh starts, bursting energy, and the potential for great achievement. It's a reminder of the limitless possibilities that await and the untapped potential within. If this card appears in a reading, it's an invitation to seize the moment. If you've been waiting for a sign to embark on a new path or endeavor, the Ace of Wands suggests that now might be the opportune moment.

This card vibrates with creative energy. It may denote a sudden burst of inspiration or a surge of artistic or creative flow. For creatives, the Ace of Wands is a beacon of encouragement, urging them to harness this energy and bring their ideas to fruition.

The wand's budding leaves and the card's overall vibrant energy speak of personal expansion and growth. It's a nudge to trust oneself, to be bold, and to act with confidence.

Reversed: *Lack of Energy, Distraction, Hesitation, Resistant to Change*
That new opportunity or beginning you've been hoping for has been delayed or has not manifested in the way you had hoped. You may have missed out on something you were looking forward to, or perhaps the timing just isn't right. You may be feeling uninspired, unmotivated, or lethargic and struggling to find your spark. This could relate to creative projects, personal endeavors, or even relationships.

If you're someone who relies on creative energy, whether as an artist, writer, musician, the reversed Ace of Wands can indicate a creative block. You might be finding it hard to come up with new ideas or to feel passionate about your work.

Perhaps there's a fear of failure, or maybe too many choices are making it hard to decide on a clear path. You might feel like you're not growing or progressing in the way you had hoped, leading to feelings of stagnation.

Upright Interpretations

General Reading: This is a time ripe with opportunities, potential, and the spark of inspiration. If you've been thinking of starting a new venture, project, or journey, now might be an auspicious time to take the plunge.

Love Reading: If you're single, this could mean the start of a fiery and exciting new relationship. For those already in relationships, the Ace suggests a rejuvenation of passion and a deeper connection. It might also indicate the potential to take a relationship to the next level.

Health Reading: If you've been feeling drained or recovering from an ailment, this card indicates a phase of improved health and well-being. It's also a great time to start a new fitness routine or health regimen. Take proactive steps toward better health.

Career Reading: New professional opportunities on the horizon. This might manifest as a new job offer, a project, or a chance to venture into a fresh field or start your own business. It's a card that urges you to take initiative, be innovative, and follow your enthusiasm. Your creative ideas are likely to be well-received, and your energy can drive you to new heights in your career.

Reversed Interpretations

General Reading: Plans or projects you were excited about could face delays or obstacles. This isn't necessarily a sign to abandon your endeavors, but rather to exercise patience and perhaps reassess your approach. It's a time to gather your energy and find new ways to rekindle your passion.

Love Reading: For singles, this could suggest potential relationships failing to take off or a lack of spark in new connections. If you're in a relationship, there might be challenges in terms of physical connection or enthusiasm. Communication is key.

Health Reading: You're entering a period of low energy or lethargy. This could also suggest setbacks in fitness goals or a potential delay in recovery from a health issue. Be sure to rest.

Career Reading: You might be feeling unenthusiastic or blocked creatively. There's a need for a fresh perspective or possibly collaboration to reignite your professional passion. Don't force things, and wait for clarity before proceeding.

In the Ace of Wands, the primary depiction features a hand emerging from a cloud, grasping a large wand adorned with leaves or blossoms, as if offering it to the viewer as a symbol of a new opportunity or spark of inspiration. The background is a picturesque landscape with a castle or home in the distance, under a radiant sky.

This image represents a divine or universal gift being bestowed upon the viewer, with the hand symbolizing a higher source of energy behind the wands. As the key symbol of the Wands suit, the wand embodies the concepts of inspiration, energy, growth, and creativity. The sprouting appearance of the wand is a symbol of new beginnings and potential, akin to the budding of a tree or plant.

The distant castle or home represents goals or the culmination of a journey, security, protection, and power. The blue river depicts freedom and the flow of life, while the lush green landscape symbolizes growth. The mound shows a goal and it also represents high attainment. Overall, the Ace of Wands is a card full of promise and potential, signifying new beginnings and opportunities for growth and creativity.

♈ **ZODIAC:** Aries (March 21 – April 19) is a Fire sign ruled by Mars. This sign embodies a determined, impulsive, and resolute energy.

♌ Leo (July 23 – August 22) is a Fire sign ruled by the Sun. Leos are known for their self-assurance and innate ability to take the center stage in most situations.

♐ Sagittarius (November 22 – December 21) is a Fire sign ruled by Jupiter. Sagittarians are often seen as the optimists of the zodiac, always looking at the brighter side of life.

△ **ELEMENT:** Fire represents energy, creativity, and power. It is the realm of love, courage, and action. It is associated with Summer, the Suit of Wands, and the South cardinal direction.

HERMETIC QABALAH Associated Hebrew Letter: Yod – Closed Hand (Deed, Work)

QABALISTIC SEPHIROT: Kether (Crown)

TIMING: Immediately; take action

TWO OF WANDS

M I N O R   A R C A N A

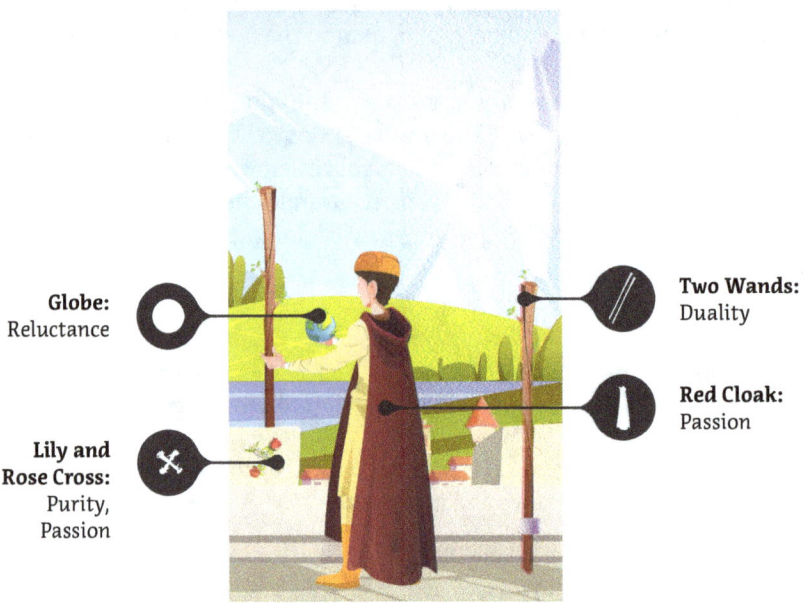

Globe:
Reluctance

Lily and Rose Cross:
Purity, Passion

Two Wands:
Duality

Red Cloak:
Passion

Yes/No Reading:

☑ ○ ○
Yes *No* *Maybe*

Names in Other Tarot Systems:
Golden Dawn: Lord of Dominion
Tarot of Marseilles: Two of Clubs
Thoth: Dominion

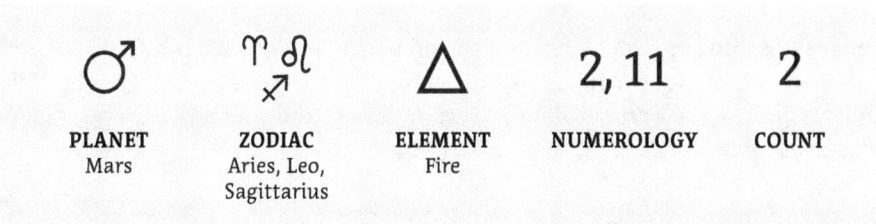

PLANET	ZODIAC	ELEMENT	NUMEROLOGY	COUNT
Mars	Aries, Leo, Sagittarius	Fire	2, 11	2

Upright: *Discovery, Potential, Future Planning, Making Decisions, Progress*

You currently hold a position of power and potential. You've already begun laying the foundation for your goals, and now you find yourself at a crossroads, contemplating the next steps to take. This card often indicates that you're considering branching out in a new direction or taking a risk, as you weigh your current situation against future aspirations.

You have a sense of control over the world around you. Think beyond your immediate surroundings and focus on long-term visions. It encourages you to explore new opportunities, whether it be a new job, moving to a different location, starting a new venture, or expanding your horizons in other ways.

Although there may be some uncertainty about future endeavors, the card instills a strong sense of empowerment. You're encouraged to trust in your own abilities, make decisions confidently, and act on them with conviction. By using careful planning and maintaining a clear vision, success is well within reach.

Reversed: *Personal Goals, Restless, Fear of the Unknown, Lack of Planning*

You're feeling stuck or uncertain about which path to take. You might have recently encountered setbacks that have caused you to question your choices or are paralyzed by the fear of making a wrong decision. Instead of exploring new opportunities, you may be turning inwards, hesitating or avoiding making a necessary decision.

Perhaps you dove into a project or situation without considering the consequences, and now you're feeling overwhelmed or regretful. You may be bogged down in the planning phase, preventing you from taking action. You might be settling for what's comfortable or familiar, instead of taking risks that could lead to greater rewards. Stepping outside of your comfort zone and confronting the unknown is sometimes necessary to achieve significant progress or transformation.

Upright Interpretations

General Reading: You're being encouraged to step out of your comfort zone and explore new territories. This card signifies that it's a time of planning, potential, and possibility. The world is literally in your hands, and you have the power to shape your path forward.

Love Reading: For singles, it may signify that someone from a different background or from abroad may enter your life. For those in a relationship, it might suggest considering a joint venture, such as traveling together or even relocating. It's a time of growth, expansion, and potentially taking a bold step together as a couple.

Health Reading: Now is a good time to try a new fitness routine, health routine, or different treatment options.

Career Reading: You have the vision and the potential for long-term success. There's an element of risk, but with careful planning and a clear vision, success is achievable. For some, it might also indicate overseas business dealings or expanding into international markets.

Reversed Interpretations

General Reading: You might be experiencing a lack of direction or a fear of moving forward, potentially due to past mistakes or uncertainties about the future. Opportunities might be missed because of procrastination or failure to act.

Love Reading: There might be hesitation about taking the next step, or perhaps both partners are not on the same page regarding the future. For singles, it can represent missed opportunities in love or sticking with what's comfortable rather than exploring new possibilities. It could also indicate a long-distance relationship that's facing challenges or not progressing as hoped.

Health Reading: You're feeling unsure about a health decision, like a treatment option or procedure. You might be second-guessing choices or feeling overwhelmed by health information.

Career Reading: You may be hesitant to take risks or are feeling overwhelmed by choices. It's a reminder not to rest on past laurels but to regain the initiative. There could also be issues with partnerships in business or projects that don't materialize as expected.

A figure stands on a battlement, holding a globe in one hand and a wand in the other. The figure's attire is typically rich, suggesting prosperity or a position of power and authority. Behind the battlement is another wand is usually affixed and standing upright. The backdrop often features a vast landscape, usually with mountains, water, and sometimes distant lands or settlements, emphasizing a sense of vast potential and far-reaching visions. It suggests that the horizon is broad, and there are many potential paths to consider.

The presence of two wands symbolizes a decision or a crossroads. It's about balancing current circumstances with future ambitions. One wand is held, representing the present and immediate concerns, while the other is usually fixed or planted, symbolizing future plans or endeavors.

Holding the globe signifies dominion and control. It represents the idea that the world is in the person's hands, emphasizing potential, ambition, and the idea of "having the world at one's fingertips." It can also signify looking outward, possibly considering travel, trade, or expansion in some form.

ZODIAC: Aries (March 21 – April 19) is a Fire sign ruled by Mars. This sign embodies a determined, impulsive, and resolute energy.

Leo (July 23 – August 22) is a Fire sign ruled by the Sun. Leos are known for their self-assurance and innate ability to take the center stage in most situations.

Sagittarius (November 22 – December 21) is a Fire sign ruled by Jupiter. Sagittarians are often seen as the optimists of the zodiac, always looking at the brighter side of life.

ELEMENT: Fire represents energy, creativity, and power. It is the realm of love, courage, and action. It is associated with Summer, the Suit of Wands, and the South cardinal direction.

HERMETIC QABALAH Associated Hebrew Letter: Yod – Closed Hand (Deed, Work)

QABALISTIC SEPHIROT: Chokmah (Wisdom)

TIMING: March 21 – March 30

THREE OF WANDS

M I N O R   A R C A N A

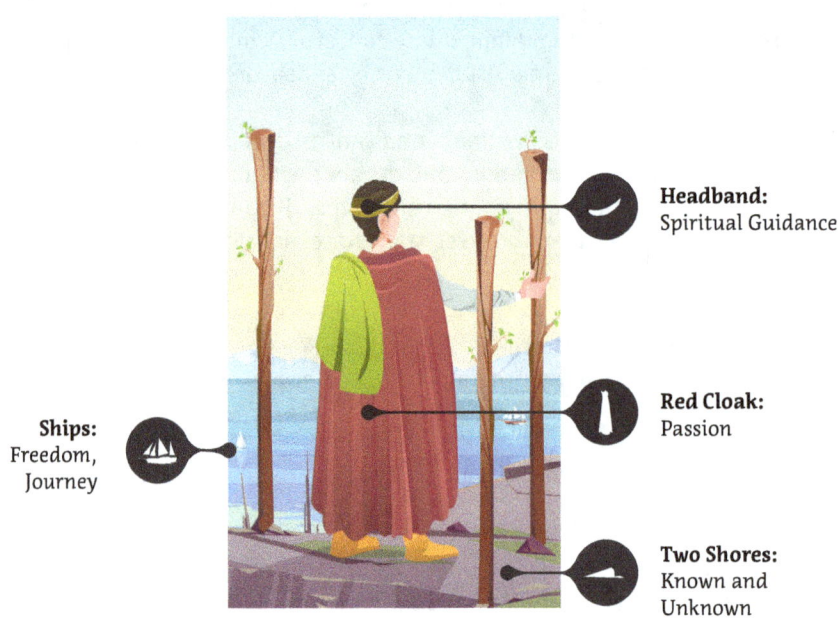

Headband:
Spiritual Guidance

Red Cloak:
Passion

Two Shores:
Known and
Unknown

Ships:
Freedom,
Journey

Yes/No Reading:

Yes   No   Maybe

Names in Other Tarot Systems:
Golden Dawn: Lord of Established Strength
Tarot of Marseilles: Three of Clubs
Thoth: Virtue

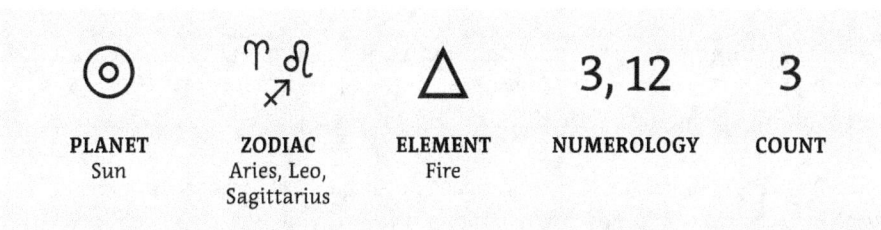

PLANET	ZODIAC	ELEMENT	NUMEROLOGY	COUNT
Sun	Aries, Leo, Sagittarius	Fire	3, 12	3

Upright: *Expansion, Accomplishment, Foresight, Adventure, Rapid Growth*
Preliminary efforts are starting to pay off and opening up opportunities for future accomplishments. The expansive horizons on the card indicate the upcoming adventures and prospects, particularly for long-term goals and big-picture thinking. Ventures with long-distance or international elements are expected to experience growth.

This card also speaks of expansion, be it in thought, venture, or physical journey. It's about taking risks and venturing into unknown territories. The world is filled with opportunities, and the Three of Wands encourages the querent to be bold, seize those opportunities, and look beyond their immediate environment. Whether it's a new business venture, a creative project, or a personal journey, the card suggests that the world is offering its riches and it's time to step out and claim them.

Reversed: *Obstacles, Dissatisfaction, Lack of Foresight, Unexpected Delays*
The feeling of stagnation you're feeling can be due to a lack of preparation or foresight, leading to missed opportunities or unrealized potentials. In all aspects of life, whether it be personal projects, career advancements, or relationships, individuals may feel unable to move forward with the same momentum and clarity they once possessed.

Perhaps there's a fear of the unknown, or maybe past failures are haunting current efforts, causing hesitation or self-doubt. This card encourages the querent to reflect on both external and internal challenges that might be stalling their progress and to consider ways to overcome these barriers. It's a reminder that while there may be obstacles on the path, with perseverance and a shift in perspective, one can navigate through them.

Upright Interpretations

General Reading: You are on the right path and are starting to see the fruits of your efforts. Now is a time of planning and looking ahead, ensuring that you're aligning your actions with your long-term goals.

Love Reading: For singles, it can indicate potential new romantic prospects on the horizon. For couples, it could suggest taking the next step in your relationship, such as engagement, marriage, or planning a future together.

Health Reading: Your efforts toward a healthier lifestyle are beginning to show results. It's also a reminder to think long-term regarding health. Whether you've started a new fitness regimen or are eating better, you're encouraged to keep looking forward and setting new health goals.

Career Reading: Your professional endeavors are on the rise. You might be considering expanding your business, collaborating on a new project, or exploring opportunities overseas. The Three of Wands in a career context indicates foresight and ambition. Your proactive efforts now will set the stage for future successes.

Reversed Interpretations

General Reading: There may be a feeling of disappointment or frustration that things aren't progressing as quickly or as positively as you had hoped.

Love Reading: There may be stagnation in a relationship, or perhaps a long-distance relationship is facing challenges. For singles, it could indicate missed romantic opportunities or potential connections that don't quite materialize.

Health Reading: You might be facing setbacks in your health goals or feeling disheartened by slow progress. It's essential to reassess your health routines, be patient, and seek guidance if necessary.

Career Reading: You might be experiencing delays or obstacles in your projects. Overseas business ventures or collaborations might face challenges. It suggests a need to reevaluate strategies, be patient, and perhaps seek additional perspectives to move forward effectively.

Standing at the peak of a hill or by the shore, an individual gazes out into a boundless body of water with their back facing the onlooker. Firmly anchored on either side of the figure are two wands, while a third is tightly held in their grasp. The expansive body of water represents the undiscovered future and remote possibilities, with the ships sailing across the waves signifying exploration, trade, and exchange of ideas. The figure's posture reflects contemplation and readiness.

The secure placement of the wands implies a sturdy foundation or starting point, and the individual's hold on the third wand signifies personal investment in the future. The water or horizon in view symbolizes boundless opportunities, unknown territories, and exciting adventures.

The figure's unwavering focus on the expanse conveys a sense of eager anticipation and forward-looking vision. These symbols, commonly seen on water, can signify ventures, trade, interactions, and the early fruits of one's labors.

♈ **ZODIAC:** Aries (March 21 – April 19) is a Fire sign ruled by Mars. This sign embodies a determined, impulsive, and resolute energy.

♌ Leo (July 23 – August 22) is a Fire sign ruled by the Sun. Leos are known for their self-assurance and innate ability to take the center stage in most situations.

♐ Sagittarius (November 22 – December 21) is a Fire sign ruled by Jupiter. Sagittarians are often seen as the optimists of the zodiac, always looking at the brighter side of life.

△ **ELEMENT:** Fire represents energy, creativity, and power. It is the realm of love, courage, and action. It is associated with Summer, the Suit of Wands, and the South cardinal direction.

〳 **HERMETIC QABALAH** Associated Hebrew Letter: Yod – Closed Hand (Deed, Work)

✤ **QABALISTIC SEPHIROT:** Binah (Understanding)

🕐 **TIMING:** March 31 – April 10

FOUR OF WANDS
M I N O R   A R C A N A

Fruit:
Fertility

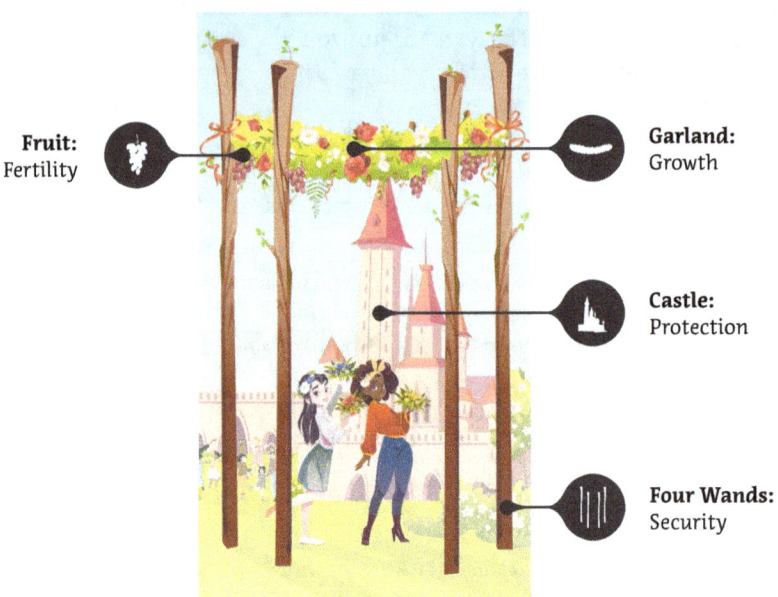

Garland:
Growth

Castle:
Protection

Four Wands:
Security

Yes/No Reading:

☑ ◯ ◯
Yes *No* *Maybe*

Names in Other Tarot Systems:
Golden Dawn: Lord of Perfected Work
Tarot of Marseilles: Four of Clubs
Thoth: Completion

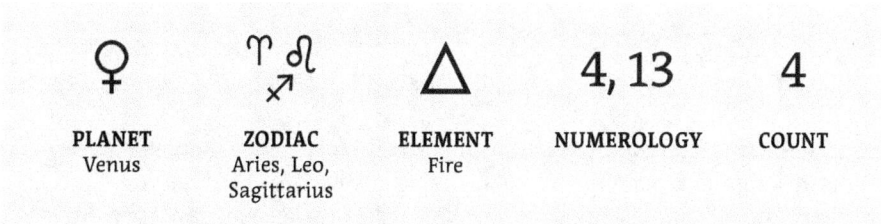

♀	♈♌♐	△	4, 13	4
PLANET	**ZODIAC**	**ELEMENT**	**NUMEROLOGY**	**COUNT**
Venus	Aries, Leo, Sagittarius	Fire		

Upright: *Harmony, Relaxation, Celebration, Homecoming, Community*
The upright Four of Wands card is an embodiment of joy, celebration, and contentment that signify the achievement of significant milestones or the attainment of specific goals that warrant rejoicing. Its essence portrays harmony and stability, which suggest that the past laid foundation is now yielding tangible rewards. This milestone marks the transition from past struggles to present success, a time to revel in the accomplishments and share the joy with others.

Additionally, the Four of Wands represents a sense of belonging and community. It implies that you have found your tribe or are surrounded by people who genuinely support and uplift you. On a broader scale, it may signify a period of peace, where past chaos and challenges have subsided, giving way to a more stable and harmonious environment. This card encourages you to take a moment to appreciate the present, acknowledging the efforts that led to such fruitful outcomes.

Reversed: *Transience, Guilt, Tension, Conflict with Others, Inner Harmony*
When the Four of Wands appears in reverse, it signifies disharmony, instability, and disruptions in various aspects of your life. This is a stark contrast to the upright card, which symbolizes celebrations and milestones. In this position, delays and obstacles may arise, making it challenging to achieve your goals. Canceled or postponed plans for important events can leave you feeling disappointed. Furthermore, the card indicates potential conflicts or misunderstandings within your community or home, creating a sense of disconnect.

Moreover, the reversed Four of Wands can also imply fear of stepping out of your comfort zone and reluctance to progress into the next phase. Impatience and restlessness may surface, leading to a need to re-evaluate your path and potentially restructure your plans. It is essential to address underlying issues to ensure that your plans are built on solid foundations. By taking the time to strengthen your plans, you can regain a sense of harmony and stability.

Upright Interpretations

General Reading: You've achieved an important milestone or are celebrating a significant event, like an engagement, wedding, housewarming, or birthday.

Love Reading: There's a joyous occasion, possibly an engagement, wedding, or another significant step forward in a relationship. This card radiates stability, harmony, and strong relationship foundations. For singles, it can indicate a festive time ahead where you may meet someone special.

Health Reading: You may have recently overcome a health hurdle and are now in the phase of celebration and relaxation. It can also indicate a time of rejuvenation or a beneficial home environment that promotes healing.

Career Reading: You might be celebrating a job well done, a promotion, or the completion of a significant project. It's a time for team celebrations and acknowledging the collaborative efforts that led to success.

Reversed Interpretations

General Reading: Events or parties might be postponed, or you might feel disconnected from your community or family. There's a sense of instability or feeling ungrounded.

Love Reading: There may be postponed weddings or relationship milestones. There might be discord or disagreements disrupting the peace in a relationship. For singles, it may point towards fleeting relationships or missed connections.

Health Reading: There are minor setbacks in recovery or healing. It could suggest that your home environment isn't as conducive to your health and well-being as it could be. Consider ways to bring more peace and balance to your living space.

Career Reading: There might be team discord or a feeling of not being appreciated for your contributions. It emphasizes the importance of finding grounding and seeking support from colleagues.

The four wands, usually depicted upright and forming a canopy or a stage-like structure, represent the solidity of the physical world. They are the four corners, giving a sense of grounding and security. The formation, often adorned with flowers or garlands, is reminiscent of a celebratory gateway or an altar, hinting at rites of passage and significant life milestones.

In many depictions, there are two figures, often dancing or celebrating amidst the structure formed by the wands. These figures represent joy, harmony, and satisfaction. Their presence emphasizes the communal or shared aspect of achievements, suggesting that the celebration or milestone is one that benefits or is recognized by more than one person.

The ground beneath the figures is often stable, hinting at solid foundations, while in the distance, one might often see a castle or a town. This distant structure suggests the idea of a long-term vision or the bigger picture. It reminds the viewer that while celebrating current successes, it's also essential to keep in mind future goals and aspirations.

♈ **ZODIAC:** Aries (March 21 – April 19) is a Fire sign ruled by Mars. This sign embodies a determined, impulsive, and resolute energy.

♌ Leo (July 23 – August 22) is a Fire sign ruled by the Sun. Leos are known for their self-assurance and innate ability to take the center stage in most situations.

♐ Sagittarius (November 22 – December 21) is a Fire sign ruled by Jupiter. Sagittarians are often seen as the optimists of the zodiac, always looking at the brighter side of life.

△ **ELEMENT:** Fire represents energy, creativity, and power. It is the realm of love, courage, and action. It is associated with Summer, the Suit of Wands, and the South cardinal direction.

� **HERMETIC QABALAH** Associated Hebrew Letter: Yod – Closed Hand (Deed, Work)

QABALISTIC SEPHIROT: Chesed (Mercy)

🕐 **TIMING:** April 11 – April 20

FIVE OF WANDS

M I N O R A R C A N A

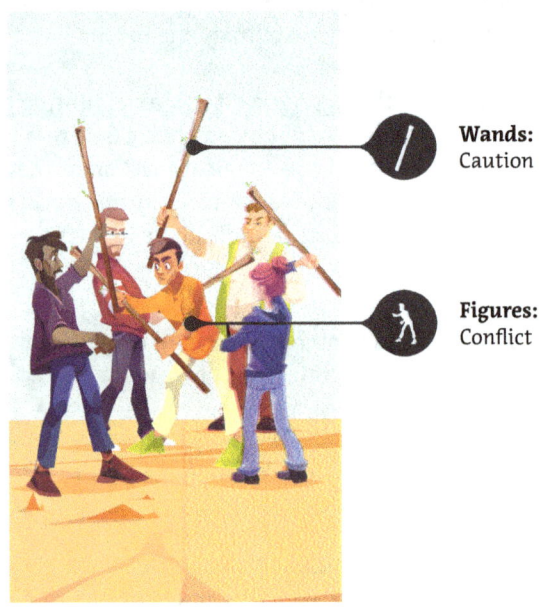

Wands:
Caution

Figures:
Conflict

Yes/No Reading:

Yes   No   Maybe

Names in Other Tarot Systems:
Golden Dawn: Lord of Strife
Tarot of Marseilles: Five of Clubs
Thoth: Strife

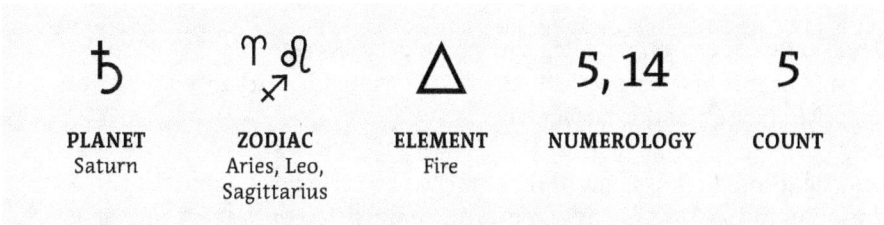

♄	♈♌♐	△	5, 14	5
PLANET	**ZODIAC**	**ELEMENT**	**NUMEROLOGY**	**COUNT**
Saturn	Aries, Leo, Sagittarius	Fire		

Upright: *Conflict, Imbalance, Competition, Tension, Rivalry, Disagreement*
The upright Five of Wands represents a time of competition, tension, and conflict. It signifies a period of clashes between different forces that hold differing opinions or goals, resulting in disagreements and struggles. These conflicts may occur in various settings, including personal, professional, or social contexts. This phase may make collaboration challenging, given the competing visions or goals. Despite the frustration and chaos that may arise, individuals should recognize that such challenges offer opportunities for growth. They encourage individuals to assert their beliefs and refine their ideas.

Although the Five of Wands portrays strife, it reminds us that conflict is a vital aspect of progress and development. By approaching these struggles constructively and considering them as opportunities to improve one's skills or beliefs, individuals can emerge stronger and more capable of dealing with future challenges. The crucial factor is to approach disagreements with an open mind, seeking to understand the opposing view, rather than merely striving for victory. This approach ensures that any solutions derived are beneficial to all parties involved.

Reversed: *Avoid Conflict, Resolution, Tension Release, Respecting Differences*
The Five of Wands in reverse signals a shift away from previously prevailing conflicts, tensions, and misunderstandings. Its presence may indicate a more harmonious atmosphere where disputes and disagreements are starting to be resolved. The card may also suggest a period of calm after the storm, with issues now confronted and settled, paving the way for improved communication and mutual understanding.

However, it is vital to remain alert to the possibility of repressed conflicts. Although everything may appear peaceful on the surface, unresolved issues could be brewing beneath, waiting to resurface. Avoidance or ignoring problems is not an effective solution. It is crucial to ensure that any disagreements are genuinely resolved and that the root causes are adequately addressed to prevent future discord.

Upright Interpretations

General Reading: You're facing challenges or disagreements. These can be internal or external, and while they may seem chaotic, they often serve to bring underlying issues to the surface.

Love Reading: Couples may find themselves bickering over minor issues. For those looking for love, it might represent competition or the feeling that you're clashing with potential partners.

Health Reading: Stress might be taking a toll, or there might be competing ideas about the right course for treatment. It can also indicate internal struggles with lifestyle choices.

Career Reading: In a career context, expect challenges or competition. This might manifest as team disagreements, competing for a position, or differing views on a project's direction. While it can be frustrating, navigating this conflict can lead to greater clarity.

Reversed Interpretations

General Reading: A a period of conflict or tension is ending. Conflicts are being suppressed or avoided, potentially leading to bigger issues later.

Love Reading: You're resolving disagreements or letting go of petty arguments. If problems are simply being brushed under the carpet rather than genuinely addressed, they might resurface later.

Health Reading: There's a reduction in stress or the resolution of conflicting health advice. It's a reminder, however, to address the root causes of tension or discomfort.

Career Reading: There's encouragement to collaborate rather than compete, but also a warning against avoiding necessary confrontations.

The heart of the card commonly shows five people each grasping a wand, embroiled in what appears to be an uncontrolled and unsynchronized battle. The central image encapsulates the essence of the struggle that arises from clashing concepts, personalities, or aspirations.

The backdrop of the card may differ depending on the deck, but it usually emphasizes the unpredictability and chaos of the situation. For example, some depictions may show a sky full of storm clouds, underscoring the idea of an external environment that is as turbulent as the internal struggle. The uneven ground upon which the figures stand indicates the unstable foundation or basis of the disagreement, pointing towards misunderstandings or a lack of clear communication as potential root causes.

The wands themselves are a crucial symbol in this card. The disorganized positioning of the wands in the card suggests that these energies are currently misdirected or not being used cohesively. It is a call for alignment, collaboration, and finding common ground amidst apparent chaos to harness the true power of these wands.

♈ **ZODIAC:** Aries (March 21 – April 19) is a Fire sign ruled by Mars. This sign embodies a determined, impulsive, and resolute energy.

♌ Leo (July 23 – August 22) is a Fire sign ruled by the Sun. Leos are known for their self-assurance and innate ability to take the center stage in most situations.

♐ Sagittarius (November 22 – December 21) is a Fire sign ruled by Jupiter. Sagittarians are often seen as the optimists of the zodiac, always looking at the brighter side of life.

△ **ELEMENT:** Fire represents energy, creativity, and power. It is the realm of love, courage, and action. It is associated with Summer, the Suit of Wands, and the South cardinal direction.

י **HERMETIC QABALAH** Associated Hebrew Letter: Yod – Closed Hand (Deed, Work)

QABALISTIC SEPHIROT: Geburah (Severity)

🕐 **TIMING:** July 22 – August 1

SIX OF WANDS

M I N O R   A R C A N A

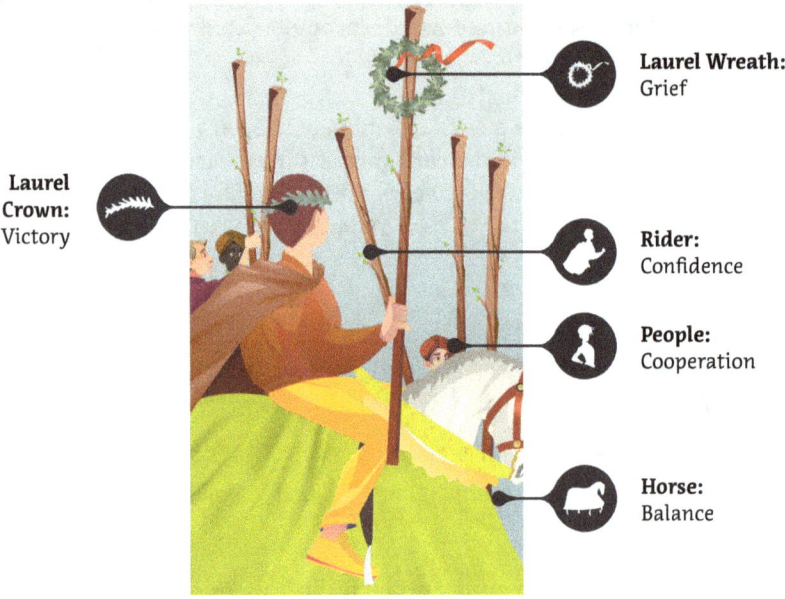

Laurel Wreath:
Grief

Laurel Crown:
Victory

Rider:
Confidence

People:
Cooperation

Horse:
Balance

Yes/No Reading:

Yes No Maybe

Names in Other Tarot Systems:
Golden Dawn: Lord of Victory
Tarot of Marseilles: Six of Clubs
Thoth: Victory

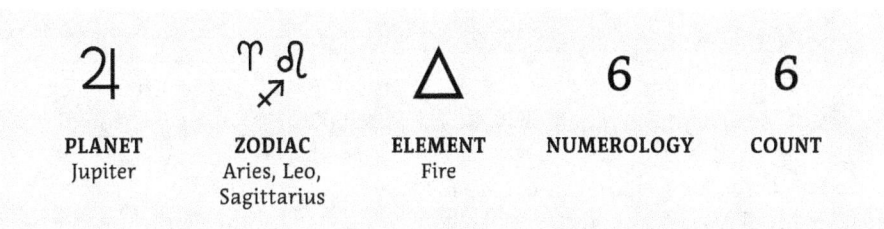

PLANET	ZODIAC	ELEMENT	NUMEROLOGY	COUNT
Jupiter	Aries, Leo, Sagittarius	Fire	6	6

Upright: *Progress, Recognition, Confidence, Victory, Public Acknowledgment*
The upright Six of Wands symbolizes a period of victory, marking the successful overcoming of challenges or competition. It represents more than just personal accomplishment, but also the affirmation that comes from others recognizing and celebrating one's achievements. The Six of Wands reminds us that the fruits of hard work, determination, and perseverance are gratifying and deserving of celebration. This triumph is not a solitary achievement, but a public occasion that draws attention and admiration from those around us.

Additionally, the Six of Wands brings an encouraging message, urging us to embrace the glow of success and allow it to boost our confidence for future pursuits. While it's important to relish the accolades and appreciation, it's equally important to reflect on the journey that led to this victory, and the lessons we learned along the way. This card's energy can serve as a motivational force for future challenges, reminding us that with unwavering dedication and self-belief, more triumphs are on the horizon.

Reversed: *Fall from Grace, Doubt, Egotism, Punishment, Imposter Syndrome*
When the Six of Wands appears in reverse, it indicates that progress towards success may have hit a roadblock or there could be a delay in receiving recognition. Instead of feeling victorious, one may experience unexpected challenges or feelings of inadequacy. Even though public validation or achievements were within reach, they may now seem out of reach. This serves as a reminder that success isn't always straightforward, and we may face obstacles that test our self-belief and resilience.

While accolades and admiration may have been received, they may have led to arrogance or complacency. This card serves as a gentle reminder to stay grounded and not let success cloud judgment. It may also indicate a fear of being in the spotlight or reluctance to share achievements. Regardless of the reason, the reversed Six of Wands encourages self-reflection to identify potential barriers to success and growth, emphasizing that true victory comes from personal growth and learning.

Upright Interpretations

General Reading: This is a time of celebration and achievement. Your efforts and hard work are now being acknowledged by others. It's a time when you can be proud of what you've accomplished and the challenges you've overcome.

Love Reading: For singles, this could mean catching the attention of someone special or enjoying a period of popularity in the dating scene. For those in a relationship, it might indicate a moment when your bond is strengthened, perhaps by overcoming challenges together.

Health Reading: Your efforts to improve your health or overcome an illness are bearing fruit, and you're feeling stronger and more energetic.

Career Reading: Whether it's a promotion, successful completion of a project, or public acknowledgment of your contributions, it's a time to enjoy the spotlight and the rewards for your efforts.

Reversed Interpretations

General Reading: You might feel like your efforts have gone unnoticed or that you're facing unexpected challenges. It's a reminder to stay resilient and not allow setbacks to diminish your self-worth.

Love Reading: Singles might experience fleeting attractions that don't materialize into anything substantial. Couples might need to address feelings of insecurity or jealousy.

Health Reading: Minor setbacks in recovery are leaving you feeling disheartened. It's essential to stay positive and seek support when needed.

Career Reading: You're feeling overlooked at work or experiencing setbacks in professional endeavors. It's a call to reassess, strategize, and keep pushing forward, understanding that every path has its ups and downs.

The Six of Wands symbolizes victory, accomplishment, and public acclaim. At the center of most representations of this card is a figure, typically mounted on a white horse, who is feted and applauded by a throng of admirers. The horse, which has traditionally been associated with strength, agility, and purity, highlights the nobility and lucidity of the achievement. The rider, adorned with a garland or a similar emblem on their head, signifies triumph and the culmination of sustained effort. This focal image not only spotlights personal success, but also the validation and esteem that one garners from others.

Encircling the main figure, the onlookers frequently brandish wands in the air, creating an atmosphere of rejoicing and endorsement. The six wands, which usually incorporate the one carried by the central character, represent harmony, equilibrium, and the harmonious integration of diverse energies or obstacles overcome in the past. Their upward trajectory conveys affirmative momentum and ascent after surmounting barriers. It is a visual depiction of surmounting difficulties and triumphing, with the community or peers bearing witness to the achievement.

♈ **ZODIAC:** Aries (March 21 – April 19) is a Fire sign ruled by Mars. This sign embodies a determined, impulsive, and resolute energy.

♌ Leo (July 23 – August 22) is a Fire sign ruled by the Sun. Leos are known for their self-assurance and innate ability to take the center stage in most situations.

♐ Sagittarius (November 22 – December 21) is a Fire sign ruled by Jupiter. Sagittarians are often seen as the optimists of the zodiac, always looking at the brighter side of life.

△ **ELEMENT:** Fire represents energy, creativity, and power. It is the realm of love, courage, and action. It is associated with Summer, the Suit of Wands, and the South cardinal direction.

ﭏ **HERMETIC QABALAH** Associated Hebrew Letter: Yod – Closed Hand (Deed, Work)

QABALISTIC SEPHIROT: Tiphareth (Beauty)

🕐 **TIMING:** August 2 – August 11

SEVEN OF WANDS

M I N O R   A R C A N A

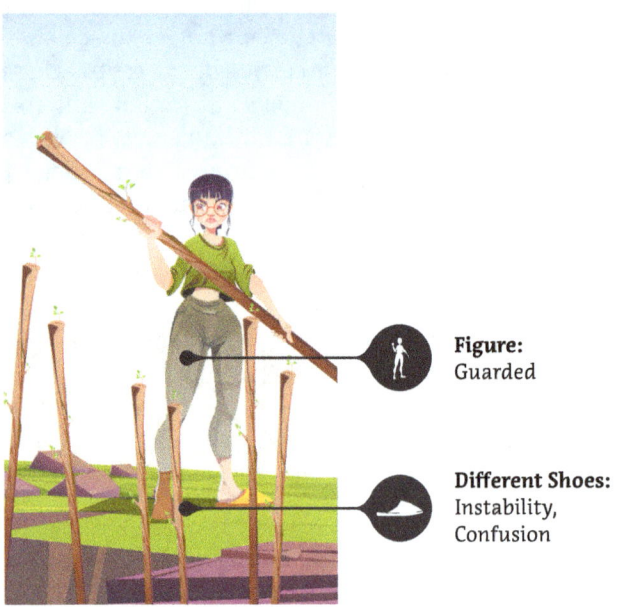

Figure: Guarded

Different Shoes: Instability, Confusion

Yes/No Reading:

○ ○ ☑
Yes   No   *Maybe*

Names in Other Tarot Systems:
Golden Dawn: Lord of Valour
Tarot of Marseilles: Seven of Clubs
Thoth: Valour

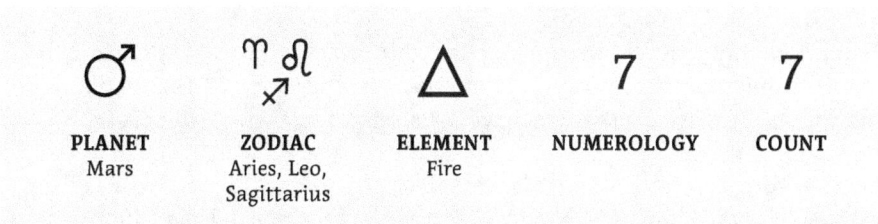

PLANET	ZODIAC	ELEMENT	NUMEROLOGY	COUNT
Mars	Aries, Leo, Sagittarius	Fire	7	7

Upright: *Challenge, Defense, Protection, Competition, Perseverance*
This is the time to stand firm and assert yourself against opposition or challenges. You may be feeling attacked or defensive, as though you're facing competitors or obstacles. You're facing external and internal battles, emphasizing the power and necessity of resilience, courage, and belief in your convictions.

By reminding you of the strength you possess within, the card encourages you to harness it to face the adversity before you. While the challenges you face may test your determination and willpower, the Seven of Wands assures you that you are capable of overcoming them. It's a call to persevere, remain steadfast and confident in your stance. If you have been considering giving up, this card urges you to do the opposite - to fight with even more passion and determination.

Reversed: *Exhaustion, Defeat, Overwhelm, Insecurity, Lack of Confidence*
When the Seven of Wands appears reversed, it can be a sign of exhaustion and overwhelm resulting from a series of difficult challenges and battles. The constant need to be on the defensive may have taken a toll, causing doubts to cloud your judgment and leading you to question the worth of continuing the struggle. At this point, retreating or reconsidering your stance may seem like the best option, as a lack of confidence and feelings of being undermined by external forces or self-sabotage take over.

However, on the other hand, the reversed Seven of Wands may also signal a shift towards lowering your defenses. You may realize that an aggressive approach isn't helping and that it's time to try a more diplomatic or collaborative approach. Rather than viewing everything as a battle, you may seek common ground and disengage from conflicts that drain your energy without producing positive results.

Upright Interpretations

General Reading: You're standing up for your beliefs, choices, or decisions and are willing to defend your point of view. There's a spirit of determination and courage, indicating that you have the strength to overcome opposition.

Love Reading: You or your partner may need to stand up for your relationship, especially if others are challenging it. There might be internal challenges within the relationship that require a firm stance and clear boundaries.

Health Reading: You might be fighting off an illness or facing challenges related to your well-being. It's essential to stay persistent and determined. Stand up for your health and well-being, making choices that are right for you even if others don't understand.

Career Reading: You may feel the need to defend your position, ideas, or projects. Opposition may come, but you are well-prepared to handle it. This is a time to stand firm, be confident, and advocate for your contributions.

Reversed Interpretations

General Reading: You might be feeling overwhelmed by challenges or opposition. It can also indicate an internal struggle, perhaps questioning if the battles you're fighting are worth the energy. You might be on the verge of giving up or feeling that you're fighting a losing battle.

Love Reading: You're avoiding confrontation or issues within the relationship. It can also mean that external pressures or conflicts are becoming too much, leading to withdrawal or reevaluation of the relationship's direction.

Health Reading: You might be feeling defeated in your health challenges or perhaps avoiding facing specific health issues head-on. It's essential to seek support if you're feeling overwhelmed and not to ignore problems hoping they will go away.

Career Reading: There might be a feeling that you're not being recognized or appreciated in your professional environment. Challenges or opposition could be taking a toll on your confidence. This card can also indicate avoiding conflicts at work or not standing up for your ideas and contributions.

The Seven of Wands depicts an individual on higher ground, wielding a wand in a defensive stance against six other wands aimed upwards towards them. This positioning accentuates the notion of being in an elevated position while being scrutinized or under attack.

The rugged terrain that often surrounds the figure represents the capriciousness of life and the difficulties that arise unexpectedly. It also highlights the necessity of being vigilant and expending effort to maintain the upper hand, even with a higher position. This person is ready to face adversity head-on, both externally and internally, often following a period of recognition or success.

Moreover, the number seven in Tarot denotes introspection and inner wisdom. The Seven of Wands suggests that to overcome opposition, one must rely on their inner strength, confidence, and conviction. The wands signify creativity, passion, and will, indicating that these battles often center around personal beliefs, values, or aspirations. The card inspires the querent to trust their inner flame and remain steadfast in their convictions, despite external pressures.

ZODIAC: Aries (March 21 – April 19) is a Fire sign ruled by Mars. This sign embodies a determined, impulsive, and resolute energy.

Leo (July 23 – August 22) is a Fire sign ruled by the Sun. Leos are known for their self-assurance and innate ability to take the center stage in most situations.

Sagittarius (November 22 – December 21) is a Fire sign ruled by Jupiter. Sagittarians are often seen as the optimists of the zodiac, always looking at the brighter side of life.

ELEMENT: Fire represents energy, creativity, and power. It is the realm of love, courage, and action. It is associated with Summer, the Suit of Wands, and the South cardinal direction.

HERMETIC QABALAH Associated Hebrew Letter: Yod – Closed Hand (Deed, Work)

QABALISTIC SEPHIROT: Netsach (Victory)

TIMING: August 12 – August 22

EIGHT OF WANDS

M I N O R   A R C A N A

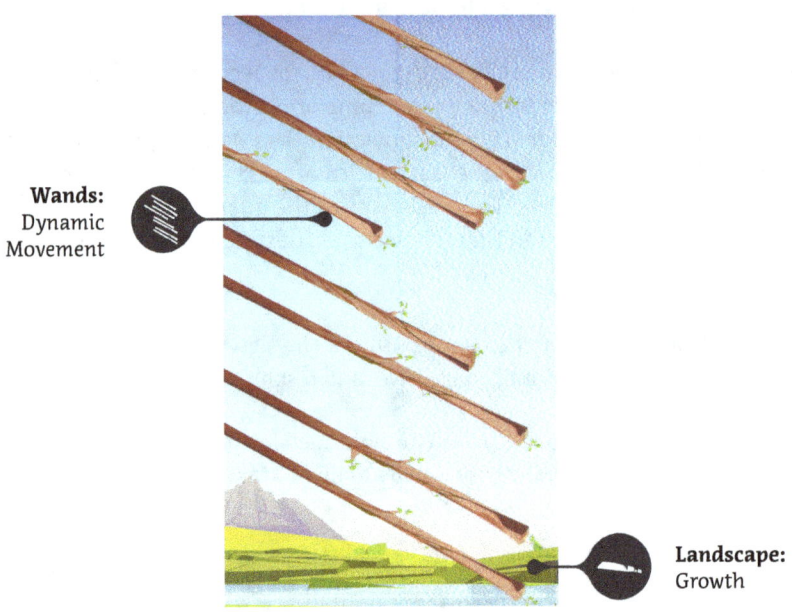

Wands:
Dynamic
Movement

Landscape:
Growth

Yes/No Reading:

☑   ○   ○

Yes   *No*   *Maybe*

Names in Other Tarot Systems:

Golden Dawn: Lord of Swiftness
Tarot of Marseilles: Eight of Clubs
Thoth: Swiftness

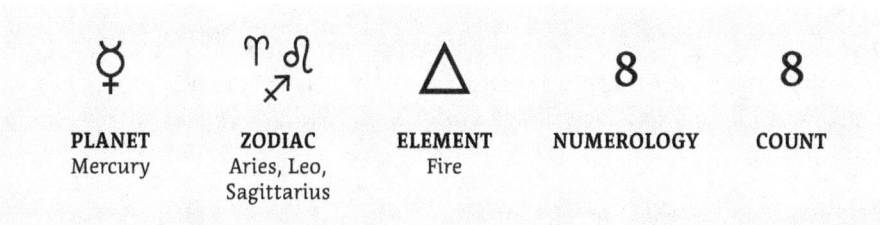

PLANET	ZODIAC	ELEMENT	NUMEROLOGY	COUNT
Mercury	Aries, Leo, Sagittarius	Fire	8	8

Upright: *Alignment, Speed, Air Travel, Action, Movement, Quick Decisions*
The upright Eight of Wands symbolizes a surge of rapid change, quick developments, and swift action. It typically appears in readings when there's a significant acceleration in events, or previously stagnant situations are suddenly gaining momentum. This card represents the powerful energy that drives individuals towards their goals and advises taking advantage of the opportunity. There's a sense of a divine alignment with the universe, with every force conspiring in favor of facilitating progress and momentum.

The Eight of Wands is associated with communication. It is an indication of receiving important news, messages, or information that can help propel matters forward. It's a period where delays and obstacles seem to disappear, and everything flows effortlessly. The card suggests that whether it's a personal endeavor, project, or relationship, the individual is on the right path, and everything is moving at remarkable speed. This time of straightforward movement and clarity signifies the alignment of one's intentions and efforts with the rhythm of the universe, and it should be embraced.

Reversed: *Panic, Slowing Down, Waiting, Frustration, Resisting Change*
The reversed Eight of Wands often signifies hindrances, stasis, and deceleration of previously dynamic energy. This can be frustrating, particularly if you were hoping for a smooth and direct path. Various external factors, unforeseeable obstacles, or even personal reluctance may be responsible for these sluggish periods, leaving you feeling trapped or uncertain.

It's possible that messages are misinterpreted or lost. It's critical during these moments to practice patience and communicate clearly. Contemplate what could be causing these obstacles or confusions. Maybe it's time to re-evaluate the direction you're headed, fine-tune your methods, or wait for a more opportune moment to act. It's important to remember that, even during periods of stasis, there is always the possibility for growth and enlightenment.

Upright Interpretations

General Reading: This is a time of swift action, movement, and rapid developments. Events that have been stagnant or delayed will now proceed at a fast pace. Communication will flow easily, and it's a time of getting things done quickly.

Love Reading: For those in relationships, there might be a sudden progression or an unexpected trip together. For singles, someone new might quickly come into your life. It's a time of fast-paced developments in your love life.

Health Reading: There's a surge of energy here, which can indicate a speedy recovery from illness or a sudden motivation to get fit and healthy. If you've been waiting for test results, they might come in sooner than expected.

Career Reading: Expect rapid developments in your professional life. This might mean a quick job change, sudden travel for work, or the fast completion of projects. If you've been waiting for a decision from superiors or responses regarding job applications, they're likely on the way.

Reversed Interpretations

General Reading: Expect delays, obstacles, and slowed momentum. What you hoped would move quickly seems to be held back. Miscommunications are also possible.

Love Reading: There might be a slowdown in progression or miscommunication between partners. Singles might experience delays in meeting someone new or face misunderstandings in the initial stages of a new relationship.

Health Reading: Recovery might take longer than anticipated. There's a need for patience and not rushing the healing process. Alternatively, expected health news or results might be delayed.

Career Reading: Career projects might not progress as quickly as hoped. There could be delays in job offers, promotions, or business deals. Communication barriers in the workplace might also become evident. It's a period to exercise patience and address any underlying issues causing the delay.

The Eight of Wands depicts eight flying wands moving rapidly through the clear sky, signifying speed, momentum, and action. These wands move purposefully without any hindrances, indicating quick events or an influx of energy and direction. The clear sky emphasizes the card's unobstructed nature, symbolizing clarity, straightforwardness, and a lack of complications or delays. There are no human or animal figures in the card, highlighting the wands and their fast movement, intensifying the themes of rapid changes and advancements.

The clear sky background serves to accentuate the unencumbered nature of the card, symbolizing clarity, straightforwardness, and an absence of complexity or delay. Devoid of human or animal figures, the card focuses solely on the wands and their swift motion, highlighting the themes of rapid changes and progress.

The wands descend from the sky, as if directed from a higher power. This could represent messages from the universe, incoming news, or sudden insights. The wands also symbolize ideas, inspiration, and projects that are about to manifest in one's life, bringing with them transformative energy.

♈ **ZODIAC:** Aries (March 21 – April 19) is a Fire sign ruled by Mars. This sign embodies a determined, impulsive, and resolute energy.

♌ Leo (July 23 – August 22) is a Fire sign ruled by the Sun. Leos are known for their self-assurance and innate ability to take the center stage in most situations.

♐ Sagittarius (November 22 – December 21) is a Fire sign ruled by Jupiter. Sagittarians are often seen as the optimists of the zodiac, always looking at the brighter side of life.

△ **ELEMENT:** Fire represents energy, creativity, and power. It is the realm of love, courage, and action. It is associated with Summer, the Suit of Wands, and the South cardinal direction.

י **HERMETIC QABALAH** Associated Hebrew Letter: Yod – Closed Hand (Deed, Work)

QABALISTIC SEPHIROT: Hod (Splendor)

🕐 **TIMING:** November 23 – December 2

NINE OF WANDS

MINOR ARCANA

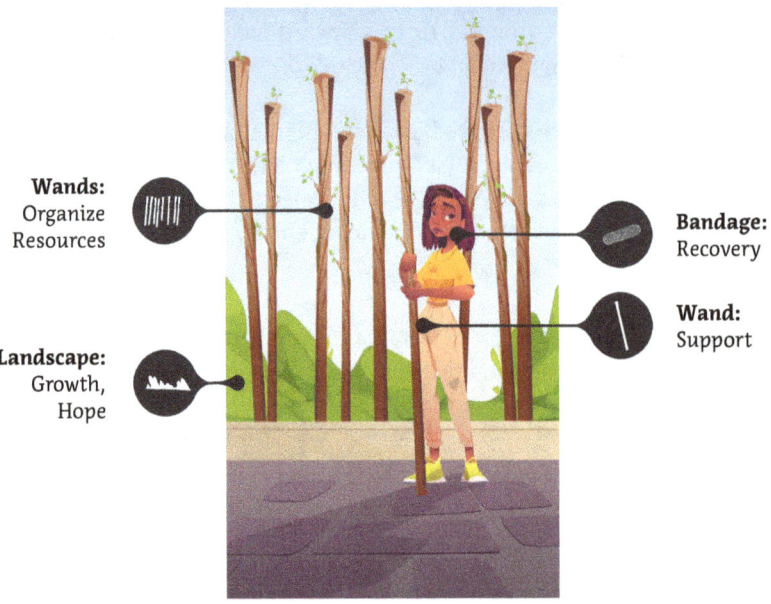

Wands:
Organize
Resources

Bandage:
Recovery

Landscape:
Growth,
Hope

Wand:
Support

Yes/No Reading:

✓ Yes ○ No ○ Maybe

Names in Other Tarot Systems:
Golden Dawn: Lord of Strength
Tarot of Marseilles: Nine of Clubs
Thoth: Strength

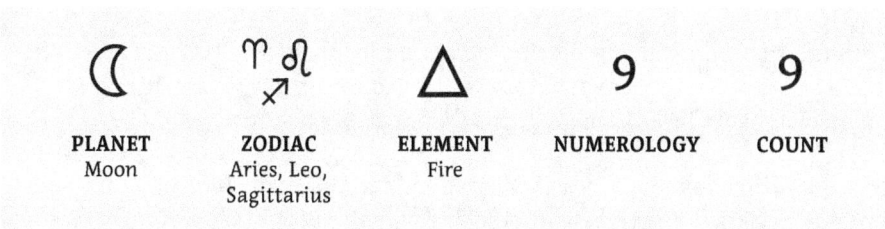

PLANET	ZODIAC	ELEMENT	NUMEROLOGY	COUNT
Moon	Aries, Leo, Sagittarius	Fire	9	9

Upright: *Resilience, Strength, Persistence, Courage, Boundaries, Grit*
When upright, the Nine of Wands represents perseverance, resilience, and the ability to endure obstacles. It appears when someone has faced many challenges and remains standing tall. This card praises the person's willpower and determination, showcasing their indomitable spirit. The querent has been shaped by their experiences and has become stronger, wiser, and more tenacious. They are now better equipped to face any adversity.

Even though the person has already overcome numerous hurdles, they must remain vigilant. There might be one final challenge to face or an unexpected twist on the horizon. The card encourages the querent not to rest on their laurels but to be ready for any forthcoming challenges, advocating for a balance between self-care and preparedness. It is a reminder that life is a series of challenges, but with resilience and a never-give-up attitude, success is attainable.

Reversed: *Exhaustion, Resentment, Fatigue, Struggle, Defensive, Paranoia*
You may be on the brink of giving up and feel unable to handle any more setbacks. This fatigue can stem from internal exhaustion or external pressures and doubts from others. The individual may become overly defensive, feeling that the world is against them, leading to a sense of isolation and paranoia. Unlike the upright position, the reversed card exposes the vulnerability and self-doubt lurking beneath the determined facade.

You might make the decision to let go of a struggle that is no longer worth the effort. You're recognizing your limitations and the ability to choose battles wisely. This might involve walking away from a situation that no longer serves them or finally accepting an outcome and moving forward. The reversed card emphasizes the importance of discernment – understanding when to persevere and when it's time to redirect one's energies to more constructive pursuits.

Upright Interpretations

General Reading: You might be trying to do too much, leading to exhaustion and a sense of being overextended. It's an encouragement to prioritize and possibly delegate tasks to manage the weight you're bearing.

Love Reading: You might be carrying more than their fair share of responsibilities or emotional baggage. It could also indicate the relationship itself has become a source of stress. Communication is key to finding balance.

Health Reading: Your physical or emotional well-being may be suffering due to excessive stress or trying to juggle too many things at once. It's essential to practice self-care, set boundaries, and possibly seek professional help if things become too challenging.

Career Reading: You're taking on more than you can handle at work. This overburdening might lead to burnout. Consider speaking to superiors about delegating tasks or setting more realistic expectations.

Reversed Interpretations

General Reading: You're releasing burdens or realizing that certain tasks are not yours to carry. It's a time of letting go, delegating, or re-prioritizing. Alternatively, it can warn against shirking responsibilities or taking shortcuts.

Love Reading: There may be a shift in relationship dynamics, with one partner realizing they've taken on too much and seeking a more equitable division of responsibilities. Alternatively, someone may be avoiding addressing crucial issues that need attention in the relationship.

Health Reading: You're entering a recovery phase after a period of stress or illness. You're learning to manage stress better. However, ensure you're not in denial about health issues that need attention.

Career Reading: You might be in a phase where you're learning to delegate tasks or prioritize better in your job. The load feels lighter. Alternatively, be cautious about neglecting responsibilities or leaving tasks unfinished.

The forefront often features a lone figure holding one wand, with eight others forming a barrier behind them. This image conveys the message that the individual possesses inner strength and is prepared to face any obstacle that comes their way. The figure may appear weary or injured, a symbol of the hardships they have overcome. Despite this, their stance is one of readiness rather than defeat, embodying perseverance and resilience.

The landscape behind the figure can further emphasize their journey, depicting a rugged terrain or undulating hills. The ground itself represents the trials of life, but the figure remains upright, demonstrating their enduring spirit. This imagery underscores the message that life is filled with challenges, but with determination and resilience, one can navigate through them and be prepared for what lies ahead. The eight wands forming a barrier represent past battles overcome, reinforcing the idea that the individual has a history of endurance.

ZODIAC: Aries (March 21 – April 19) is a Fire sign ruled by Mars. This sign embodies a determined, impulsive, and resolute energy.

Leo (July 23 – August 22) is a Fire sign ruled by the Sun. Leos are known for their self-assurance and innate ability to take the center stage in most situations.

Sagittarius (November 22 – December 21) is a Fire sign ruled by Jupiter. Sagittarians are often seen as the optimists of the zodiac, always looking at the brighter side of life.

ELEMENT: Fire represents energy, creativity, and power. It is the realm of love, courage, and action. It is associated with Summer, the Suit of Wands, and the South cardinal direction.

HERMETIC QABALAH Associated Hebrew Letter: Yod – Closed Hand (Deed, Work)

QABALISTIC SEPHIROT: Yesod (Foundation)

TIMING: December 3 – December 12

TEN OF WANDS

M I N O R   A R C A N A

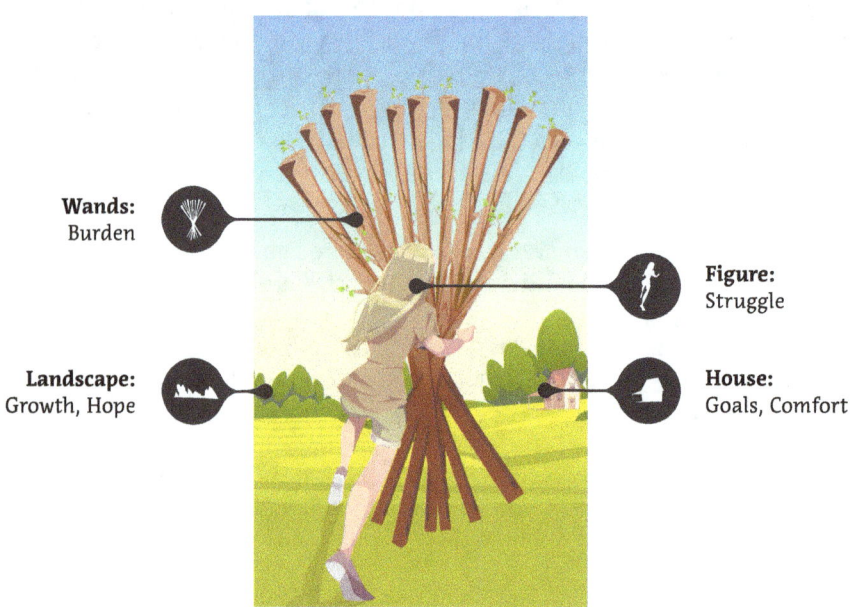

Wands:
Burden

Figure:
Struggle

Landscape:
Growth, Hope

House:
Goals, Comfort

Yes/No Reading:

○   ✔   ○

Yes   *No*   *Maybe*

Names in Other Tarot Systems:

Golden Dawn: Lord of Oppression
Tarot of Marseilles: Ten of Clubs
Thoth: Oppression

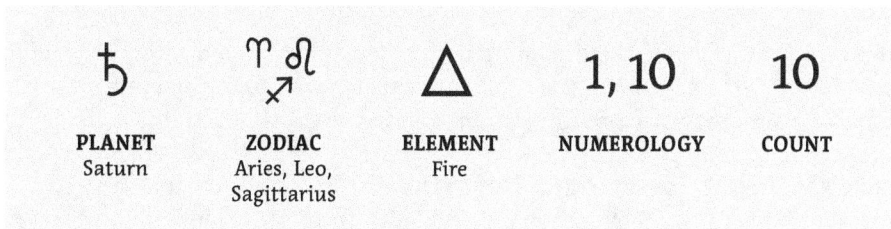

♄	♈♌♐	△	1, 10	10
PLANET	**ZODIAC**	**ELEMENT**	**NUMEROLOGY**	**COUNT**
Saturn	Aries, Leo, Sagittarius	Fire		

Upright: *Accomplishment, Responsibility, Burden, Completion, Hard Work*
You've taken on too much either by choice or due to necessity, and the weight of these responsibilities is beginning to take a toll. It indicates a situation where ambition, commitment, or external pressures have led to a sense of being overstretched or approaching a breaking point. You may be pushing through with sheer willpower driven by a sense of duty, even at the cost of personal well-being and balance.

Nevertheless, the Ten of Wands provides a glimmer of hope and perspective. The heavy load suggests that the journey or challenge is nearing its conclusion, and relief or the end of a task is on the horizon. Although one may feel exhausted or overwhelmed, this card also serves as a reminder of the resilience of the human spirit. There is strength in perseverance, and the current struggles will lead to valuable lessons and personal growth. It may also signal a time to re-evaluate responsibilities, consider seeking assistance, delegate tasks, or establish boundaries to ensure a sustainable life balance.

Reversed: *Burnt Out, Overstressed, Delegation, Exhaustion, Release*
This is a time of liberation, where burdens can be lifted and certain responsibilities can be reassessed or delegated. You may be shedding weighty obligations, re-evaluating the necessity of tasks, or experiencing freedom from past struggles. Learning to delegate, set limits, and say 'no' when needed are all possible outcomes. This card urges a shift towards a more balanced, relaxed approach to life's challenges, providing a break from constant pressure and the drive to achieve.

Neglecting one's obligations or taking shortcuts may result in unfinished business or repercussions. It's crucial to distinguish whether the lightening of your load is a genuine release from unnecessary burdens or a potentially harmful avoidance of responsibility. Therefore, the reversed Ten of Wands should be interpreted with caution and careful consideration.

Upright Interpretations

General Reading: You've faced numerous obstacles but remain standing, ready to confront whatever comes next. This card encourages you to persevere and draw on your inner strength to push through to the end.

Love Reading: You or your partner might have been hurt before and are now cautious about opening up again. It could indicate a relationship that has faced its fair share of challenges but is still enduring. For singles, it might mean being careful and protective of your heart, having been burned before.

Health Reading: You might be in the final stretch of a long recovery or health challenge. The card asks you to keep pushing forward and not give up, even if you feel tired or discouraged. It could also suggest being vigilant and proactive about your health.

Career Reading: You might feel fatigued or like you're constantly fighting battles, but success is within reach if you keep pushing. It might also suggest a need to stand your ground and protect what you've built.

Reversed Interpretations

General Reading: You're experiencing feelings of weariness, overwhelm, or a sense of defeat. It can also suggest being overly defensive or paranoid. On the flip side, it might indicate a decision to release a burden or walk away from a struggle that isn't worth your energy anymore.

Love Reading: There may be issues of mistrust, defensiveness, or past trauma affecting your relationship. One party might be overly cautious due to past hurts. For singles, it suggests letting go of past heartbreaks to move forward.

Health Reading: You might be feeling burnt out or overly stressed about health matters. There's a need to pay attention to warning signs and possibly seek rest or professional guidance. Alternatively, you may be on the path to healing and releasing past health burdens.

Career Reading: You're feeling defeated or wanting to give up after facing constant challenges at work. However, it could also mean recognizing when it's time to walk away from an unproductive situation or job.

The Ten of Wands depicts an individual struggling under the weight of ten heavy wands, which represent the accumulation of challenges, duties, and obligations they have taken upon themselves. The central figure is bent under the weight of the wands, emphasizing the concept of being overwhelmed and possibly having taken on more than they can handle. This figure's stooped and struggling posture highlights the state of exhaustion or near-breaking point that can result from ambition, responsibility, or commitment.

Contrasting with the figure's burdened state, the background of the card in many depictions shows a home or destination in sight, indicating that relief or the end of a journey is near. While they might feel overwhelmed at the moment, it's important to remember that there's a purpose or reason for the current struggles. This serves as a reminder that it's necessary to reassess one's responsibilities, delegate where possible, and recognize one's limits.

ZODIAC: Aries (March 21 – April 19) is a Fire sign ruled by Mars. This sign embodies a determined, impulsive, and resolute energy.

Leo (July 23 – August 22) is a Fire sign ruled by the Sun. Leos are known for their self-assurance and innate ability to take the center stage in most situations.

Sagittarius (November 22 – December 21) is a Fire sign ruled by Jupiter. Sagittarians are often seen as the optimists of the zodiac, always looking at the brighter side of life.

ELEMENT: Fire represents energy, creativity, and power. It is the realm of love, courage, and action. It is associated with Summer, the Suit of Wands, and the South cardinal direction.

HERMETIC QABALAH Associated Hebrew Letter: Yod – Closed Hand (Deed, Work)

QABALISTIC SEPHIROT: Malkuth (Kingdom)

TIMING: December 13 – December 21

PAGE OF WANDS

MINOR ARCANA

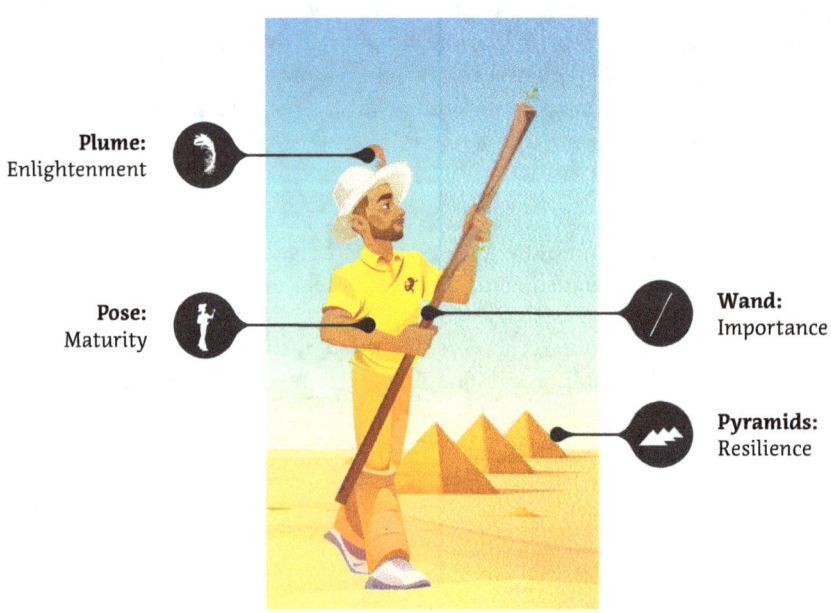

Plume:
Enlightenment

Pose:
Maturity

Wand:
Importance

Pyramids:
Resilience

Yes/No Reading:

☑ ⚪ ⚪
Yes *No* *Maybe*

Names in Other Tarot Systems:
Golden Dawn: Princess of Wands
Tarot of Marseilles: Valet of Clubs
Thoth: Princess of Wands

♈♌ ♐	△	2, 11	7
PLANET	**ZODIAC**	**ELEMENT**	**NUMEROLOGY** **COUNT**
	Aries, Leo, Sagittarius	Fire	

Upright: *Inspiration, Ambition, Freedom, Limitless Potential, Exploration*
The upright Page of Wands brings forth a burst of enthusiasm, energy, and inspiration. This card symbolizes the beginning of a creative project, a new phase of life, or the ignition of a fresh idea. The youthful energy embodied in this card inspires you to take a leap of faith, maintain a positive outlook, and believe in your potential. Opportunities lie ahead, and this card urges you to seize them with both hands, even if the path seems uncertain or challenging.

Furthermore, the Page of Wands can indicate the arrival of a message or communication, particularly concerning new opportunities or ventures. This card nudges you to embrace your uniqueness, make bold decisions, and trust your intuition. Whether you are exploring a new hobby, making a career change, or undergoing a personal transformation, the Page of Wands assures you that now is the time to explore and that the universe is supporting your efforts. Adopt the curiosity of a child and the spirit of an adventurer as you approach the world, for it is yours to discover.

Reversed: *Lack of Direction, Impatience, Spiritual Path, Procrastination*
You're feeling a sense of disorder both internally and externally. This suggests a block in creativity and inspiration, resulting in ideas that fail to take hold. Your enthusiasm may be dampened, leaving you with a sense that all your efforts are in vain. This card also signifies unfulfilled potential, due to self-doubt, overthinking, or hesitation, preventing you from taking action on your bright ideas.

The message or communication you were expecting is delayed or not as positive as anticipated. It also warns against impulsiveness or reckless behavior, urging you to step back, analyze the situation with clarity, and ensure that your goals are not overly ambitious. Before taking the next step, it is essential to ground yourself, seek guidance, and reassess your approach.

Upright Interpretations

General Reading: You have an energetic, enthusiastic, and adventurous approach to life, and entering a phase where you're encouraged to express yourself and start new undertakings.

Love Reading: If you're in a relationship, it might mean rekindling the spark or trying new things together. For singles, it indicates the potential for a new, passionate encounter or the beginning of a spirited relationship.

Health Reading: Your energy levels are high, and it's an excellent time to embark on new fitness routines or explore alternative health practices. However, remember that, like the youthful Page, it's essential to know your limits and not to overexert yourself.

Career Reading: You're likely to experience new professional opportunities or tasks that allow for creative expression. This card suggests being open to learning and approaching challenges with eagerness and enthusiasm.

Reversed Interpretations

General Reading: There's a possibility of blocked creativity or a lack of direction. It can also indicate bad news or delays in messages.

Love Reading: In the realm of relationships, this card reversed might hint at immature attitudes, lack of commitment, or fleeting attractions. It can also suggest a lack of chemistry or that the initial spark in a relationship is starting to fade.

Health Reading: Low energy levels or a lack of motivation might be present. There may be a need to assess whether your actions are harming your health in the long run or if you're neglecting your well-being.

Career Reading: Professionally, there might be a feeling of being stuck or lacking direction. Projects could be stalling, or you might be experiencing a lack of inspiration. It's essential to reassess and perhaps look at things from a different angle.

Depicted as a young figure standing in a barren desert with a firm grasp on a wand, the Page of Wands embodies the spirit of exploration and adventure. As a Tarot card, Pages often symbolize new phases or messages, and in the realm of wands associated with fire and inspiration, this represents a phase of enthusiasm, creativity, and the urge to embark on a new venture. With a youthful energy, the Page's eagerness to learn and purity of passion underscores the idea of a beginner's spirit.

The desert background of many Page of Wands renditions serves as a symbolic representation of untapped potential and uncharted territories. Despite the challenges that may come with such an open canvas, it also presents a wealth of opportunities to explore and conquer. The distant mountains in the backdrop signify both challenges and achievements, beckoning the adventurous spirit of the Page to embark on new endeavors.

♈ **ZODIAC:** Aries (March 21 – April 19) is a Fire sign ruled by Mars. This sign embodies a determined, impulsive, and resolute energy.

♌ Leo (July 23 – August 22) is a Fire sign ruled by the Sun. Leos are known for their self-assurance and innate ability to take the center stage in most situations.

♐ Sagittarius (November 22 – December 21) is a Fire sign ruled by Jupiter. Sagittarians are often seen as the optimists of the zodiac, always looking at the brighter side of life.

△ **ELEMENT:** Fire represents energy, creativity, and power. It is the realm of love, courage, and action. It is associated with Summer, the Suit of Wands, and the South cardinal direction.

ᛁ **HERMETIC QABALAH** Associated Hebrew Letter: Yod – Closed Hand (Deed, Work)

QABALISTIC SEPHIROT: Malkuth (Kingdom)

◑ **TIMING:** June 21 – September 20

KNIGHT OF WANDS

MINOR ARCANA

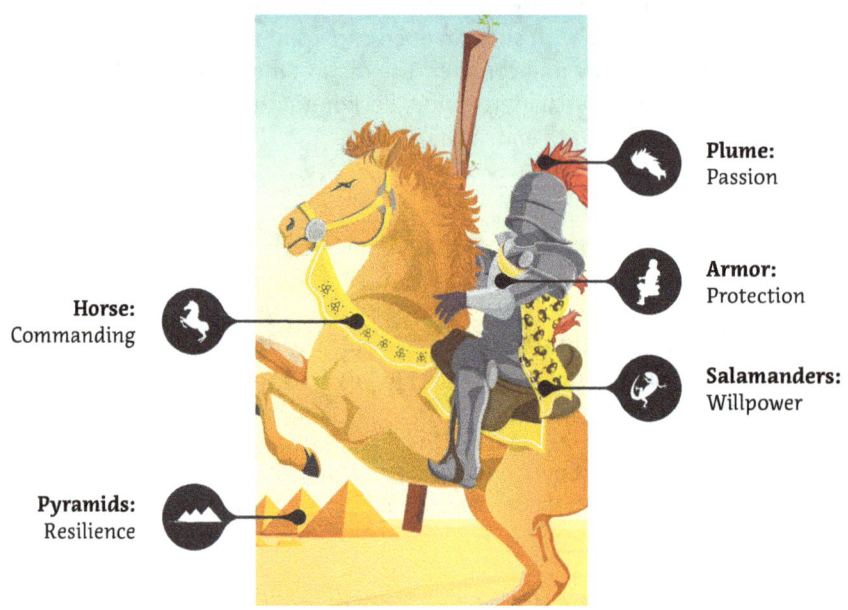

Horse:
Commanding

Pyramids:
Resilience

Plume:
Passion

Armor:
Protection

Salamanders:
Willpower

Yes/No Reading:

Yes   No   Maybe

Names in Other Tarot Systems:
Golden Dawn: Prince of Wands
Tarot of Marseilles: Cavalier of Clubs
Thoth: Prince of Wands

PLANET	ZODIAC	ELEMENT	NUMEROLOGY	COUNT
	Aries, Leo, Sagittarius	Fire	3, 12	4

Upright: *Passion, Courageous, Energy, Adventure, Impulsiveness, Action*
The Knight of Wands embodies a period of fervor, exploration, and bravery. Its appearance typically indicates an individual or energy that is charged with vitality and a zest for life. They are motivated to take risks, delve into new opportunities, and actualize dreams into existence.

Nevertheless, while the Knight of Wands radiates self-assurance and vibrancy, there's a warning about rash decision-making. This Knight can sometimes undertake more than they can manage, propelled by their adventurous nature. Despite the commendable enthusiasm, there's a necessity to temper it with forethought and planning. For those who receive this card, it serves as a reminder to channel their vivacious outlook towards a purposeful path while still being open to unexpected events and the excitement of the unknown.

Reversed: *Anger, Arrogance, Impulsiveness, Recklessness, Haste, Delays*
When the Knight of Wands appears in a reversed position, it is indicative of extreme impulsiveness and recklessness. Such behavior can lead to unwanted consequences, as the actions taken are often without sufficient forethought. This Knight carries an overbearing energy that causes them to jump headlong into situations, driven by misdirected passion or impatience, without considering the repercussions of their choices. This can also result in feeling scattered or spread too thin, as they attempt to take on numerous endeavors without completing any of them.

Additionally, the reversed Knight of Wands may display traits of arrogance, unpredictability, or aggression. Such behavior may appear flighty, with a lack of commitment or responsibility. This card can serve as a reminder to check one's ego and avoid steamrolling over others in pursuit of personal goals. Conversely, for those feeling stagnant or timid, the reversed Knight encourages them to take action with careful consideration and a balanced approach. In essence, this card urges one to harness their inner fire but to use it judiciously.

Upright Interpretations

General Reading: There might be a significant journey or a change in residence. This card can also indicate someone who is passionate, daring, and loves challenges.

Love Reading: Passion and spontaneity are key themes with the Knight of Wands. If single, an exciting, adventurous individual might sweep you off your feet. For those in a relationship, it can suggest a resurgence of romance, or even a spontaneous trip or adventure together.

Health Reading: You might feel an increase in vitality and energy. It's a good time to start a new workout regime or engage in physical activities. However, take care not to overextend yourself or be reckless in your endeavors.

Career Reading: Expect rapid developments, perhaps a new job offer, business trip, or an unexpected opportunity. You're encouraged to take the initiative and be proactive. However, ensure that your actions are well-calculated and not just impulsive.

Reversed Interpretations

General Reading: Beware of hasty actions, impulsiveness, and potential recklessness. There might be delays in travel or a lack of direction. It can also indicate someone who starts things but doesn't finish them.

Love Reading: There might be a tendency to rush into relationships or make impulsive decisions in love, which could lead to regret later. For those in relationships, there could be heated arguments or misunderstandings caused by one or both partners acting without thinking.

Health Reading: Watch out for accidents due to carelessness or rushing. It's essential to listen to your body and not overexert yourself. There might also be a tendency to act impulsively without considering the consequences to your health.

Career Reading: Beware of making hasty decisions in your professional life. There might be a temptation to jump into a new opportunity without proper consideration, which could backfire. It's essential to think things through and not act solely on impulse.

The fiery and spirited horse upon which the Knight of Wands is frequently depicted riding is an emblem of the energy, passion, and impulsiveness embodied by this card. The dynamic stance of the horse, often rearing up or galloping at full speed, reflects the Knight's eagerness for action. Often, their attire is adorned with salamanders, creatures associated with fire, and a plume of feathers on their helmet. The salamanders, particularly when shown eating their tails in a nod to the Ouroboros, symbolize cyclical transformation, endurance, and the continual renewal of energy.

The backdrop of a desert or barren land serves as a reminder of the Knight's occasional recklessness and tendency to act without considering the consequences. Fueled by passion and confidence, they may overlook details or rush into situations without fully understanding them. The desert scenery may hint at the potential outcomes of such haste, suggesting that while the Knight possesses the enthusiasm to start ventures, they may not always see them through to fertile completion.

ZODIAC: Aries (March 21 – April 19) is a Fire sign ruled by Mars. This sign embodies a determined, impulsive, and resolute energy.

Leo (July 23 – August 22) is a Fire sign ruled by the Sun. Leos are known for their self-assurance and innate ability to take the center stage in most situations.

Sagittarius (November 22 – December 21) is a Fire sign ruled by Jupiter. Sagittarians are often seen as the optimists of the zodiac, always looking at the brighter side of life.

ELEMENT: Fire represents energy, creativity, and power. It is the realm of love, courage, and action. It is associated with Summer, the Suit of Wands, and the South cardinal direction.

HERMETIC QABALAH Associated Hebrew Letter: Yod – Closed Hand (Deed, Work)

QABALISTIC SEPHIROT: Tiphareth (Beauty)

TIMING: July 12 – August 11

QUEEN OF WANDS

M I N O R   A R C A N A

Crown:
Honor, Power

Throne:
Power

Cat: Cunning,
Wisdom, Mystery

Sunflower:
Life

Grey Platform:
Neutrality

Yes/No Reading:

☑   ◯   ◯

Yes   *No*   *Maybe*

Names in Other Tarot Systems:

Golden Dawn: Queen of Wands
Tarot of Marseilles: Dame of Clubs
Thoth: Queen of Wands

♈ ♌ ♐	△	4, 13	4
PLANET	**ZODIAC**	**ELEMENT**	**NUMEROLOGY**	**COUNT**
	Aries, Leo, Sagittarius	Fire		

Upright: *Optimistic, Vivacious, Determination, Independent, Social, Warmth*
When upright, the Queen of Wands exudes vibrancy, confidence, and charisma. They personify passion, warmth, and an unyielding enthusiasm for life. Upon entering a room, they have an innate ability to light it up. The Queen is fiercely independent and energetic, and excels at managing and nurturing the growth of their projects and relationships. Their presence brings positive energy, motivation, and encouragement.

Drawing this card can indicate that you are adopting the Queen's qualities or that they represent someone you may encounter or already know. This encourages you to tap into your own inner fire and confidence, and take charge of situations with fierce determination. Believing in yourself and your abilities, like the Queen, will inspire and attract those around you. The card empowers you to unleash your potential and approach life with grace, passion, and purpose.

Reversed: *Jealousy, Introversion, Vengeful, Selfish, Insecure, Moodiness*
When in a reversed position, the Queen of Wands can indicate a lack of confidence and vibrancy that they usually exude when upright. It may signify insecurity, a reduced sense of self-worth, or an excessive need for attention and approval. Instead of their usual radiant and inspiring figure, they may become quick-tempered, jealous, and overly aggressive, with their passionate nature becoming overwhelming and potentially leading to drama or conflict in interactions.

On the other hand, a reversed Queen of Wands may indicate an internal conflict where one suppresses their energetic nature out of fear of judgment or past rejection. This could suggest holding back from realizing one's full potential and inner fire, reminding oneself not to let insecurities or external influences dampen their light. By reflecting on the reasons behind these emotions, it can lead to personal growth and a renewed sense of the Queen's positive qualities.

Upright Interpretations

General Reading: The Queen of Wands represents someone who is full of energy, confidence, and charisma. They suggest that now is a time to be determined, take charge of a situation, and bring warmth and vibrancy to your everyday life.

Love Reading: You're in a place where you feel confident and secure in your relationship. Alternatively, if you're single, it can indicate that you're radiating a magnetic charm that's attracting potential partners. It's a time to embrace your inner passion.

Health Reading: You're in a phase where you're feeling energetic and lively. It's an excellent time to pick up a new physical activity or health routine. Alternatively, this card could also symbolize recovering from an illness or health setback with renewed vigor.

Career Reading: You might be in a leadership position or stepping into one. Your charisma and determination make you stand out, and you have the ability to inspire those around you. It's a time to take charge and lead with enthusiasm.

Reversed Interpretations

General Reading: The reversed Queen of Wands can indicate a lack of energy or confidence. It suggests periods of self-doubt, or trying too hard to seek attention or approval. You might be feeling out of touch with your inner fire and enthusiasm.

Love Reading: You or your partner might be experiencing jealousy or a need for constant validation. There's a possibility of coming on too strong or being overly dramatic in relationship matters. For singles, this might indicate attracting or being attracted to individuals with these traits.

Health Reading: There might be a feeling of lethargy or lack of motivation to maintain health routines. It's a time to reignite your passion for well-being, even if it means seeking external motivation or support.

Career Reading: You may face challenges in leadership or find it hard to assert yourself. There's a possibility of feeling overshadowed or not being recognized for your contributions. Alternatively, it could indicate trying too hard to stand out, leading to conflicts.

The Queen of Wands sits regally on their throne, which is adorned with sunflowers and lions, symbolizing their fiery nature and leadership qualities. The sunflowers, turned towards the sun, represent their positive and determined outlook on life. A black cat rests at their feet, highlighting their deep intuition and connection to the esoteric, while contrasting their fierce lion-like qualities.

In one hand, the Queen of Wands holds a blooming sunflower, representing their ability to find joy and warmth in all situations. In the other hand, they hold a wand sprouting with leaves, symbolizing their fertility, creativity, and potential for growth. Their energetic approach to life is underscored by the warm yellows and fiery golds that dominate the Queen of Wands card, representing their association with the fire element.

The Queen of Wands exudes a contagious energy that inspires those around them to pursue their passions with confidence and enthusiasm. Their ability to channel their energies productively and manifest their vision into reality makes them a force to be reckoned with.

♈ **ZODIAC:** Aries (March 21 – April 19) is a Fire sign ruled by Mars. This sign embodies a determined, impulsive, and resolute energy.

♌ Leo (July 23 – August 22) is a Fire sign ruled by the Sun. Leos are known for their self-assurance and innate ability to take the center stage in most situations.

♐ Sagittarius (November 22 – December 21) is a Fire sign ruled by Jupiter. Sagittarians are often seen as the optimists of the zodiac, always looking at the brighter side of life.

△ **ELEMENT:** Fire represents energy, creativity, and power. It is the realm of love, courage, and action. It is associated with Summer, the Suit of Wands, and the South cardinal direction.

HERMETIC QABALAH Associated Hebrew Letter: Yod – Closed Hand (Deed, Work)

QABALISTIC SEPHIROT: Binah (Understanding)

TIMING: March 11 – April 10

KING OF WANDS

MINOR ARCANA

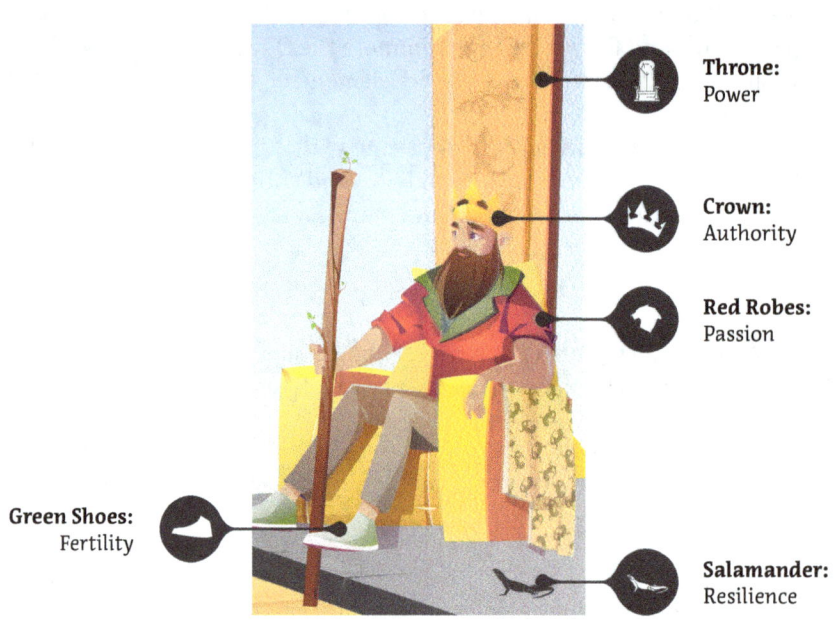

Throne: Power

Crown: Authority

Red Robes: Passion

Green Shoes: Fertility

Salamander: Resilience

Yes/No Reading:

☑ Yes   ○ No   ○ Maybe

Names in Other Tarot Systems:
Golden Dawn: King of Wands
Tarot of Marseilles: Roi of Clubs
Thoth: Knight of Wands

♈♌♐	△	5, 14	4
PLANET	**ELEMENT**	**NUMEROLOGY**	**COUNT**
ZODIAC Aries, Leo, Sagittarius	Fire		

Upright: *Experience, Charm, Dependable, Leadership, Entrepreneurship*

The King of Wands personifies leadership that is driven by passion and inspiration. Its appearance in an upright reading indicates a charismatic, confident, and action-oriented individual who is a natural leader. This person not only dreams big but actively works towards achieving their goals with an infectious energy, inspiring others to join them on their journey. They are unafraid to take risks to fulfill their ambitions and possess an inner fire that drives them to overcome obstacles with determination and courage.

Beyond being a representation of a person, the King of Wands also signifies a period in one's life where they step into their power, take charge, and feel confident in their decisions. It's a call to tap into your inner strength, be bold in your endeavors, and trust your instincts. When this card appears, it encourages you to lead with confidence, unleash your creative potential, and approach challenges with a combination of optimism and pragmatism. Whether you're starting a new project, taking on a leadership role, or simply navigating life's journey, the King of Wands reminds you to do so with passion, conviction, and a zest for life.

Reversed: *Possessiveness, Dominant, Rude, Bully, Controlling, Impulsiveness*

Those represented by this card are high-energy and captivating but can be hasty and unthinking in their decision-making, leading to irascible behavior and an inability to recognize the emotions and perspectives of others.

On a personal level, the reversed King of Wands might suggest uncertainty or a lack of direction. Rather than emanating confidence and lucidity, one might be uncertain of their direction, reluctant to take action, or hampered by fear of failure. It's also a warning against becoming overly self-centered or letting one's ego interfere with sensible decision-making. This card urges self-reflection, encouraging the reassessment of one's motivations, finding a balance between confidence and modesty, and channeling inner passion in a way that is both impassioned and thoughtful towards others.

Upright Interpretations

General Reading: The King of Wands embodies ambition, vision, and leadership. This is a sign that you're in a position of confidence and have the energy and enthusiasm to achieve your goals. Trust in your instincts and experiences.

Love Reading: In relationships, the King of Wands represents a partnership where both parties encourage each other's ambitions. If you're single, you might attract or be attracted to someone with leadership qualities, someone who is charismatic and confident.

Health Reading: You're in a phase where you're feeling strong, both mentally and physically. The King encourages you to take the lead in your health journey, whether it's trying a new fitness regimen or leading others in a wellness challenge.

Career Reading: This card often signals a time of professional growth. You might be stepping into a leadership role or starting a new entrepreneurial venture. Your vision and charisma will guide you, but remember to act decisively.

Reversed Interpretations

General Reading: The reversed King of Wands can indicate impulsiveness, haste, or arrogance. It might be a sign of someone who's overconfident, leading to potential mistakes.

Love Reading: In a relationship context, this card might suggest that one person is being overly dominant or impulsive. There might be issues related to arrogance or an overbearing nature. If you're single, be wary of potential partners who come off as too aggressive or domineering.

Health Reading: Be careful not to overexert oneself or to become overly confident about one's health. It can also be a reminder not to ignore medical advice out of arrogance.

Career Reading: Be cautious of taking on more than you can handle. The reversed King may indicate someone who promises more than they can deliver, or someone in a leadership position who's not leading effectively. It can also suggest conflicts at work due to ego clashes.

Sitting atop a grandiose throne adorned with symbols of lions and salamanders, the King of Wands embodies strength and authority. The lions represent courageous leadership qualities while the salamanders symbolize the ability to transform challenges into opportunities through the cycle of life, death, and rebirth. Despite their regal presence, the King is not detached but actively engaged and ready to take action.

Their robes, often depicted in vivid hues of red and gold, amplify their dynamic force and further reinforce their position as a passionate leader and visionary. While often depicted against an arid desert landscape, this only highlights the King's ability to thrive in challenging conditions. They have a unique ability to utilize their resources, passion, and creativity to make the best out of any situation. The desert landscape underlines their resilience, adaptability, and unwavering strength of character.

♈ **ZODIAC:** Aries (March 21 – April 19) is a Fire sign ruled by Mars. This sign embodies a determined, impulsive, and resolute energy.

♌ Leo (July 23 – August 22) is a Fire sign ruled by the Sun. Leos are known for their self-assurance and innate ability to take the center stage in most situations.

♐ Sagittarius (November 22 – December 21) is a Fire sign ruled by Jupiter. Sagittarians are often seen as the optimists of the zodiac, always looking at the brighter side of life.

△ **ELEMENT:** Fire represents energy, creativity, and power. It is the realm of love, courage, and action. It is associated with Summer, the Suit of Wands, and the South cardinal direction.

י **HERMETIC QABALAH** Associated Hebrew Letter: Yod – Closed Hand (Deed, Work)

QABALISTIC SEPHIROT: Chokmah (Wisdom)

🕐 **TIMING:** November 13 – December 12

ACE OF SWORDS

M I N O R   A R C A N A

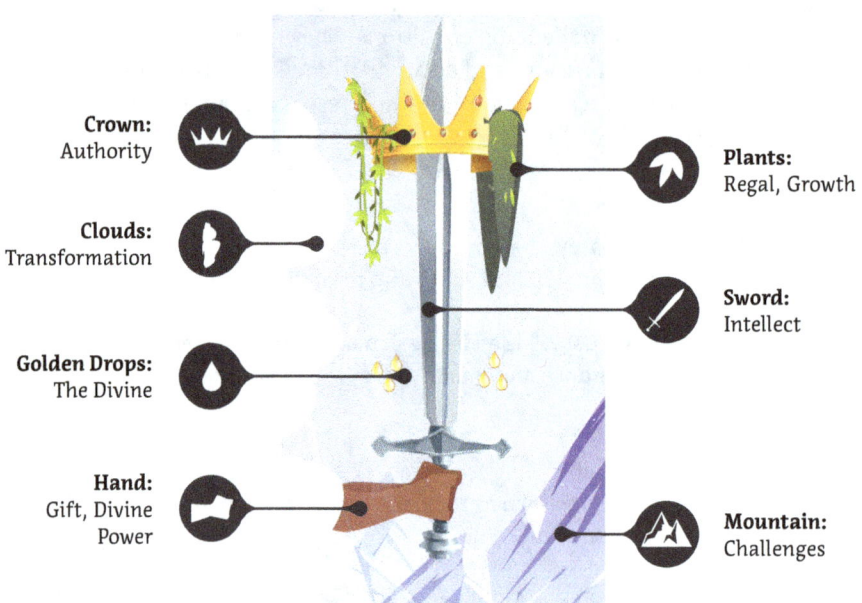

Crown:
Authority

Clouds:
Transformation

Golden Drops:
The Divine

Hand:
Gift, Divine
Power

Plants:
Regal, Growth

Sword:
Intellect

Mountain:
Challenges

Yes/No Reading:

Yes   No   Maybe

Names in Other Tarot Systems:
Golden Dawn: The Radix of the Powers of Air
Tarot of Marseilles: Ace of Swords
Thoth: The Root of the Powers of Air

♊ ♎ ♒	△	1, 10	5, 11
PLANET	**ZODIAC**	**ELEMENT**	**NUMEROLOGY**	**COUNT**
	Gemini, Libra, Aquarius	Air		

Upright: *Focus, Intellect, Breakthrough, New Ideas, Success, Sharp Mind*
You're having a moment of revelation, intellectual power, and clarity. The confusion is dissipating, providing clear comprehension. This period calls for distinguishing between truth and falsehood, perceiving things as they are. Like a sharp sword, this card cuts through illusions, offers lucidity, and facilitates well-informed choices. It recommends that the querent depend on their intelligence and logic to maneuver through the situation, signifying they have the necessary tools to solve the problem or make an important decision.

Moreover, the upright Ace of Swords represents the triumph of justice or truth. It can be shown as someone standing up for their beliefs, revealing the truth, or serving justice. The card's vigor is assertive and straightforward, highlighting the significance of open communication, honesty, and integrity. It reminds the querent that while truth and clarity are empowering, they also require the judicious use of power. This is the time to be decisive and equitable, to express oneself while recognizing the ramifications and effects of one's words and deeds.

Reversed: *Insults, Frustration, Brutality, Chaos, Clouded Judgment*
There's a state of confusion or miscommunication. The card's usual attributes of insight and intellectual clarity become obscured, resulting in misunderstandings, misinterpretations, or an inability to see the truth. Inverted, the sword loses its symbolism of piercing clarity and instead suggests a delay in understanding or the presence of misinformation. This position indicates mental scatter or feeling overwhelmed, making it challenging to arrive at a clear conclusion or make sense of one's circumstances.

There may be a misuse of intellectual power in contrast to the upright position's representation of truth and clarity. Misapplied, the sword can cause harm, and as a result, it is a warning against speaking or acting without full knowledge or using words as weapons. One is urged to be cautious in their beliefs.

Upright Interpretations

General Reading: You may gain a new understanding or see the truth in a situation. This is a time for clear thinking and honest communication.

Love Reading: Focus on clear communication with a partner and to understand the truth about your relationship. You may need a fresh start or a moment of realization regarding your feelings or your partner's feelings.

Health Reading: Clarity regarding a health issue might emerge. This could be a diagnosis that finally provides answers or a newfound mental clarity that supports your overall well-being.

Career Reading: You are likely to experience a breakthrough in your career. This could be a new project, idea, or a fresh start. Clear communication and understanding will lead you to success.

Reversed Interpretations

General Reading: You might be feeling confused, misinformed, or mentally scattered. There may be misunderstandings or a lack of clear communication, causing hurdles in progress.

Love Reading: Misunderstandings, lack of clarity, or miscommunication may strain the relationship. It's also possible that someone isn't being entirely truthful or transparent about their feelings or intentions.

Health Reading: You might be facing misdiagnoses, or unclear information regarding health. It could also indicate mental fog or confusion, impacting mental well-being.

Career Reading: Misunderstandings or miscommunication might cause obstacles in your professional life. It's essential to verify all information and ensure you're clear in your professional interactions. Alternatively, there could be a delay in a new start or project.

The Ace of Swords prominently features an upright sword as its primary symbol, representing the potency of intellect, transparency, and authenticity. Its double edge conveys the twofold nature of the mind, serving as an instrument for fairness and coherence or as a weapon of destruction and confusion. A crown frequently adorns or is punctured by the sword, connoting victory, power, and a divine mandate, which suggests that the wisdom or decisions attributed to this card transcend individual significance and bear cosmic weight.

Clouds or tumultuous skies surround the sword, emphasizing that clarity often stems from disarray or turbulence. The hand that grasps the sword from the clouds reinforces the notion of divine or universal guidance, imparting this insight or veracity. The inclusion of mountainous backgrounds in some Tarot decks signifies challenges or impediments, implying that the truth uncovered by the Ace of Swords can surmount any obstacle. The Ace of Swords' imagery collectively communicates a potent message concerning the transformative and illuminating influence of truth, discernment, and transparency.

ZODIAC: Gemini (May 21 – June 20) is an Air sign ruled by Mercury. The dual nature of Gemini embodies a mix of yin and yang, and Geminis often feel as though they have two distinct sides.

Libra (September 23 – October 22) is an Air sign ruled by Venus. Libras often strive for harmony and balance in their lives.

Aquarius (January 20 – February 18) is an Air sign ruled by Uranus. Aquarians are self-reliant, analytical, independent, clever, and optimistic.

ELEMENT: Air represents logic, intellect, and communication. The intangible element is considered to be active, masculine energy. It is associated with Spring, the Suit of Wands, and the East cardinal direction.

HERMETIC QABALAH Associated Hebrew Letter: Waw – Hook, Nail (Connections, Secure)

QABALISTIC SEPHIROT: Kether (Crown)

TIMING: December 23 – March 20

TWO OF SWORDS

M I N O R   A R C A N A

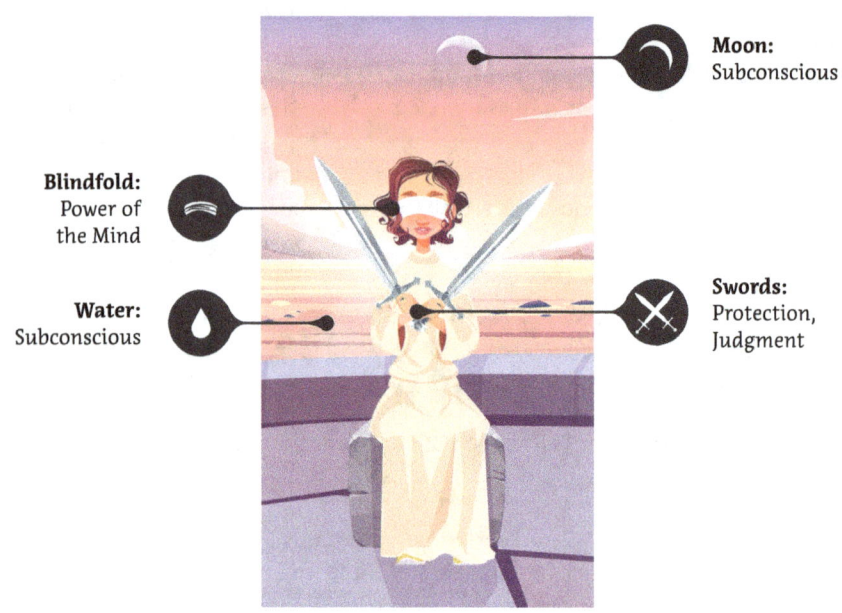

Moon:
Subconscious

Blindfold:
Power of
the Mind

Water:
Subconscious

Swords:
Protection,
Judgment

Yes/No Reading:

Yes   No   *Maybe*

Names in Other Tarot Systems:
Golden Dawn: Lord of Peace Restored
Tarot of Marseilles: Two of Swords
Thoth: Peace

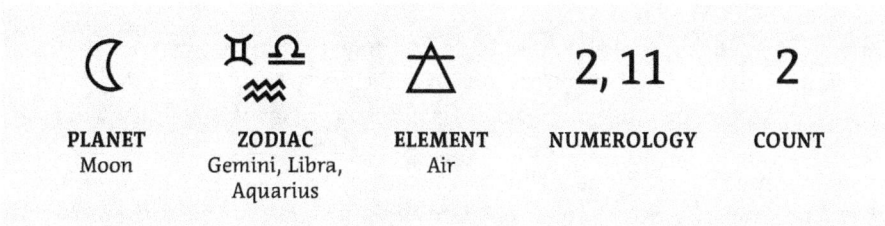

PLANET	ZODIAC	ELEMENT	NUMEROLOGY	COUNT
Moon	Gemini, Libra, Aquarius	Air	2, 11	2

Upright: *Indecision, Difficult Decisions, Impasse, Avoidance, Weighing Options*
The Two of Swords is a card that speaks to conflicts both inside and outside of oneself, a struggle with indecision, and a moment of choice. Its appearance often signifies being stuck between two equally compelling options, resulting in a deadlock when deciding. The blindfold worn by the figure in the card suggests that one may be unwilling to face the truth about a situation, either out of fear or feeling overwhelmed by the weight of the decision. During this time, the card encourages stepping back and reflecting before moving.

Furthermore, the Two of Swords may also represent the need for mental and emotional balance and boundaries. The defensive stance taken by the figure holding the swords implies the need to protect oneself from external pressures and trust one's inner wisdom. It's a reminder that while seeking external advice can be helpful, ultimately, one's final decision should resonate with one's inner truth. Though the path ahead may not be clear, this card advises approaching the situation thoughtfully, removing any blindfold of denial, and facing it with courage.

Reversed: *Confusion, Disruption, Anxiety, Worry, Information Overload*
You're in the early stages of progress or resolution following a period of indecisiveness or stagnation. The inner or outer conflicts that were previously crippling may start to unwind, indicating that you are either being compelled to make a decision or gaining greater clarity on the path ahead. This inverted card implies that the time for avoidance or denial is ending, and while the decision may be uncomfortable or challenging, taking action is unavoidable.

There is a risk of acting impulsively without fully comprehending the implications of the decision. There may be a tendency to be reactive, driven by the discomfort of being in a state of limbo. Ensure you're not rushing to a decision to bring an end to the situation. Evaluate all aspects of the circumstances before moving forward.

Upright Interpretations

General Reading: You're at a crossroads and may feel torn between two paths or decisions. There's a need for introspection and clarity. Avoidance or denial won't serve you; facing the situation head-on is necessary, even if it feels challenging.

Love Reading: You might be feeling conflicted or unsure about a relationship or a critical decision related to love. There might be a need to protect one's emotions or maintain boundaries, but open communication is essential.

Health Reading: You might be in denial about a situation or facing a difficult choice regarding treatment or lifestyle. It's essential to gather all information and consult professionals, but ultimately, the decision should align with your feelings and intuition.

Career Reading: You might be facing a decision about a job offer, project direction, or a business relationship. There's a need for careful consideration and perhaps seeking counsel from mentors or colleagues. Protect your professional interests, but avoid being overly defensive.

Reversed Interpretations

General Reading: A decision or resolution is on the horizon, but ensure it isn't made in haste. The period of indecision is ending, and it's time to move forward, but careful deliberation is still advised.

Love Reading: There might be a forthcoming revelation or decision in your love life. Whether it's deciding to commit, break up, or address an issue, ensure that the choice is well-considered and not reactive.

Health Reading: You might soon gain clarity about a health issue or decide on a course of treatment. While movement towards resolution is positive, don't rush into decisions without thoroughly understanding the implications.

Career Reading: A career decision is looming. Whether it's about changing jobs, taking on a new project, or navigating office dynamics, it's essential to make choices rooted in a thorough understanding and not merely out of urgency or pressure.

The blindfold symbolizes a lack of clarity or an unwillingness to confront the truth. It could indicate denial, a conscious decision to avoid a crucial issue or uncertainty about which path to take. The two swords are positioned in a way that indicates a stalemate or an equilibrium, reflecting the realm of thoughts and communication. Their crossed positions suggest conflicting ideas.

The calm waters in the background signify present but not turbulent emotions. This implies that the internal conflict might be more of a mental or logical challenge than an emotional one. The crescent moon, on the other hand, represents intuition, cycles, and the unknown.

The position of the person is significant and varies from deck to deck. If seated, it could indicate introspection and contemplation, indicating the need to look within for answers. If standing, it may suggest a more active stance, a readiness to confront whatever challenge lies ahead, even if they are still uncertain about which direction to take.

ZODIAC: Gemini (May 21 – June 20) is an Air sign ruled by Mercury. The dual nature of Gemini embodies a mix of yin and yang, and Geminis often feel as though they have two distinct sides.

Libra (September 23 – October 22) is an Air sign ruled by Venus. Libras often strive for harmony and balance in their lives.

Aquarius (January 20 – February 18) is an Air sign ruled by Uranus. Aquarians are self-reliant, analytical, independent, clever, and optimistic.

ELEMENT: Air represents logic, intellect, and communication. The intangible element is considered to be active, masculine energy. It is associated with Spring, the Suit of Wands, and the East cardinal direction.

HERMETIC QABALAH Associated Hebrew Letter: Waw – Hook, Nail (Connections, Secure)

QABALISTIC SEPHIROT: Chokmah (Wisdom)

TIMING: September 23 – October 2

THREE OF SWORDS

MINOR ARCANA

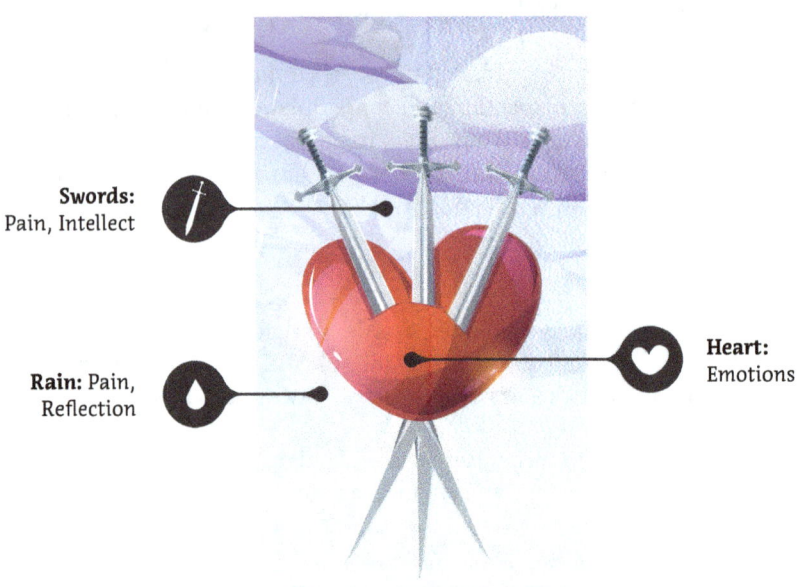

Swords:
Pain, Intellect

Rain: Pain,
Reflection

Heart:
Emotions

Yes/No Reading:

Yes   No   Maybe

Names in Other Tarot Systems:
Golden Dawn: Lord of Sorrow
Tarot of Marseilles: Three of Swords
Thoth: Sorrow

♄	♊ ♎ ♒	△	3, 12	3
PLANET	**ZODIAC**	**ELEMENT**	**NUMEROLOGY**	**COUNT**
Saturn	Gemini, Libra, Aquarius	Air		

Upright: *Grief, Separation, Heartbreak, Sorrow, Emotional Pain, Alienation*
The upright Three of Swords embodies themes of sorrow, heartbreak, and emotional pain, signifying a difficult period marked by grief, disappointment, or the sting of betrayal. This card reveals the hurtful words, actions, or realizations that have cut to the heart and left wounds that might be raw and fresh. It underscores the emotional toll such experiences take on our spirit, resulting in loneliness, loss, or anguish.

Despite its negative connotation, the Three of Swords conveys a deeper message of healing and growth. Although painful, these experiences often lead to profound personal insight and eventual healing. Though the wounds are evident, they mark the beginning of the healing process and moving through the hurt toward eventual recovery and understanding. Essentially, this card encourages acknowledgment of the pain, its origins, and the importance of processing and moving forward. Ultimately, the stormy clouds will give way to clearer skies, leaving a deeper understanding and insight behind.

Reversed: *Recovery, Forgiveness, Optimism, Letting Go of Pain, Compromise*
You're in a period of healing and reconciliation. There's a transition from acute grief to a more reflective and understanding state. When reversed, this card signifies the release of past hurts, forgiveness, or the strength to move on from a painful situation. The downward movement of the swords represents the removal of emotional burdens and the start of the healing process.

However, the reversed Three of Swords should also be a caution against suppressing or avoiding emotions. While it does indicate healing, there is a risk of prematurely pushing aside feelings without fully processing them, which can result in unresolved emotional baggage. It is essential to ensure that the recovery process is genuine and not just a superficial avoidance of emotional pain. Sometimes, it suggests lingering resentments or unresolved issues that need addressing before true healing can occur. The card emphasizes deep introspection, acceptance, and genuine emotional release for true recovery.

Upright Interpretations

General Reading: You might be experiencing a period of sorrow, disappointment, or heartbreak. This could be due to unforeseen events, betrayals, or realizations that challenge your emotions deeply. It's a time to acknowledge your feelings, process them, and find ways to heal.

Love Reading: You're experiencing heartbreak, separation, or misunderstandings in a relationship. There might be a betrayal or the surfacing of painful truths. For singles, it may suggest lingering pain from past relationships that affects current emotions or readiness for new love.

Health Reading: You might be feeling emotional stress that's impacting your physical health, or perhaps the mental strain of dealing with a health issue. Ensure you address both emotional and physical well-being, seeking support when needed.

Career Reading: There could be disagreements, unexpected setbacks, or the realization of hard truths about your job or colleagues.

Reversed Interpretations

General Reading: You are entering a phase of healing and recovery, potentially mending from past hurts. Alternatively, you might be avoiding or suppressing certain emotions, which could lead to unresolved issues. It's essential to ensure emotional processing is genuine.

Love Reading: Healing is on the horizon for relationships that have experienced turbulence. Forgiveness and reconciliation might be possible. For those single, it indicates moving past previous heartaches and becoming open to new romantic possibilities. However, ensure you're not overlooking unresolved emotions.

Health Reading: There's a potential for improved emotional well-being or recovery from a health-related setback. Stay mindful of repressed emotions, as they can resurface in the form of physical ailments.

Career Reading: Resolution and healing from previous workplace issues or conflicts are indicated. There's potential for improving work relationships and mending bridges. On the other hand, ensure you're not in denial about workplace challenges or issues that need to be addressed

The Three of Swords depicts three swords piercing a heart, evoking pain, heartbreak, and sorrow. The heart-piercing imagery reflects the emotional anguish that hurtful words, thoughts, or revelations can cause. It could signify a betrayal, separation, or a hard truth that cuts to the core.

The card's backdrop often portrays rain and stormy clouds, emphasizing the themes of grief and sadness. Rain represents tears and emotional release, while tumultuous clouds symbolize heartbreak and emotional turmoil. The setting accentuates the sense of a trying period fraught with despair and sorrow.

The swords' arrangement, usually directly and straightforwardly, represents the blunt and unequivocal nature of the pain or realization. The arrangement leaves no room for ambiguity; the hurt is apparent and undeniable. In Tarot, the number three indicates growth, expression, and expansion. Personal growth and more profound understanding are possible through experiencing pain, even if it initially feels heart-wrenching.

ZODIAC: Gemini (May 21 – June 20) is an Air sign ruled by Mercury. The dual nature of Gemini embodies a mix of yin and yang, and Geminis often feel as though they have two distinct sides.

Libra (September 23 – October 22) is an Air sign ruled by Venus. Libras often strive for harmony and balance in their lives.

Aquarius (January 20 – February 18) is an Air sign ruled by Uranus. Aquarians are self-reliant, analytical, independent, clever, and optimistic.

ELEMENT: Air represents logic, intellect, and communication. The intangible element is considered to be active, masculine energy. It is associated with Spring, the Suit of Wands, and the East cardinal direction.

HERMETIC QABALAH Associated Hebrew Letter: Waw – Hook, Nail (Connections, Secure)

QABALISTIC SEPHIROT: Binah (Understanding)

TIMING: October 3 – October 12

FOUR OF SWORDS

MINOR ARCANA

PAX:
"Peace" in
Latin

Stained Glass:
Fragmented

Prone Figure:
Stagnation

Swords:
Hardships

Sword:
Tenacity

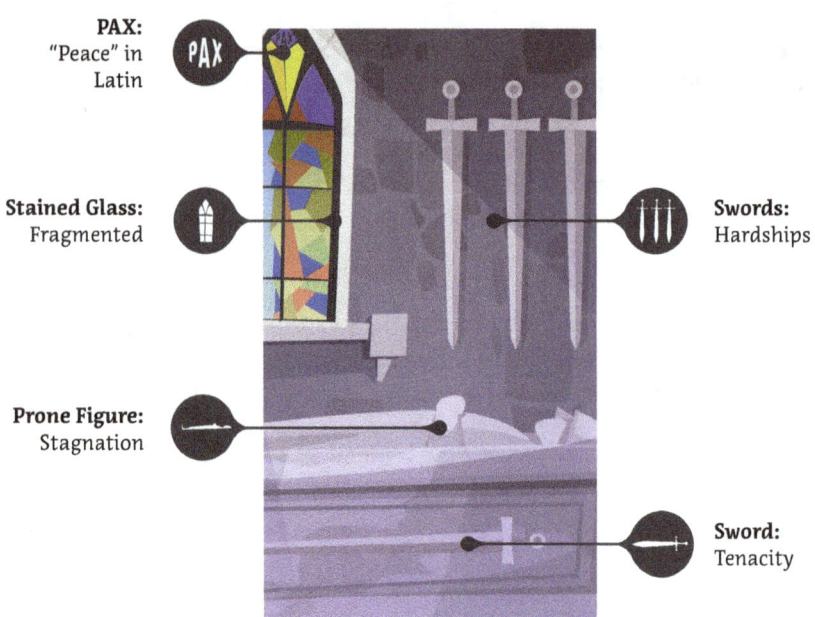

Yes/No Reading:

Yes   No   **Maybe**

Names in Other Tarot Systems:
Golden Dawn: Lord of Rest from Strife
Tarot of Marseilles: Four of Swords
Thoth: Truce

♃	♊ ♎ ♒	△	4, 13	4
PLANET	**ZODIAC**	**ELEMENT**	**NUMEROLOGY**	**COUNT**
Jupiter	Gemini, Libra, Aquarius	Air		

Upright: *Relaxation, Exhaustion, Mental Overload, Contemplation, Restoration*
Whether following a period of strife, emotional turmoil, or relentless activity, this card advises a deliberate break to recharge mentally, emotionally, and physically. This isn't about passivity or aimlessness; it's about actively choosing solitude and calm to achieve clarity, heal wounds, and prepare for the next phase of one's journey.

Some of life's greatest insights and resolutions come during moments of quietude. In a world that often demands continuous action and engagement, this card stands as an affirmation of the importance of personal sanctuary, meditation, and the deep rejuvenation that can only be found in stillness. It counsels patience and understanding, suggesting that sometimes, true strength is found not in action, but in thoughtful retreat.

Reversed: *Restlessness, Burnout, Stress, Slow Recovery, Stagnation*
The once peaceful haven for contemplation and repose has been disrupted, signaling that the need for rest and recuperation, which may have been previously ignored or delayed, can no longer be brushed aside. However, there is a sense of unease and confinement in this necessary pause, creating a tension between the desire to act and the need to rest.

One is forced into retreat or isolation, not by choice but by circumstance, perhaps due to recovery after an illness or feeling left out and eager to re-enter the active bustle of life. The focus of the card shifts from the benefits of rest to the frustrations of inactivity or the challenges of reintegration.

Additionally, this reversed card serves as a warning against potential burnout, highlighting the dangers of consistently neglecting the body and mind's need for downtime, which could result in exhaustion or even more significant setbacks. The card's core message is to prioritize balance and recognize that moments of inactivity are not setbacks but instead critical for long-term well-being and success.

Upright Interpretations

General Reading: You're entering a period of rest, recovery, and contemplation. After battling through challenges, it's time to step back, rejuvenate, and reflect. This pause allows for mental clarity and healing.

Love Reading: Take a step back to reflect on the relationship or to give each other space. For singles, it's a time of self-reflection before entering a new relationship.

Health Reading: This card suggests a recovery period, whether from physical illness or mental exhaustion. It emphasizes the need for relaxation and perhaps seeking solitude for healing.

Career Reading: It's a period of retreat from active projects, maybe due to burnout. Take this time to strategize and plan for the future.

Reversed Interpretations

General Reading: The reversed position indicates a restless period or an urgent need to come out of isolation. It might also suggest a forced period of inactivity or stagnation where the rest isn't by choice.

Love Reading: Tensions might be rising due to inaction or avoidance in the relationship. For singles, it may indicate rushing into love without adequate self-reflection.

Health Reading: You might be feeling restless during a recovery phase or pushing yourself too hard without allowing proper healing time.

Career Reading: Delays or stagnation in career endeavors may be frustrating There might be an urgency to act but circumstances are forcing you to wait.

The Four of Swords often depicts a figure in a horizontal position, reminiscent of a tomb effigy, indicating a state of profound rest or meditation. This representation reinforces the card's withdrawal, recovery, and contemplation themes.

Typically, the card features three swords suspended above or behind the resting figure, while one is positioned horizontally beneath or beside them. These swords symbolize the challenges or stresses left behind or set aside. The lone sword, distinct from the others, may denote clarity or a single-minded focus arising from the rest and reflection period.

The background highlights a stained glass window or a church or temple setting in numerous decks. This spiritual atmosphere emphasizes the card's connection to introspection, healing, and potentially seeking spiritual or divine guidance during the retreat. It conveys the idea of sanctuary and the tranquility that can be discovered in personal or sacred spaces.

♊ **ZODIAC:** Gemini (May 21 – June 20) is an Air sign ruled by Mercury. The dual nature of Gemini embodies a mix of yin and yang, and Geminis often feel as though they have two distinct sides.

♎ Libra (September 23 – October 22) is an Air sign ruled by Venus. Libras often strive for harmony and balance in their lives.

♒ Aquarius (January 20 – February 18) is an Air sign ruled by Uranus. Aquarians are self-reliant, analytical, independent, clever, and optimistic.

△ **ELEMENT:** Air represents logic, intellect, and communication. The intangible element is considered to be active, masculine energy. It is associated with Spring, the Suit of Wands, and the East cardinal direction.

ו **HERMETIC QABALAH** Associated Hebrew Letter: Waw – Hook, Nail (Connections, Secure)

❦ **QABALISTIC SEPHIROT:** Chesed (Mercy)

🕐 **TIMING:** October 13 – October 22

FIVE OF SWORDS

M I N O R   A R C A N A

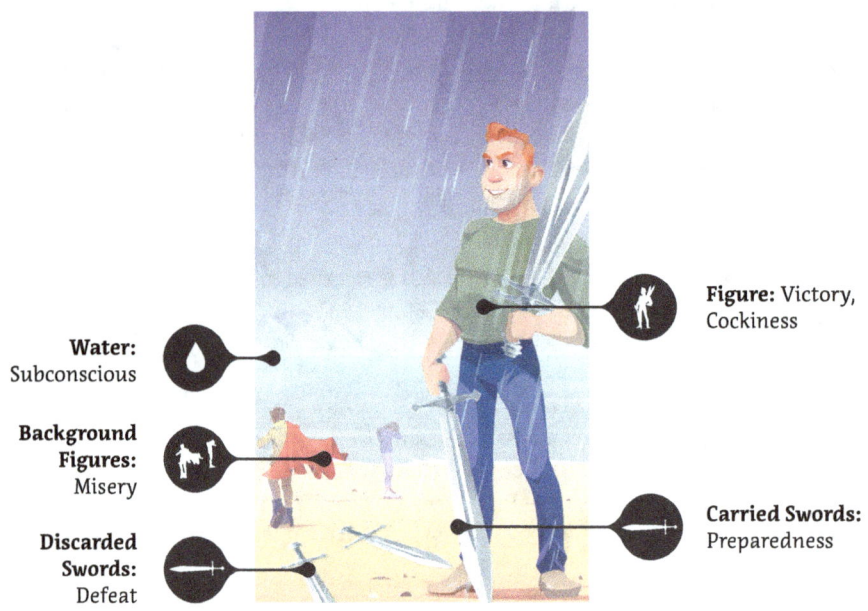

Figure: Victory, Cockiness

Water: Subconscious

Background Figures: Misery

Discarded Swords: Defeat

Carried Swords: Preparedness

Yes/No Reading:

○   ✓   ○

Yes   No   Maybe

Names in Other Tarot Systems:
Golden Dawn: Lord of Defeat
Tarot of Marseilles: Five of Swords
Thoth: Defeat

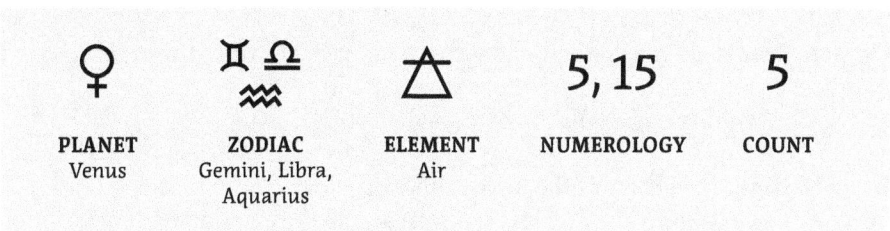

PLANET	ZODIAC	ELEMENT	NUMEROLOGY	COUNT
Venus	Gemini, Libra, Aquarius	Air		

Upright: *Dishonesty, Failure, Conflict, Deception, Defeat, Competition, Ego*
The Five of Swords speaks to the complexities of conflict, personal ambition, and the consequences of pursuing victory at any cost. This card suggests triumph, but it's a triumph that often feels hollow, marked by strained relationships, tension, or a nagging sense of regret. It warns about the pitfalls of unchecked ambition, highlighting the difference between achieving success and maintaining integrity.

Moreover, the card prompts introspection about one's motives and actions. It asks: Are you pursuing your goals with respect for others, or are you stepping on toes and burning bridges in the process? The Five of Swords is a reminder that victories achieved at the expense of others or one's principles may not be as satisfying or long-lasting as they first appear.

Reversed: *Past Resentment, Compromise, Reconciliation, Making Amends*
The reversed Five of Swords suggests that they are experiencing the aftermath of a conflict or dispute and may be dealing with regret, shame, or guilt. While they might have initially thought they'd achieved a victory or had the upper hand, upon reflection, they realize the win might have come at a significant personal or moral cost. Their actions or decisions might not align with their values or the person they aspire to be. They might question whether the perceived victory was worth the relationships or integrity that were compromised in the process.

On another note, the reversed Five of Swords can also indicate a desire to reconcile or make amends after tension or disagreement. They may recognize the importance of compromise and the value of relationships over personal pride or winning at any cost. It's a moment of introspection, understanding that sometimes it's better to lose a battle to preserve the greater peace or a meaningful relationship. They are urged to seek resolution, open lines of communication, and work towards rebuilding trust.

Upright Interpretations

General Reading: There's a sense of victory, but it might be at the expense of others or one's own inner peace. It can also point to empty triumphs where the cost of winning outweighs the perceived benefits.

Love Reading: In matters of the heart, this card may point to tension, disagreements, or one-sided victories in a relationship. One partner might feel like they're constantly "winning" arguments, but at the cost of the relationship's health.

Health Reading: This card can indicate mental strain due to conflicts or aggressive pursuit of goals without considering one's well-being. It's essential to understand the toll that constant strife can take on health.

Career Reading: The Five of Swords could hint at workplace conflicts, competitive environments, or achieving goals through cutthroat methods. It's a reminder to consider if the means truly justify the end.

Reversed Interpretations

General Reading: This card reversed implies moving past conflicts and seeking reconciliation. It might also signify a realization about the hollowness of certain victories or an attempt to avoid further conflicts and confrontations.

Love Reading: There might be attempts to mend fences after conflicts or an understanding that winning battles in a relationship isn't as important as mutual respect and harmony.

Health Reading: The reversed card suggests healing from past stresses or a shift towards a more peaceful and balanced lifestyle to benefit overall well-being.

Career Reading: In a career context, this might mean seeking mediation after disputes or understanding that cooperation and teamwork yield better results than personal aggrandizement.

The Five of Swords depicts a figure holding three swords, standing triumphantly, while two other swords lie on the ground. Nearby, two more figures are shown retreating, suggesting they've been defeated or have surrendered. This central imagery speaks to victory but hints at the costs and repercussions of such a win.

The backdrop is barren or tumultuous, mirroring conflict and strife's emotional and environmental consequences. It underscores the idea that, while battles may be won, the aftermath can be lonely or fraught with tension.

In many decks, the main figure has a smug or satisfied expression, emphasizing the idea of personal victory. However, this satisfaction might seem shallow, hinting at the internal reflection about whether the victory was worth the cost.

ZODIAC: Gemini (May 21 – June 20) is an Air sign ruled by Mercury. The dual nature of Gemini embodies a mix of yin and yang, and Geminis often feel as though they have two distinct sides.

Libra (September 23 – October 22) is an Air sign ruled by Venus. Libras often strive for harmony and balance in their lives.

Aquarius (January 20 – February 18) is an Air sign ruled by Uranus. Aquarians are self-reliant, analytical, independent, clever, and optimistic.

ELEMENT: Air represents logic, intellect, and communication. The intangible element is considered to be active, masculine energy. It is associated with Spring, the Suit of Wands, and the East cardinal direction.

HERMETIC QABALAH Associated Hebrew Letter: Waw – Hook, Nail (Connections, Secure)

QABALISTIC SEPHIROT: Geburah (Severity)

TIMING: January 20 – January 29

SIX OF SWORDS

M I N O R   A R C A N A

Mountains: Challenges

Calm Water: Subconscious

Boat Operator: Control

Child: Indecision

Boat: Transition

Swords: Blockage, Baggage

Adult Passenger: Optimism

Rough Water: Paradox

Yes/No Reading:

◯ Yes   ◯ No   ☑ Maybe

Names in Other Tarot Systems:
Golden Dawn: Lord of Earned Success
Tarot of Marseilles: Six of Swords
Thoth: Science

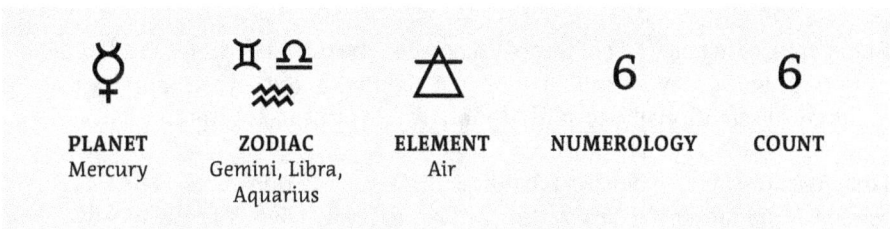

PLANET	ZODIAC	ELEMENT	NUMEROLOGY	COUNT
Mercury	Gemini, Libra, Aquarius	Air	6	6

Upright: *Transition, Progress, Travel, Change, Rite of Passage, Release*
The upright Six of Swords embodies the theme of transition and moving towards better times. It signifies a phase where one is leaving behind difficulties, challenges, or turmoil, embarking on a journey towards tranquility, clarity, and resolution. This journey can be literal, like a physical relocation, or more metaphorical, representing an emotional or mental shift.

Furthermore, while the card denotes change and movement, it also emphasizes that this transition is deliberate and necessary. It's not about running away but about consciously choosing to move towards environments or states of being that are more conducive to growth and peace. The Six of Swords reminds us that while transitions can be challenging, they're often crucial for our well-being and personal evolution.

Reversed: *Resistance to Change, Unfinished Business, Resisting, Overwhelm*
The reversed Six of Swords suggests that they encounter obstacles or resistance in trying to escape challenging circumstances. They may be stuck in a situation or mindset, finding it hard to progress and transition into a more positive phase. The hope and relief typically associated with the upright position of this card seem elusive, causing frustration. Their desire for change and to transition to a better situation is clear, but something, possibly internal barriers or external complications, is hindering this progression.

Additionally, this card can signify that they might be avoiding necessary change or evading critical transitions, perhaps due to fear of the unknown or a reluctance to leave behind the familiar, no matter how tumultuous. They may be clinging to the past, not quite ready to let go, even if they know deep down that moving on is for the best. The reversed Six of Swords serves as a reminder that growth often requires leaving behind what no longer does them, and while the journey might be fraught with challenges, facing them head-on will eventually lead to smoother waters.

Upright Interpretations

General Reading: The Six of Swords represents transition, change, and moving from turbulent waters to calmer shores. It signifies a journey, either physically, mentally, or emotionally, towards a more stable or peaceful state.

Love Reading: You're moving past difficulties in a relationship and heading towards a smoother phase. Or, this card could imply physically moving or traveling with a partner. For singles, it may mean leaving past heartaches behind and moving towards a new romantic phase.

Health Reading: This card denotes recovery and moving away from health challenges. It suggests improvement and heading towards a better phase of well-being.

Career Reading: Professionally, the Six of Swords indicates transitioning to a better job, moving towards a more fulfilling role, or even physically relocating for work. It represents positive changes in one's career trajectory.

Reversed Interpretations

General Reading: When reversed, it may indicate delays in transitions, resistance to change, or being stuck in a challenging situation. There's a sense of feeling trapped or unable to move forward.

Love Reading: You may have unresolved issues in a relationship or you're stuck in old patterns that prevent you from finding love. There might be an unwillingness or inability to leave a challenging relationship.

Health Reading: There might be delays in recovery or difficulties in transitioning to a healthier lifestyle. Past health issues might still be causing problems.

Career Reading: There are setbacks in your career advancements, challenges in adapting to a new job, or delays in plans to relocate for professional reasons.

A figure or figures are shown in a boat, ferrying across waters with swords placed in the vessel. The boat represents the vessel of transition, while the water's condition—from turbulent to calm—symbolizes the journey from chaos or difficulty toward peace and resolution.

The figures in the boat have their backs turned to the viewer, looking ahead or down. This posture emphasizes leaving the past behind and focusing on the future. The forward-facing orientation suggests optimism and the hope of better horizons.

The presence of swords in the boat, even during transition, reminds us that we carry our experiences, lessons, and challenges with us. They are a part of our story, and while we move towards better times, we don't entirely leave our past behind but rather integrate those experiences into our evolving journey.

ZODIAC: Gemini (May 21 – June 20) is an Air sign ruled by Mercury. The dual nature of Gemini embodies a mix of yin and yang, and Geminis often feel as though they have two distinct sides.

Libra (September 23 – October 22) is an Air sign ruled by Venus. Libras often strive for harmony and balance in their lives.

Aquarius (January 20 – February 18) is an Air sign ruled by Uranus. Aquarians are self-reliant, analytical, independent, clever, and optimistic.

ELEMENT: Air represents logic, intellect, and communication. The intangible element is considered to be active, masculine energy. It is associated with Spring, the Suit of Wands, and the East cardinal direction.

HERMETIC QABALAH Associated Hebrew Letter: Waw – Hook, Nail (Connections, Secure)

QABALISTIC SEPHIROT: Tiphareth (Beauty)

TIMING: January 30 – February 8

SEVEN OF SWORDS
M I N O R   A R C A N A

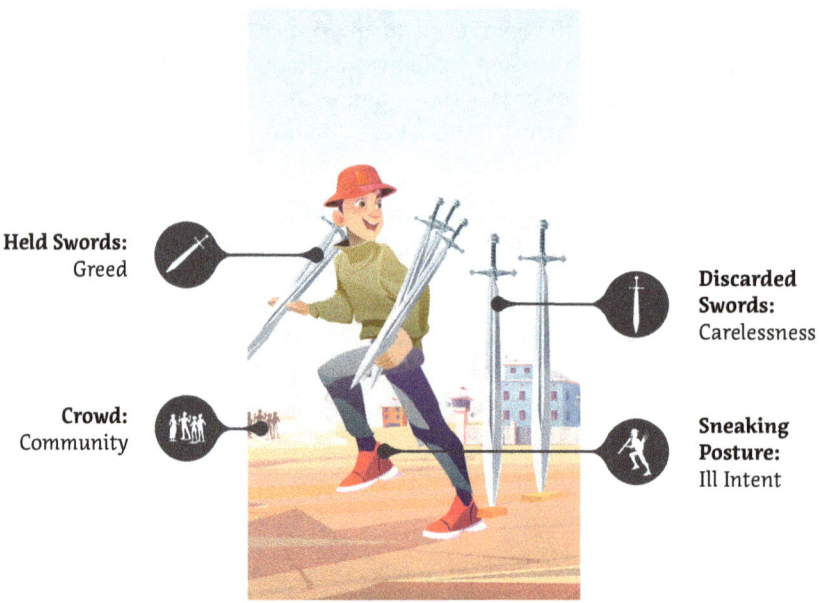

Held Swords:
Greed

Discarded Swords:
Carelessness

Crowd:
Community

Sneaking Posture:
Ill Intent

Yes/No Reading:

○   ☑   ○

Yes   *No*   *Maybe*

Names in Other Tarot Systems:
Golden Dawn: Lord of Futility
Tarot of Marseilles: Seven of Swords
Thoth: Futility

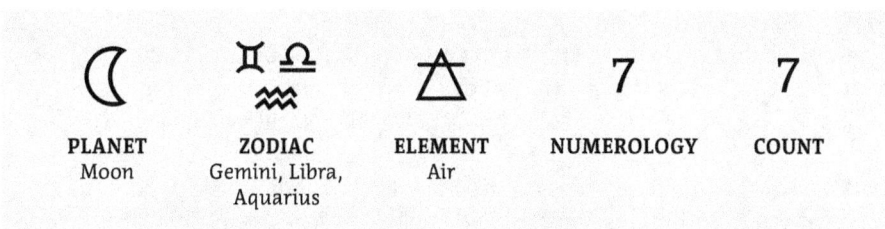

PLANET	ZODIAC	ELEMENT	NUMEROLOGY	COUNT
Moon	Gemini, Libra, Aquarius	Air	7	7

Upright: *Lying, Theft, Adaptability, Deception, Betrayal, Sneaking Around*
The Seven of Swords advises caution due to its embodiment of themes such as tact, cunning, and, occasionally, deception. This signifies that things may not be as simple as they appear and that more could be happening beneath the surface. It should be noted, however, that this does not always entail malicious intent. Instead, it often indicates the need for intelligence and strategy when dealing with complex situations.

Nonetheless, the Seven of Swords often warns of potential betrayal or the necessity to be cautious around those who may not have one's best interests at heart. It serves as a reminder to rely on one's intuition, remain vigilant, and understand that not everything or everyone is transparent.

Reversed: *Imposter Syndrome, Confession, Malevolence, Ineffective, Affair*
The reversed Seven of Swords suggests a period where deceit, betrayal, or underhanded tactics might be coming to light. When this card shows up changed, it often implies that they are becoming aware of the truth, uncovering hidden information, or discovering that someone's intentions weren't as genuine as once believed. Alternatively, it can also indicate their feelings of guilt or shame for having acted dishonestly or taken shortcuts that were not in alignment with their core values. The card speaks to realizing and exposing truths that may have been hidden or avoided.

This card also prompts reflection on motives and actions, both theirs and those of others around them. While the upright position usually suggests sneaky behavior or a hidden agenda, the reversed position highlights the aftermath of such actions or the recognition of their consequences. It may be a time for them to come clean about their indiscretions, make amends, or address the actions of others who have impacted them. Facing the reality of the situation, acknowledging wrongdoings, and seeking resolution are critical steps encouraged by the reversed Seven of Swords.

Upright Interpretations

General Reading: The Seven of Swords often indicates deception, cunning, or a strategy that may not be entirely above board. It can suggest using tact and diplomacy over force but may also imply betrayal or sneaky behavior.

Love Reading: Beware of secrets or deceit within the relationship, potential unfaithfulness, or hidden agendas. For singles, it suggests caution, as someone might not be entirely transparent with their intentions.

Health Reading: The card can indicate that someone might be in denial about their health or avoiding a necessary medical check-up. It implies a need for transparency and honesty regarding well-being.

Career Reading: In career readings, the Seven of Swords might suggest office politics, hidden agendas, or someone working behind the scenes for personal gain. It implies a need for vigilance and discretion.

Reversed Interpretations

General Reading: Secrets are being exposed, or there's a realization that deceit is not the way forward. It might also indicate a feeling of guilt over past underhanded actions or an attempt to make amends.

Love Reading: This card reversed might reveal truths previously hidden in a relationship. There's an energy of coming clean or confronting past deceitful actions.

Health Reading: There might be a realization about the importance of health transparency or confronting health issues head-on instead of avoiding them.

Career Reading: The card can hint at deception being unveiled in the workplace or a realization that sneaky tactics aren't beneficial in the long run.

The card usually displays a person sneaking away from a camp or society while clutching multiple swords, indicating dishonesty or theft. Leaving behind some swords while taking others may signify obtaining whatever is feasible covertly and leaving a trail or proof of the act.

The tent, or community, that the individual leaves behind represents a place of security, camaraderie, or established norms. Moving away stealthily with the swords stresses the themes of disloyalty, secrecy, or deviating from established conventions.

Frequently, the person is depicted stepping on unsteady ground, highlighting the uncertain and demanding nature of their path. This terrain reinforces the idea that deceitful or shrewd actions may offer a quicker route, but they come with their challenges.

ZODIAC: Gemini (May 21 – June 20) is an Air sign ruled by Mercury. The dual nature of Gemini embodies a mix of yin and yang, and Geminis often feel as though they have two distinct sides.

Libra (September 23 – October 22) is an Air sign ruled by Venus. Libras often strive for harmony and balance in their lives.

Aquarius (January 20 – February 18) is an Air sign ruled by Uranus. Aquarians are self-reliant, analytical, independent, clever, and optimistic.

ELEMENT: Air represents logic, intellect, and communication. The intangible element is considered to be active, masculine energy. It is associated with Spring, the Suit of Wands, and the East cardinal direction.

HERMETIC QABALAH Associated Hebrew Letter: Waw – Hook, Nail (Connections, Secure)

QABALISTIC SEPHIROT: Netsach (Victory)

TIMING: February 9 – February 18

EIGHT OF SWORDS

M I N O R   A R C A N A

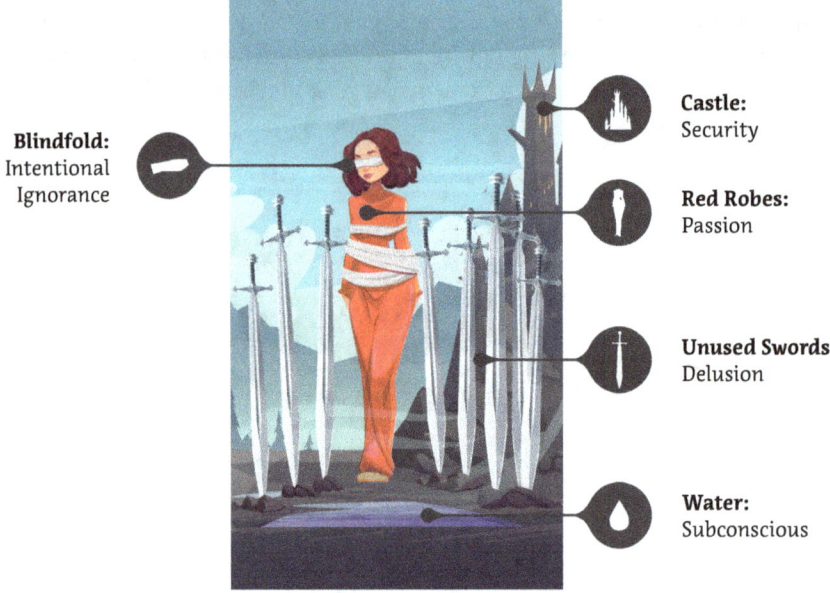

Blindfold:
Intentional
Ignorance

Castle:
Security

Red Robes:
Passion

Unused Swords:
Delusion

Water:
Subconscious

Yes/No Reading:

○　✓　○

Yes　*No*　*Maybe*

Names in Other Tarot Systems:
Golden Dawn: Lord of Shortened Force
Tarot of Marseilles: Eight of Swords
Thoth: Interference

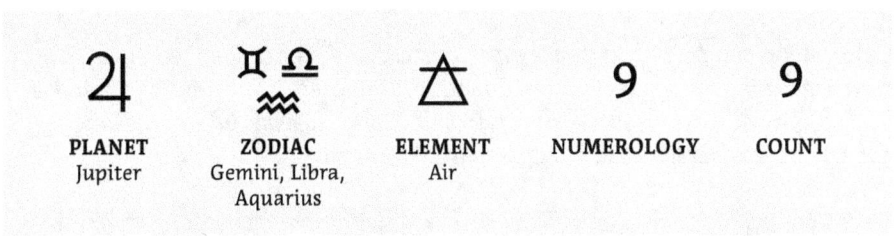

♃	♊ ♎ ♒	△	9	9
PLANET	**ZODIAC**	**ELEMENT**	**NUMEROLOGY**	**COUNT**
Jupiter	Gemini, Libra, Aquarius	Air		

Upright: *Entrapment, Bound, Weak, Imprisonment, Victim, Negative Thoughts*
The upright Eight of Swords depicts a scenario where someone feels trapped or restricted, often by their thoughts, beliefs, or fears. When this card appears, it points to situations where the individual might believe they are bound by circumstances, seeing no way out. However, it's essential to note that these perceived barriers are often more mental than actual. They might be holding onto limiting beliefs or negative self-talk that prevents them from seeing solutions or paths to freedom that are readily available.

In many ways, the Eight of Swords is a gentle reminder that the person's perception of a situation plays a significant role in their reality. Instead of seeking alternatives or solutions, they may focus on what they can't do. The card encourages introspection, urging them to question why they feel trapped and to challenge these feelings.

Reversed: *Inner Critic, Escape, Release, Open to New Perspectives, Freedom*
When the Eight of Swords appears reversed in a reading, it often signifies a significant shift in perspective, hinting that the individual is beginning to recognize that the constraints and limitations they've felt were largely self-imposed. They might be in the process of breaking free from past patterns of thinking and self-imposed barriers that have held them back. This card can indicate a newfound awareness and empowerment, suggesting that they have either found or are seeking ways to liberate themselves from their previous mental confines and situations they felt trapped in.

However, while the reversed Eight of Swords hints at a potential liberation, it also reminds them that freeing oneself takes conscious effort. Merely recognizing the chains doesn't automatically dissolve them. They must actively challenge their beliefs, confront their fears, and take deliberate steps toward change. The card encourages them to trust themselves, be patient, and understand that real liberation often requires internal and external work.

Upright Interpretations

General Reading: The Eight of Swords suggests feeling trapped, confined, or restricted by circumstances, often due to self-imposed limitations or a mindset of victimhood. It represents a situation where one feels powerless to change, even if the real barriers are more perceived than real.

Love Reading: In the realm of love, this card might indicate feeling trapped or confined in a relationship. There might be a perceived inability to change or escape the situation. For singles, it could suggest a mindset that prevents one from finding or accepting love.

Health Reading: When it comes to health, the Eight of Swords can imply a mental block or being in denial about a health issue. It might also suggest feeling trapped by a health condition, without seeing a way out.

Career Reading: Professionally, the Eight of Swords can indicate feeling trapped in a job or career path. There's a sensation of being stuck without any visible options for advancement or change.

Reversed Interpretations

General Reading: When reversed, the Eight of Swords points to a growing awareness or realization that the chains binding you are breakable. It indicates a potential for liberation, breakthroughs, and newfound clarity.

Love Reading: The card indicates a personal awakening, realizing that one has more power in their love life than previously thought. It could mean breaking free from unhealthy relationship patterns or gaining clarity in love matters.

Health Reading: This card might suggest a change in perspective regarding health. It can denote realizing the power of the mind over the body or seeking alternative treatments that once seemed out of reach.

Career Reading: It signals a potential realization of untapped opportunities or paths in one's career. There's an energy of empowerment, understanding that there are more options available than initially perceived.

At the center is a person wearing a blindfold, suggesting a lack of clarity or understanding. This blindness is self-imposed, representing denial or refusal to see the truth. The swords that encircle or stand near the figure signify the perceived barriers or challenges. Even though they form a cage, there's typically enough space between them, hinting that the confinement is more a product of perception than reality. In many renditions, the person's hands or wrists are bound, emphasizing the sensation of powerlessness or confinement. However, these bindings are often loose enough, suggesting that they could free themselves with some effort or change in perspective.

The Eight of Swords paints a striking picture of self-imprisonment, emphasizing the power of mindset and perception in shaping our realities. It's a call to recognize our internal barriers and understand that we often hold the key to our liberation.

ZODIAC: Gemini (May 21 – June 20) is an Air sign ruled by Mercury. The dual nature of Gemini embodies a mix of yin and yang, and Geminis often feel as though they have two distinct sides.

Libra (September 23 – October 22) is an Air sign ruled by Venus. Libras often strive for harmony and balance in their lives.

Aquarius (January 20 – February 18) is an Air sign ruled by Uranus. Aquarians are self-reliant, analytical, independent, clever, and optimistic.

ELEMENT: Air represents logic, intellect, and communication. The intangible element is considered to be active, masculine energy. It is associated with Spring, the Suit of Wands, and the East cardinal direction.

HERMETIC QABALAH Associated Hebrew Letter: Waw – Hook, Nail (Connections, Secure)

QABALISTIC SEPHIROT: Hod (Splendor)

TIMING: May 21 – May 31

NINE OF SWORDS

MINOR ARCANA

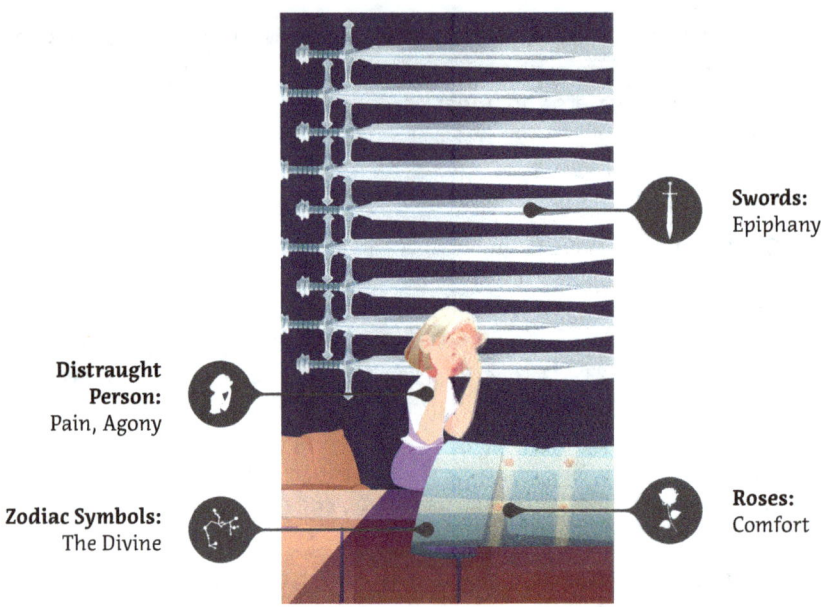

Swords:
Epiphany

Distraught Person:
Pain, Agony

Zodiac Symbols:
The Divine

Roses:
Comfort

Yes/No Reading:

○　☑　○

Yes　*No*　*Maybe*

Names in Other Tarot Systems:

Golden Dawn: Lord of Despair and Cruelty
Tarot of Marseilles: Nine of Swords
Thoth: Cruelty

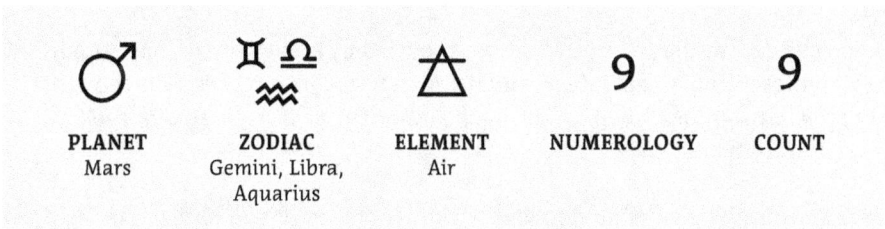

PLANET	ZODIAC	ELEMENT	NUMEROLOGY	COUNT
Mars	Gemini, Libra, Aquarius	Air	9	9

Upright: *Hopelessness, Anxiety, Panic, Guilt, Trauma, Worry, Fear, Nightmares*
This card paints a picture of deep psychological turmoil. It embodies the dark night of the soul, where worries, regrets, and fears seem to amplify, often out of proportion to the actual situation. This card represents the harsh grip of anxiety, sleepless nights, and the mental spirals that can feel inescapable.

However, as dire as it sounds, the Nine of Swords also serves as a potent reminder that much of this torment is internal and self-created. While the concerns may be based on real issues, they are often exaggerated by the mind. It's a call to seek support, counseling, or healing to address these internal struggles.

The Nine of Swords offers a poignant visualization of the internal battleground where fears, regrets, and anxieties wage war, making clear the profound effects of mental and emotional turmoil.

Reversed: *Secrets, Deep-Concern, Inner Turmoil, Recovery, Improvement*
When the Nine of Swords appears reversed in a reading, it often signals a potential release from overwhelming anxiety and fears plaguing someone. They may be on the cusp of moving beyond the sleepless nights and distressing thoughts haunting them toward a place of clarity and healing. This card can serve as a reminder that the worst of their worries might be an illusion, and that the reality of their situation is not as dire as they imagine it to be.

However, the reversed Nine of Swords can also indicate a tendency to repress or avoid dealing with the root causes of their anxieties. Instead of confronting their worries and addressing them head-on, they may be burying them deep down, only to have them resurface later. This card urges them to seek help or find coping mechanisms that allow them to face their fears and concerns directly. Only by acknowledging the sources of their stress can they truly begin the healing process and find the peace they seek.

Upright Interpretations

General Reading: The Nine of Swords is commonly known as the "nightmare" card, representing anxiety, fear, and being overwhelmed by negative thoughts or regrets. It signifies a mental torment that might be exaggerated or more perceived than real.

Love Reading: When related to love, the Nine of Swords can indicate intense worry about a relationship or harboring deep-seated insecurities. For some, it might suggest sleepless nights due to relationship problems or fear of commitment.

Health Reading: In terms of health, this card may imply sleepless nights, stress-related illnesses, or mental health issues. It's a sign to seek support and not let anxieties fester.

Career Reading: Professionally, the Nine of Swords can signify stress and anxiety over job security, workplace conflicts, or fear of failure. It can represent an overwhelming pressure to perform.

Reversed Interpretations

General Reading: In its reversed position, the Nine of Swords suggests a potential release from anxiety or beginning to see the light at the end of the tunnel. It can also indicate confronting fears, understanding them, and starting the process of healing.

Love Reading: This card can signal a gradual overcoming of relationship anxieties or resolving miscommunications. It speaks of learning to trust and letting go of baseless fears in love.

Health Reading: Healing is on the horizon. This can denote improvement in mental health, getting better sleep, or finding coping strategies that work.

Career Reading: This card can point to a period of recovery after a stressful professional phase or the realization that workplace anxieties were unfounded or exaggerated.

A central figure sits upright in bed with their hands covering their face, seemingly in deep despair, anguish, and grief. The bed, which is meant to be a place of respite, becomes instead a site of torment, highlighting the intrusion of tormenting thoughts into the sanctity of personal space.

The dark or cold setting of the card, whether through the apparent nighttime or the bleak color palette, contrasts sharply with the usual safety and warmth associated with a bedroom. This contrast serves as a symbol of the mental anguish that can transform even the most peaceful of havens into landscapes of suffering. The nine swords typically depicted above the central figure or on the wall are pointed reminders of the card's intellectual and mental domain. Swords are traditionally associated with the realm of thought in Tarot symbolism, and in this card, they represent the oppressive nature of mental struggles, fears, regrets, and anxieties.

The dark background or atmosphere, devoid of light, captures the sensation of being trapped in the overwhelming grip of night, literally and metaphorically. This interpretation emphasizes the depth of emotional and psychological crisis.

ZODIAC: Gemini (May 21 – June 20) is an Air sign ruled by Mercury. The dual nature of Gemini embodies a mix of yin and yang, and Geminis often feel as though they have two distinct sides.

Libra (September 23 – October 22) is an Air sign ruled by Venus. Libras often strive for harmony and balance in their lives.

Aquarius (January 20 – February 18) is an Air sign ruled by Uranus. Aquarians are self-reliant, analytical, independent, clever, and optimistic.

ELEMENT: Air represents logic, intellect, and communication. The intangible element is considered to be active, masculine energy. It is associated with Spring, the Suit of Wands, and the East cardinal direction.

HERMETIC QABALAH Associated Hebrew Letter: Waw – Hook, Nail (Connections, Secure)

QABALISTIC SEPHIROT: Yesod (Foundation)

TIMING: June 1 – June 10

TEN OF SWORDS

M I N O R   A R C A N A

Dark Sky:
Gloom

Calm Water:
Peace

Hand Gesture:
Divine Blessing

Yellow Sky:
Hope

Prone Figure:
Defeat

Yes/No Reading:

Yes   No   Maybe

Names in Other Tarot Systems:
Golden Dawn: Lord of Ruin
Tarot of Marseilles: Ten of Swords
Thoth: Ruin

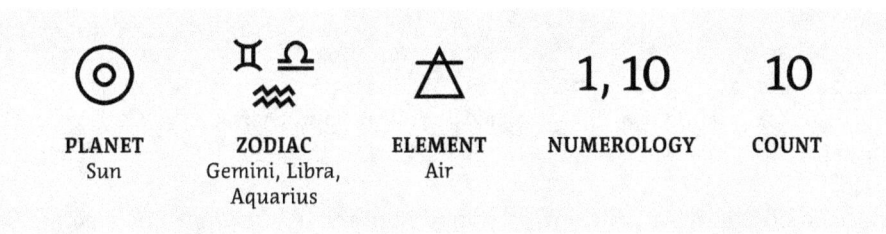

PLANET	ZODIAC	ELEMENT	NUMEROLOGY	COUNT
Sun	Gemini, Libra, Aquarius	Air	1, 10	10

Upright: *Defeat, Laziness, Rock Bottom, Deep Wounds, Loss, Crisis, Betrayal*
The Ten of Swords is a card of endings — often painful, sudden, and unexpected. It represents a situation that has reached rock bottom, where things seemingly can't get worse. This card embodies betrayal, loss, or the culmination of unfortunate events.

Despite the initial gloom, this card also signals release. The worst is over, and there's a surrender to the universe, an acceptance of what has occurred. This acknowledgment is the first step towards healing and moving forward.

While the card speaks of harsh realities, it also points out that once something has concluded, there's space for a new beginning. It's a reminder that after every ending comes a new dawn, even if it isn't visible immediately.

Reversed: *Recovery, Survival, Regeneration, Mending, Moving Upwards*
The Ten of Swords reversed heralds a time of recovery. The darkness and pain that once seemed all-consuming begin to lift, and there's a palpable sense of hope. The weight of past betrayals or disappointments no longer pins down the individual. Instead, there's a newfound strength and determination to rise above.

This position often suggests a period of introspection. There's an understanding that while one may have faced betrayals or hardships, these experiences are also teachers. It signifies the journey of processing pain, understanding its origins, and working towards preventing future heartaches.

The reversed Ten of Swords is like the first light after a long, treacherous night. While scars may remain, one realizes that one has survived the worst. It embodies the adage, "What doesn't kill you makes you stronger."

Upright Interpretations

General Reading: The Ten of Swords indicates a painful ending, betrayal, or the realization that a situation has reached its lowest point. It is the culmination of hardships, signaling that things cannot get worse and there's only a way up from here.

Love Reading: In love, this card can signify the end of a relationship, feeling backstabbed or deeply hurt by a partner. It's a realization that things may have come to an irrevocable end.

Health Reading: The Ten of Swords might point to feeling mentally or physically at a low point, possibly due to stress or other health complications. It's a strong indication to seek help or make necessary changes.

Career Reading: Career-wise, the Ten of Swords can suggest a significant setback, end of a job or project, or feeling betrayed in the professional sphere.

Reversed Interpretations

General Reading: This position suggests recovery and the potential for rebirth. While the pain of the past may linger, there is hope and an opportunity to rise from the ashes and move forward.

Love Reading: The Ten of Swords reversed in love could indicate the beginning of healing after a heartbreak or the chance for reconciliation. Past wounds start to heal, and there's potential for a fresh start.

Health Reading: Healing and recovery are the key themes. This might signify recuperation, improved mental well-being, or finding effective treatments.

Career Reading: There's potential for new beginnings or unexpected opportunities following a career disappointment. It indicates resilience and bouncing back after a setback.

At the center is a prone figure, with ten swords penetrating their back. This graphic portrayal serves to symbolize betrayal, defeat, or treachery. The figure's posture indicates surrender and the conclusion of a conflict, whether internal or external. The swords that immobilize the figure highlight the cognitive or psychological aspect of this defeat. They could signify thoughts, beliefs, or external statements that have inflicted harm. The number ten, signifying the final stage of the suit, implies a culmination or completion of a cycle.

Frequently, the upper part of the card features a bleak or stormy sky, indicating the despair and despondency associated with this card. Nevertheless, numerous interpretations also integrate a brightening horizon or a suggestion of a sunrise in the distance — a sign of optimism and fresh starts that follow after a tumultuous time. The environment depicted is generally desolate or barren, reinforcing the themes of conclusion, emptiness, and devastation. However, this desolation can also connote a blank slate, ready for new beginnings to sprout once healing commences.

ZODIAC: Gemini (May 21 – June 20) is an Air sign ruled by Mercury. The dual nature of Gemini embodies a mix of yin and yang, and Geminis often feel as though they have two distinct sides.

Libra (September 23 – October 22) is an Air sign ruled by Venus. Libras often strive for harmony and balance in their lives.

Aquarius (January 20 – February 18) is an Air sign ruled by Uranus. Aquarians are self-reliant, analytical, independent, clever, and optimistic.

ELEMENT: Air represents logic, intellect, and communication. The intangible element is considered to be active, masculine energy. It is associated with Spring, the Suit of Wands, and the East cardinal direction.

HERMETIC QABALAH Associated Hebrew Letter: Waw – Hook, Nail (Connections, Secure)

QABALISTIC SEPHIROT: Malkuth (Kingdom)

TIMING: June 11 – June 20

PAGE OF SWORDS
M I N O R   A R C A N A

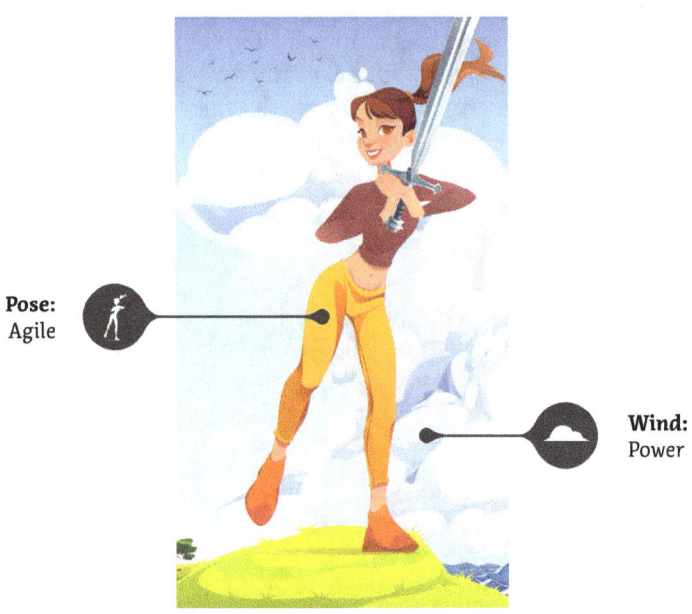

Pose:
Agile

Wind:
Power

Yes/No Reading:

Yes   No   Maybe

Names in Other Tarot Systems:
Golden Dawn: Princess of Swords
Tarot of Marseilles: Valet of Swords
Thoth: Princess of Swords

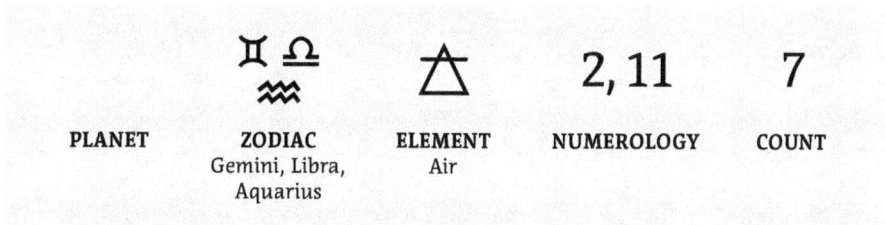

PLANET	ZODIAC	ELEMENT	NUMEROLOGY	COUNT
	Gemini, Libra, Aquarius	Air	2, 11	7

Upright: *Curiosity, Mental Energy, Innovation, Thirst for Knowledge, Caution*
The upright Page of Swords embodies the spirit of inquiry. It represents an eager mind seeking truth and clarity to understand the world. This quest for knowledge is driven by pure intent and an insatiable curiosity.

The Page of Swords can also act as a harbinger, bringing messages about challenges, conflicts, or the need to stand one's ground. While the news might be unexpected, it comes as a call to prepare, arm oneself with information, and face the challenge head-on. The card radiates youthful energy, symbolizing someone not afraid to ask questions, challenge the status quo, or bring a fresh perspective to old problems. It encourages tapping into one's youthful energy, being bold, and approaching situations with a keen and analytical mind.

Reversed: *Manipulation, Stupidity, Paranoia, Haste, Haphazard Action*
The Page of Swords is depicted as a youthful figure standing tall with a sword held upright, symbolizing their thirst for knowledge and curiosity about the world. They represent the early stages of intellectual exploration, where the energy is fresh, and the desire to learn and communicate is intense. The windswept landscape often present in this card's imagery reflects the turbulent waters of the young mind, eager to challenge, question, and understand. They are analytical, constantly questioning the status quo, and have a keen sense of justice. Their sharp intellect and nimble mind allow them to see through deceptions, making them excellent problem solvers.

However, like many in the initial stages of a journey, the Page of Swords may sometimes speak or act without fully considering the implications, leading to potential misunderstandings or conflicts. Their eagerness can lead them to be hasty or impulsive. Despite this, their intentions are pure. They bring forth a message of using one's intellect and communication skills to navigate challenges, and their appearance often suggests that a new phase of learning or a fresh perspective is on the horizon.

Upright Interpretations

General Reading: The Page of Swords represents a thirst for knowledge, a curious mind, and a quest for truth. It may also symbolize a message, often related to challenges or conflicts, or a person who's analytical and perhaps a bit impulsive.

Love Reading: In a love context, this card might suggest open communication about feelings or concerns. It could also indicate a curious or analytical partner who seeks clarity in the relationship.

Health Reading: The Page of Swords may hint at the need to gather more information about a health issue or to approach health with curiosity and openness. It's a prompt to ask questions and seek understanding.

Career Reading: In career, the Page of Swords can indicate a new project that requires keen research and sharp intellect. It can also signify constructive criticism or the need to communicate more effectively at work.

Reversed Interpretations

General Reading: In its reversed position, the Page of Swords can indicate gossip, deceit, or a lack of direction. It suggests hasty decisions or speaking without thinking and can represent someone who is scatterbrained or not trustworthy.

Love Reading: This could point to misunderstandings, dishonesty, or communication barriers in a relationship. It might also suggest that someone isn't being entirely open or truthful.

Health Reading: There might be misdiagnosis, misinformation, or denial regarding a health issue. It's crucial to be cautious about getting swayed by unreliable health advice.

Career Reading: This suggests potential misunderstandings at work, gossip, or being underprepared for a task or project. It's a warning against rushing into things without adequate preparation.

The background features clouds and birds, suggesting the element of air which is associated with the suit of Swords. This represents thoughts, communication, and the intellectual realm.

The Page holds a sword upright, symbolizing a readiness to face challenges and a desire for truth. The way the sword is held, often with both ease and confidence, shows the Page's dedication to clarity and justice. They're standing on higher ground or a hill, indicating a position of observation and perspective. This reinforces the idea of seeking clarity, overviewing situations, and the quest for knowledge.

The youthful appearance of the Page represents the early stages of intellectual and communicative development. It indicates freshness, new ideas, and the beginning phase of a journey towards mastering the realm of thought and communication.

♊ **ZODIAC:** Gemini (May 21 – June 20) is an Air sign ruled by Mercury. The dual nature of Gemini embodies a mix of yin and yang, and Geminis often feel as though they have two distinct sides.

♎ Libra (September 23 – October 22) is an Air sign ruled by Venus. Libras often strive for harmony and balance in their lives.

♒ Aquarius (January 20 – February 18) is an Air sign ruled by Uranus. Aquarians are self-reliant, analytical, independent, clever, and optimistic.

△ **ELEMENT:** Air represents logic, intellect, and communication. The intangible element is considered to be active, masculine energy. It is associated with Spring, the Suit of Wands, and the East cardinal direction.

ו **HERMETIC QABALAH** Associated Hebrew Letter: Waw – Hook, Nail (Connections, Secure)

QABALISTIC SEPHIROT: Malkuth (Kingdom)

TIMING: December 21 – March 20

KNIGHT OF SWORDS

M I N O R   A R C A N A

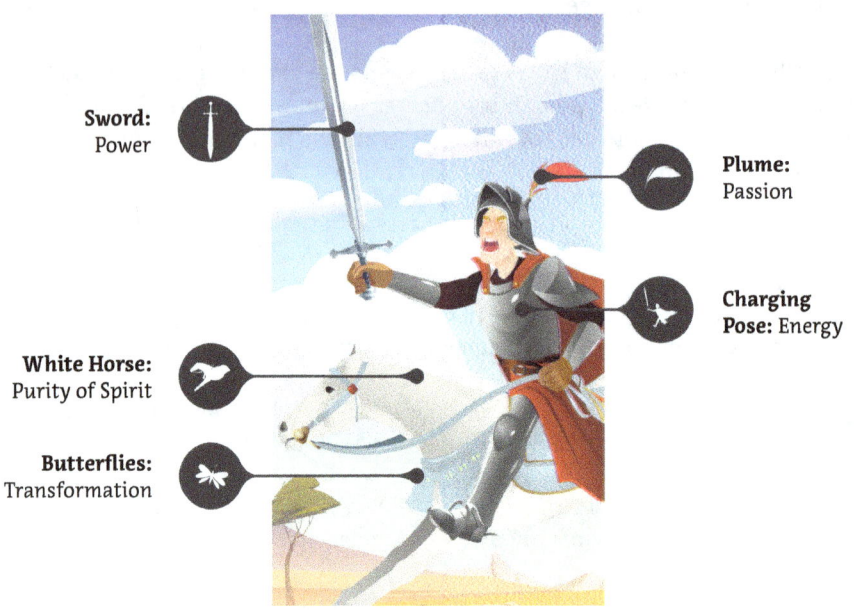

Sword:
Power

Plume:
Passion

Charging Pose: Energy

White Horse:
Purity of Spirit

Butterflies:
Transformation

Yes/No Reading:

☑   ◯   ◯

Yes   *No*   *Maybe*

Names in Other Tarot Systems:
Golden Dawn: Prince of Swords
Tarot of Marseilles: Cavalier of Swords
Thoth: Prince of Swords

♊︎ ♎︎ ♒︎	△	3, 12	4
PLANET	ZODIAC	ELEMENT	NUMEROLOGY	COUNT

PLANET	ZODIAC	ELEMENT	NUMEROLOGY	COUNT
	Gemini, Libra, Aquarius	Air		

Upright: *Big Changes, Rebellion, Direct, Impulse, Defense of Beliefs, Ambitious*
The Knight of Swords represents someone with a sharp intellect, unyielding determination, and a readiness to tackle challenges head-on. When they set their sights on a goal, little can deter them from their path. Their mind operates precisely, and they can cut through confusion or deceit to get to the truth. They are fearless advocates for their beliefs and are not afraid to voice their opinions or stand up for what they deem right. Their approach is often direct and operates with a sense of urgency, sometimes coming across as impatient or hasty.

However, their admirable assertiveness can sometimes verge on aggression, and their quickness to act might lead them to overlook crucial details. They may benefit from pausing, gathering more information, and considering the consequences of their actions. While they are undeniably effective in pursuing their goals, a touch of caution and strategy can lead to more sustainable successes.

Reversed: *Lack of Direction, Restless, Unpredictable, Impulsive, Losing Control*
When the Knight of Swords appears reversed in a reading, it indicates someone acting impulsively, with a recklessness that can lead to mistakes or unintended consequences. They may need to be speaking without thinking, rushing into situations without a proper plan, or charging forward without considering the feelings and perspectives of others. This card suggests that their haste, impulsiveness, and potentially aggressive approach may result in conflicts, misunderstandings, or missed opportunities.

The reversed Knight of Swords also serves as a reminder to slow down, reassess, and think things through. While they may be passionate about their cause or eager to make a point, finding balance is essential. It's an invitation to harness their energy and intellect more constructively, ensuring that decisions are made with a clearer mind. They can approach challenges with more wisdom and foresight by taking a moment to pause, reflect, and strategize, leading to more favorable outcomes.

Upright Interpretations

General Reading: The Knight of Swords represents boldness, ambition, and swift action. This card suggests that someone is charging forward with determination and clarity of purpose, sometimes even with a hint of recklessness.

Love Reading: In the realm of love, the Knight of Swords may symbolize an intense and passionate relationship or someone who pursues their romantic interest aggressively. The energy is thrilling but might also be fleeting.

Health Reading: In health readings, this card might indicate a need for quick action or a proactive approach. There's a determination to tackle health issues head-on.

Career Reading: The Knight of Swords in a career context signifies swift actions, aggressive strategies, and the drive to succeed. It can also point to an upcoming challenge that requires decisiveness.

Reversed Interpretations

General Reading: In its reversed position, the Knight of Swords can signify impulsivity, rash decisions, or a lack of strategy. It warns of the potential pitfalls of acting without considering the consequences.

Love Reading: This card reversed suggests conflicts, arguments, or impulsiveness in a relationship. It may also warn of a partner who is hasty or inconsiderate.

Health Reading: It can signify neglecting health warnings, being careless about one's well-being, or rushing into treatments without proper research.

Career Reading: This suggests potential hasty decisions that might backfire, conflicts at work, or being ill-prepared for challenges.

The Knight of Swords card showcases a knight charging forward on their steed with a drawn sword, symbolizing determination, ambition, and action. The winds blow fiercely around them, perhaps indicating the challenges or conflicts they are rushing into or the speed at which they move. The turbulent sky in the background further underscores their mission's urgency and potential recklessness. Their armor suggests they are prepared for battle, and their focused gaze indicates a single-minded pursuit of their objective.

This card embodies a powerful energy of swift movement and determination. They don't wait for things to happen; they make them happen. The Knight of Swords represents someone highly driven, often jumping into situations headfirst without fully gauging the consequences. Their passion and ambition can be commendable, but it can also lead them into unnecessary trouble. While they are known for their directness and sharp intellect, there's also a warning here: the need to temper haste with wisdom to ensure that the path of action taken is swift, just, and well-considered.

♊ **ZODIAC:** Gemini (May 21 – June 20) is an Air sign ruled by Mercury. The dual nature of Gemini embodies a mix of yin and yang, and Geminis often feel as though they have two distinct sides.

♎ Libra (September 23 – October 22) is an Air sign ruled by Venus. Libras often strive for harmony and balance in their lives.

♒ Aquarius (January 20 – February 18) is an Air sign ruled by Uranus. Aquarians are self-reliant, analytical, independent, clever, and optimistic.

△ **ELEMENT:** Air represents logic, intellect, and communication. The intangible element is considered to be active, masculine energy. It is associated with Spring, the Suit of Wands, and the East cardinal direction.

ו **HERMETIC QABALAH** Associated Hebrew Letter: Waw – Hook, Nail (Connections, Secure)

✵ **QABALISTIC SEPHIROT:** Tiphareth (Beauty)

🕐 **TIMING:** January 10 – February 8

QUEEN OF SWORDS

M I N O R   A R C A N A

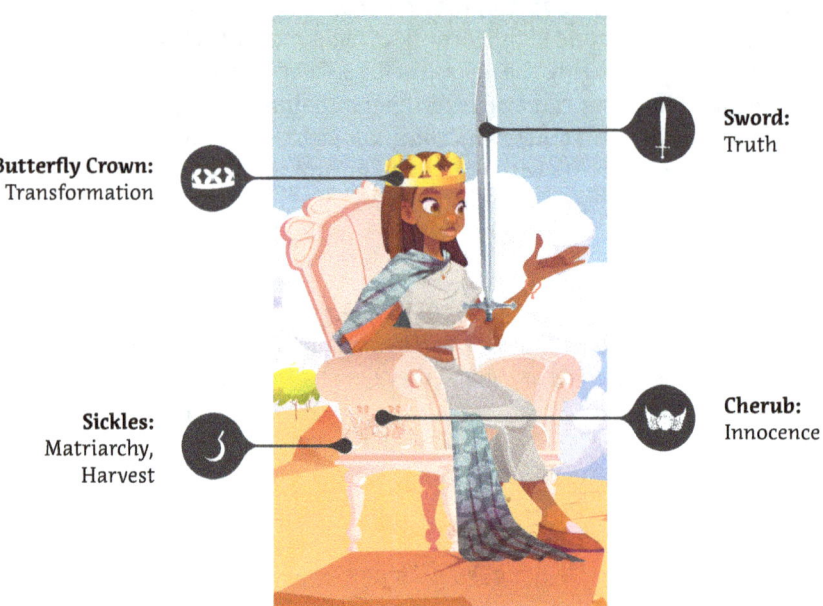

Butterfly Crown:
Transformation

Sword:
Truth

Sickles:
Matriarchy,
Harvest

Cherub:
Innocence

Yes/No Reading:

Yes   No   **Maybe**

Names in Other Tarot Systems:
Golden Dawn: Queen of Swords
Tarot of Marseilles: Dame of Swords
Thoth: Queen of Swords

♊ ♎ ♒	△	4, 13	4
PLANET	ZODIAC	ELEMENT	NUMEROLOGY	COUNT
	Gemini, Libra, Aquarius	Air		

Upright: *Perceptive, Morals, Eccentric, Discernment, Complexity, Sharp Wit*
The upright Queen of Swords embodies the essence of intellectual clarity, sharp intuition, and unwavering honesty. They are a figure who, through experiences, has learned the value of clear boundaries and direct communication. Their wisdom comes from knowledge and their lived experiences, often marked by hardships and challenges. These trials have honed their judgment and allowed them to discern truth from falsehood easily. They are not swayed by emotional manipulation, preferring to see situations clearly and discerningly.

In conversations, they are straightforward and value transparency. While they may sometimes be perceived as detached or cold, it's their way of ensuring objectivity. The Queen of Swords encourages individuals to seek clarity in their thoughts and approach situations rationally. Drawing this card might be a sign that one needs to cut through illusions, see things as they are, and communicate their truth without hesitation. It's a reminder that sometimes, embracing the energy of the Queen of Swords can lead to the most authentic and clear outcomes.

Reversed: *Cold-Hearted, Vindictive, Cruel, Bitter, Resentful, Mental Fog*
When the Queen of Swords appears reversed, they symbolize a person who may be allowing their intellect and analytical abilities to cloud their judgment, leading to decisions made from a place of bitterness or cynicism. They could represent someone who has let past traumas or betrayals influence their present interactions, causing them to be overly critical, sharp-tongued, or unnecessarily harsh in their judgments. Their keen insight becomes a potential pitfall as they may use it to dissect and criticize without offering constructive feedback.

The reversed Queen of Swords can also indicate someone struggling to set clear boundaries or unable to communicate their thoughts and feelings effectively. They are reminded of the importance of regaining their clarity and purpose.

Upright Interpretations

General Reading: The Queen of Swords embodies clarity, independence, and intellect. They possess keen perception and is often known for their sharp wit and ability to communicate ideas effectively. They represent someone who values truth and is direct in their dealings.

Love Reading: In the realm of love, the Queen of Swords speaks to straightforward communication. This may indicate a relationship where both parties value transparency. For singles, it suggests they know what they want and are clear about their boundaries.

Health Reading: The Queen of Swords advises using intellect and clear thinking when approaching health issues. It may also suggest seeking expert opinions or doing thorough research.

Career Reading: In a career context, the Queen of Swords indicates clear communication, decisiveness, and strategic planning. It suggests taking a logical approach to career decisions.

Reversed Interpretations

General Reading: In the reversed position, the Queen of Swords can indicate a person who is overly critical, emotionally detached, or someone who uses their intellect to manipulate or harm.

Love Reading: This card can suggest coldness, barriers in communication, or a feeling of emotional distance in a relationship. It might also indicate past wounds affecting the present.

Health Reading: Potential neglect of mental health, not listening to professional advice, or overthinking health issues to the point of anxiety.

Career Reading: It could signify workplace conflicts, miscommunication, or being overly critical or detached from colleagues.

The Queen of Swords card depicts a regal figure seated on a throne, with a clear sky behind them. They hold a sword upright in one hand, symbolizing their clarity of thought and intellectual prowess. Their other hand often gestures as if they are ready to communicate or deliver a message. The clouds at the base of the card signify the challenges and emotional turmoil they have surmounted, and the birds in the sky can represent their high-flying thoughts and ability to see the bigger picture. The crown they wear, often adorned with butterflies, speaks to their transformation and growth through life's adversities.

They embody intellectual independence, clear communication, and insightful judgment. As a master of objectivity and analysis, the Queen of Swords represents someone who can cut through confusion and see the truth of a situation. They value honesty and directness, often coming off as forthright or even blunt. Yet, their intentions are pure, driven by a desire to understand and be understood. They are not easily swayed by emotion, making decisions based on logic and understanding, and they expect the same clarity and straightforwardness from others.

♊ **ZODIAC:** Gemini (May 21 – June 20) is an Air sign ruled by Mercury. The dual nature of Gemini embodies a mix of yin and yang, and Geminis often feel as though they have two distinct sides.

♎ Libra (September 23 – October 22) is an Air sign ruled by Venus. Libras often strive for harmony and balance in their lives.

♒ Aquarius (January 20 – February 18) is an Air sign ruled by Uranus. Aquarians are self-reliant, analytical, independent, clever, and optimistic.

🜁 **ELEMENT:** Air represents logic, intellect, and communication. The intangible element is considered to be active, masculine energy. It is associated with Spring, the Suit of Wands, and the East cardinal direction.

ו **HERMETIC QABALAH** Associated Hebrew Letter: Waw – Hook, Nail (Connections, Secure)

QABALISTIC SEPHIROT: Binah (Understanding)

🕐 **TIMING:** September 12 – October 12

KING OF SWORDS

M I N O R A R C A N A

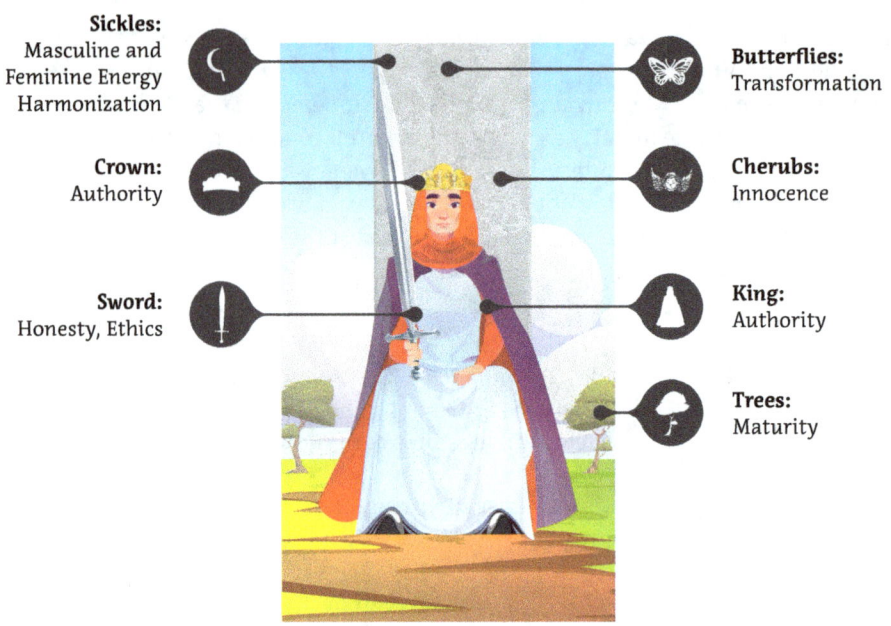

Sickles:
Masculine and
Feminine Energy
Harmonization

Crown:
Authority

Sword:
Honesty, Ethics

Butterflies:
Transformation

Cherubs:
Innocence

King:
Authority

Trees:
Maturity

Yes/No Reading:

○ ○ ☑
Yes *No* *Maybe*

Names in Other Tarot Systems:
Golden Dawn: King of Swords
Tarot of Marseilles: Roi of Swords
Thoth: Knight of Swords

♊ ♎ ♒	△	5, 14	4
PLANET	**ZODIAC**	**ELEMENT**	**NUMEROLOGY**	**COUNT**
	Gemini, Libra, Aquarius	Air		

Upright: *Routine, Truth, Integrity, Discipline, Authority, Intellect*
The King of Swords embodies intellectual clarity, logic, and understanding. When this card emerges in a reading, it signifies a presence or need for decision-making based on facts, reason, and clear thought. They stand as a beacon of truth, cutting through ambiguity with their sharp insights and unwavering focus. Their decisions are made after careful analysis, ensuring that each step taken is well-calculated and just. Those who encounter the King of Swords know them to be fair, transparent, and consistent in their actions. They earn respect not just because of their position but because of their integrity, honesty, and commitment to ethical principles.

The King of Swords also represents effective communication. They have a gift for articulating their thoughts clearly, making them an excellent advisor, mentor, or spokesperson. They can be relied upon for wise counsel, offering a balanced and well-informed perspective on complex issues. This card encourages individuals to seek out knowledge, engage in open dialogue, and, like the King, always strive for a deeper understanding.

Reversed: *Manipulative, Cruel, Weak, Aggressive, Cynical, Abuse of Power*
When the King of Swords appears reversed in a reading, it often points to a potential misuse of intellectual prowess. They might be harnessing their keen intellect for manipulative tactics, cunning schemes, or deceitful actions. Their once-clear vision could be clouded by personal biases, leading them to twist facts or create false narratives. This card serves as a warning to be wary of those who may present themselves as knowledgeable but have ulterior motives or hidden agendas.

The King of Swords can indicate a tendency to become emotionally distant or even cold-hearted. Instead of guiding with wisdom and compassion, they might dismiss or belittle others without proper consideration. They can become overly analytical, often missing the emotional nuances of situations and failing to connect with others on a deeper, empathetic level.

Upright Interpretations

General Reading: Clear, rational thinking is needed. Base your decisions on logic, facts, and reason rather than your heart. The King of Swords encourages you to approach situations with a clear head, to seek the truth, and to communicate with honesty and precision.

Love Reading: The King of Swords suggests a relationship grounded in mutual respect and clear communication. It can also signify a partner who is rational and provides wise counsel.

Health Reading: When the King of Swords appears in a health reading, it advises a logical and researched approach to health issues. Seek expert opinions and make informed decisions.

Career Reading: The King of Swords indicates clear leadership, strategic planning, and effective communication. It embodies the qualities of a fair, wise, and rational leader who serves the best interests of all.

Reversed Interpretations

General Reading: The King of Swords can signify manipulation, harsh judgment, or a misuse of intellectual power. Be wary of those that may be overly critical. Keep a close eye on your affairs to ensure that no one is taking advantage.

Love Reading: The reversed King in a love reading may indicate a partner who is emotionally detached, overly critical, or controlling. There may be communication barriers or an imbalance of power in the relationship.

Health Reading: It may suggest being closed off to professional advice, neglecting mental well-being, or over-rationalizing health issues.

Career Reading: The reversed King might indicate a boss or colleague who is overly authoritative, manipulative, or dismissive of others' ideas.

The King is usually depicted holding a long, upright sword, symbolizing their authority, clarity of thought, and the power of truth. The upright position of the sword emphasizes justice, fairness, and balanced judgment.

The King's throne, often adorned with butterflies, clouds, and sometimes cherub faces signifies their high intellectual position and dominion over thought.

In many decks, the King is set against a backdrop of mountains, suggesting challenges they have overcome and their elevated perspective and clarity of vision.

The King of Swords often wears armor beneath their robe, indicating their readiness for any intellectual battle or challenge. Their attire, often blue or in cool tones, aligns them with the element of air, further emphasizing their intellectual and communicative prowess.

♊ **ZODIAC:** Gemini (May 21 – June 20) is an Air sign ruled by Mercury. The dual nature of Gemini embodies a mix of yin and yang, and Geminis often feel as though they have two distinct sides.

♎ Libra (September 23 – October 22) is an Air sign ruled by Venus. Libras often strive for harmony and balance in their lives.

♒ Aquarius (January 20 – February 18) is an Air sign ruled by Uranus. Aquarians are self-reliant, analytical, independent, clever, and optimistic.

△ **ELEMENT:** Air represents logic, intellect, and communication. The intangible element is considered to be active, masculine energy. It is associated with Spring, the Suit of Wands, and the East cardinal direction.

ו **HERMETIC QABALAH** Associated Hebrew Letter: Waw – Hook, Nail (Connections, Secure)

QABALISTIC SEPHIROT: Chokmah (Wisdom)

🕐 **TIMING:** May 11 – June 10

ACE OF CUPS

MINOR ARCANA

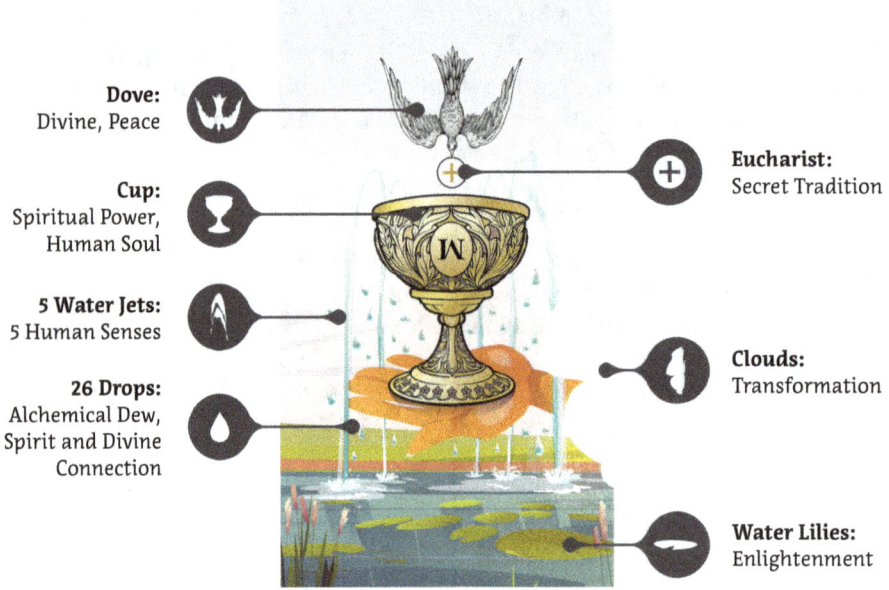

Dove:
Divine, Peace

Cup:
Spiritual Power,
Human Soul

5 Water Jets:
5 Human Senses

26 Drops:
Alchemical Dew,
Spirit and Divine
Connection

Eucharist:
Secret Tradition

Clouds:
Transformation

Water Lilies:
Enlightenment

Yes/No Reading:

✓   ○   ○

Yes   No   Maybe

Names in Other Tarot Systems:

Golden Dawn: The Radix of the Powers of Water
Tarot of Marseilles: Ace of Cups
Thoth: The Root of the Powers of Water

☽	⯰ ♏︎ ♋︎	▽	1, 10	5, 11
PLANET	**ZODIAC**	**ELEMENT**	**NUMEROLOGY**	**COUNT**
Moon	Pisces, Scorpio, Cancer	Water		

Upright: *Proposal, Conception, Marriage, Intuition, Spirituality, New Feelings*
When the Ace of Cups appears in a reading, it represents a fresh start for emotional and spiritual growth. This card suggests a time of sincerity, clearness, and a profusion of feelings, be it love, compassion, or creativity.

The Ace of Cups symbolizes the potential for establishing profound bonds with others or oneself. It's an era where the heart is vulnerable to both giving and receiving love without reservations. Additionally, this card reflects an intuitive understanding of one's emotional self and its hidden depths.

Furthermore, the Ace of Cups may signal an evolution in awareness or a spiritual awakening. It's an attachment to the soul, the emotional essence, and embodies a stream of inner peace, delight, and contentment.

Reversed: *Emotional Loss, Anguish, Infertility, Emptiness, Blocked Creativity*
When the Ace of Cups is reversed, it may indicate that emotions are not flowing freely. This can manifest as unmet emotional needs, disappointment, or missed opportunities for spiritual growth. In addition, this position can signify emotional exhaustion or feelings of emptiness, often caused by holding onto past hurts or refusing to forgive. Fear or past traumas can also prevent new connections or experiences from being pursued.

Therefore, the reversed Ace of Cups is an invitation for self-reflection and introspection. It prompts individuals to explore the reasons for emotional stagnation and to seek ways to open their hearts once again. This may involve practices such as healing, self-love, therapy, or spiritual exploration.

Upright Interpretations

General Reading: The Ace of Cups represents a new beginning in the emotional realm, a fresh start filled with compassion, love, and intuition. It signifies an open heart, receptivity to deep feelings, and the potential for emotional or spiritual fulfillment.

Love Reading: For those in relationships, the Ace of Cups suggests a deepening of emotional bonds or entering a new, harmonious phase. For singles, it might indicate the blossoming of a new romance or a period where one becomes open to the possibility of love.

Health Reading: The Ace of Cups is a positive sign, suggesting emotional healing and well-being. It can indicate a period of rejuvenation, healing from emotional wounds, or finding inner peace.

Career Reading: In a career context, the Ace of Cups may point to a job or project that you feel passionate about. It could also signify harmonious work relationships and tasks that align with your emotional or spiritual values.

Reversed Interpretations

General Reading: The reversed Ace of Cups might indicate missed opportunities in emotional connections or feelings of emptiness. There may be a blockage in expressing genuine emotions, leading to bottled-up feelings.

Love Reading: This card reversed can suggest emotional barriers in a relationship, unreciprocated feelings, or missed opportunities in love. For singles, it might indicate hesitation in opening up to potential partners.

Health Reading: It can point to emotional or spiritual imbalances. Past traumas or unresolved feelings might be affecting one's well-being.

Career Reading: In terms of career, the reversed Ace of Cups may signify a lack of passion for your job or a project. It might also indicate discord or emotional detachment from coworkers.

The Ace of Cups symbolizes emotional and spiritual abundance, highlighting the universe's offering of love and inner peace. The card shows an overflowing cup with five water streams, representing the abundance of emotions and the five senses. The full cup is representative of an open heart that is prepared to share its emotional depth. A descending dove, which signifies peace, love, and the Holy Spirit, is often present above the cup, indicating divine intervention in the spiritual and emotional realms.

Additionally, a hand emerging from a cloud holding the cup serves as a gift or offering from the divine. This heavenly nudge encourages individuals to embrace the available emotional and spiritual wealth. Furthermore, the water body depicted below, whether a river or a pond, mirrors the vastness of emotions and the subconscious. The lotuses or water lilies surrounding the cup suggest spiritual enlightenment and emotional purity.

♓ **ZODIAC:** Pisces (February 19 – March 20) is a Water sign ruled by Neptune. Pisceans are known for their emotional depth and keen intuition.

♏ Scorpio (October 23 – November 21) is a Water sign ruled by Pluto. Scorpios are known for their intensity and depth.

♋ Cancer (June 21 – July 22) is a Water sign ruled by the Moon. Cancers are highly empathetic, although they can be initially perceived as cold and distant. They're often caregivers and nurturing.

▽ **ELEMENT:** Water rules emotions and is a symbol of healing, peace, dreams, and compassion. It is associated with Winter, the Suit of Cups, and the West cardinal direction.

ה **HERMETIC QABALAH** Associated Hebrew Letter: Heh – Window (Vision, Reasoning)

QABALISTIC SEPHIROT: Kether (Crown)

TIMING: September 23 – December 20

TWO OF CUPS

MINOR ARCANA

Red Lion: Passion, Sexual Energy

Staff of Hermes/ Caduceus: Healing

Cup: Spiritual Power, Human Soul

Two People: Masculine and Feminine Energy, Unity, Partnership

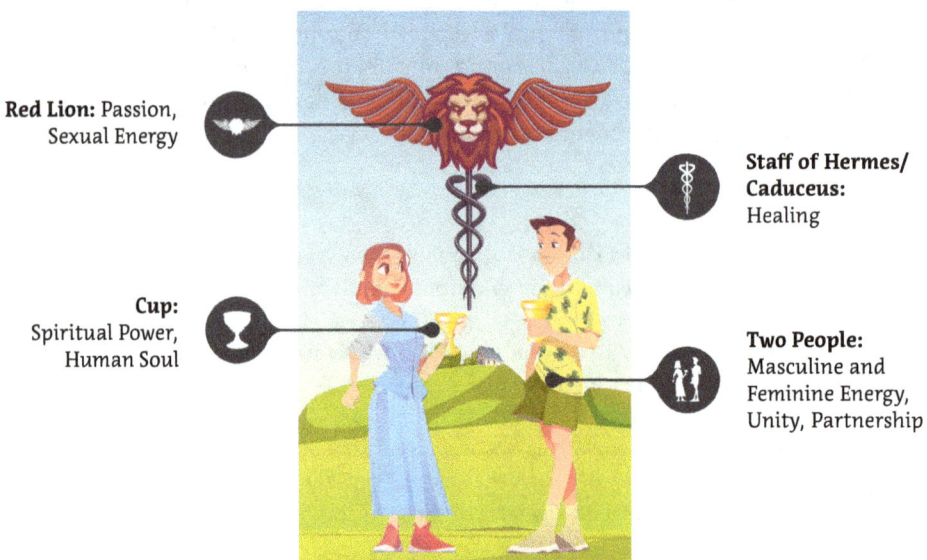

Yes/No Reading:

☑ ○ ○
Yes   No   Maybe

Names in Other Tarot Systems:
Golden Dawn: Lord of Love
Tarot of Marseilles: Two of Cups
Thoth: Love

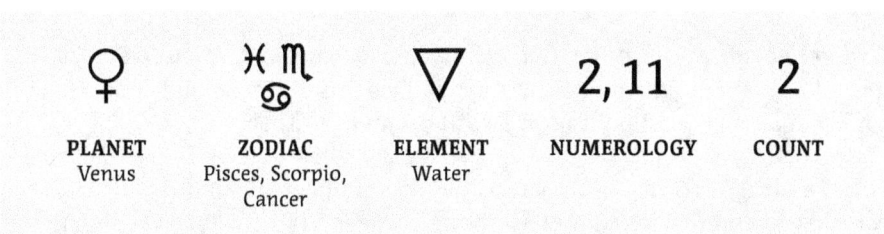

PLANET	ZODIAC	ELEMENT	NUMEROLOGY	COUNT
Venus	Pisces, Scorpio, Cancer	Water	2, 11	2

Upright: *Fairness, Peace, Romantic Love, Unity, Partnership, Connection*
The Two of Cups symbolizes a significant and profound bond between two individuals, based on mutual respect, comprehension, and a shared emotional frequency. When this card appears, whether in a platonic, romantic, or professional relationship, it usually indicates the potential of teamwork and harmony.

The Two of Cups is more than just a superficial link; it often implies a soulful relationship or a connection through fate. Additionally, the card alludes to balance, not only in terms of an external relationship but also in the harmony between one's masculine and feminine energy or rational and emotional nature.

Reversed: *Imbalance, Separation, Broken Connection, Tension, Inequity, Fights*
The reversed Two of Cups typically signifies a disruption in harmony and mutual understanding. It can represent a relationship where there's a lack of reciprocity, or where one party feels undervalued or misunderstood.

This position might also indicate external factors that strain a relationship, such as interference from others, or situations where shared goals and values start to diverge, causing tensions.

In some cases, the reversed Two of Cups can also suggest a need for personal boundaries, or a period where individuals might need to focus on their personal growth before they can successfully collaborate or bond with others.

Upright Interpretations

General Reading: The Two of Cups symbolizes partnership, mutual respect, and a harmonious balance between two individuals. It often points to a deep connection or a bond that is both emotional and spiritual.

Love Reading: This card is a very positive omen, indicating mutual attraction, commitment, and a deep emotional bond between partners. It can represent the early stages of a romantic relationship or the deepening of an existing one.

Health Reading: The Two of Cups suggests emotional balance and harmony, which can lead to physical well-being. It might also indicate a healing partnership, such as a beneficial therapist-patient relationship.

Career Reading: In a professional context, the card signifies partnerships and collaborations that are built on mutual respect and shared goals. It can point to a successful business partnership or teamwork.

Reversed Interpretations

General Reading: The reversed Two of Cups might indicate a disharmony or imbalance in a relationship. There could be misunderstandings, miscommunications, or a disconnect between two individuals.

Love Reading: This card reversed can suggest a strain in a romantic relationship, a potential breakup, or feelings of being out of sync with your partner. It can also indicate a one-sided relationship.

Health Reading: For health, it might suggest emotional imbalances or stress due to relationship issues. It could also imply a lack of mutual understanding in a therapeutic relationship

Career Reading: The reversed Two of Cups can indicate disagreements, conflicts, or a partnership that's not yielding desired results.

The Two of Cups embodies the profound nature of human connections, whether romantic, platonic, or business-oriented. When this card appears, whether in a romantic, platonic, or professional context, it signifies the potential for teamwork and harmonious collaboration.

The card showcases two people, usually depicted as a man and a woman, who symbolize unity and partnership. Their equal stance and the way they face each other indicate mutual respect and the balanced nature of their relationship. They hold two cups, which symbolize the emotional and spiritual gifts that each brings to the relationship.

Typically appearing between the two figures, the caduceus - a staff with two snakes winding around it - symbolizes commerce, negotiation, and balance. This emphasizes the theme of partnership and mutual exchange in the relationship. Often seen above the caduceus, the lion represents strength, passion, and courage. In the context of this card, it suggests a robust and passionate bond between the individuals.

♓ **ZODIAC:** Pisces (February 19 – March 20) is a Water sign ruled by Neptune. Pisceans are known for their emotional depth and keen intuition.

♏ Scorpio (October 23 – November 21) is a Water sign ruled by Pluto. Scorpios are known for their intensity and depth.

♋ Cancer (June 21 – July 22) is a Water sign ruled by the Moon. Cancers are highly empathetic, although they can be initially perceived as cold and distant. They're often caregivers and nurturing.

▽ **ELEMENT:** Water rules emotions and is a symbol of healing, peace, dreams, and compassion. It is associated with Winter, the Suit of Cups, and the West cardinal direction.

ה **HERMETIC QABALAH** Associated Hebrew Letter: Heh – Window (Vision, Reasoning)

QABALISTIC SEPHIROT: Chokmah (Wisdom)

TIMING: June 21 – July 1

THREE OF CUPS

MINOR ARCANA

Cups:
Spiritual Power,
Celebration

Three People:
Community

Plants:
Abundance

Yes/No Reading:

☑   ○   ○

Yes   *No*   *Maybe*

Names in Other Tarot Systems:

Golden Dawn: Lord of Abundance
Tarot of Marseilles: Three of Cups
Thoth: Abundance

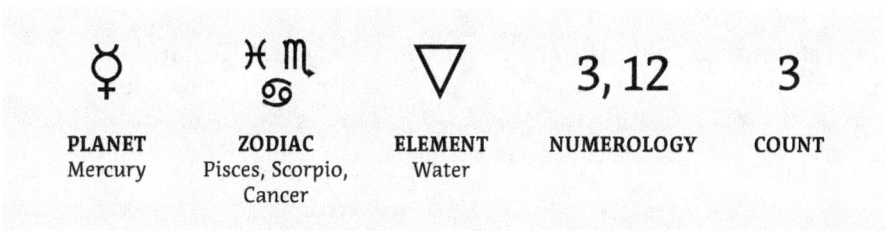

☿	⋈ ♏ ♋	▽	3, 12	3
PLANET	**ZODIAC**	**ELEMENT**	**NUMEROLOGY**	**COUNT**
Mercury	Pisces, Scorpio, Cancer	Water		

Upright: *Friendship, Community, Gatherings, Support, Happiness, Celebration*
The Three of Cups stands tall and radiates a message of communal joy, celebration, and unity. It symbolizes an upcoming period where social connections, shared laughter, and the essence of togetherness are paramount.

This card often appears in readings that suggest upcoming celebrations, gatherings, or reunions. It could be a joyous occasion like a wedding, birth announcement, or a simple get-together with loved ones. It represents deeper emotional bonds in relationships, such as harmonious connections and close friendships. These connections rejuvenate our spirits and remind us of the happiness of shared memories and mutual appreciation.

The Three of Cups symbolizes collaboration and teamwork, especially in creative endeavors. It may signify successful projects or merging talents to create something beautiful and significant. It represents that coming together as a collective often enhances our abilities and results in more magnificent outcomes than we might achieve alone.

Reversed: *Overindulgence, Loneliness, Termination, Isolation, Gossip, Affair*
The Three of Cups in reverse suggests disharmony, miscommunication, and potential conflicts within a group. Fractures may arise due to either external circumstances or internal dynamics. Celebrations may be delayed, relationships may experience misunderstandings, or a once harmonious group could face internal strife or competition. It may also indicate feelings of isolation or isolation from one's social circle. It can allude to times when one feels left out or when celebrations seem insincere.

It may highlight the dangers of excessive indulgence, warning against excessive partying or neglecting responsibilities for short-lived pleasures. This card serves as a reminder to balance social interactions, communicate effectively, and approach situations with understanding and empathy.

Upright Interpretations

General Reading: The Three of Cups embodies celebration, community, and collective joy. It speaks to the beauty of shared experiences, coming together with others, and reveling in the moment. This card can represent a gathering, party, or any event where camaraderie and happiness abound.

Love Reading: In terms of romance, the Three of Cups suggests a joyful time – this could be an engagement, a wedding, or just a time of happiness and bonding in a relationship. For singles, it might indicate that they'll meet potential partners in social settings or through mutual friends.

Health Reading: For health, the Three of Cups is a favorable sign, hinting at rejuvenation and recovery. It could also indicate a time of relaxation, taking breaks with friends, or perhaps attending therapeutic group sessions.

Career Reading: In the professional realm, this card can signify a team's success, a project's completion, or just a time for the team to celebrate and bond. It emphasizes collaboration and shared achievements.

Reversed Interpretations

General Reading: The reversed Three of Cups might signify celebrations gone awry, conflicts in social circles, or overindulgence. It can hint at the need to curb excesses or to reconsider the company one keeps.

Love Reading: In romance, this card reversed can indicate a third-party situation, or complications arising from external influences. It might also suggest temporary separations or conflicts in a relationship.

Health Reading: From a health perspective, overindulgence, particularly in terms of substances, might be a concern. It encourages one to maintain moderation and be wary of peer pressure.

Career Reading: In work and career situations, the reversed Three of Cups could indicate team disagreements, unsuccessful projects, or missed opportunities to celebrate due to setbacks.

The Three of Cups commemorates moments when we unite with our loved ones, family, or community to revel in mutual joy, be it an accomplishment, marking milestones, or simply basking in the company of one another.

At the card's core, we see three figures, often women, depicted dancing in a circle or raising their cups to toast. Their happy expressions and harmonious dance or gestures convey mutual respect, friendship, and a profound sense of belonging. The figures are often dressed in flowing dresses or robes, capturing a sense of freedom, movement, and unbridled happiness. Their attire underpins the card's festive essence and emotions' fluidity. Each figure holds a cup, raised high in jubilation, representing emotional contentment and the delight of shared experiences. Raising these cups is an indication of giving and sharing positive emotions.

The card's setting typically boasts an abundance of flowers or fruits, either on the ground or in the surrounding area, symbolizing the tangible rewards of life and the physical representation of abundance and prosperity. The background of the card, frequently a clear sky or a lush landscape, amplifies the positive and unrestricted moment, suggesting a time unburdened by limitations.

ZODIAC: Pisces (February 19 – March 20) is a Water sign ruled by Neptune. Pisceans are known for their emotional depth and keen intuition.

Scorpio (October 23 – November 21) is a Water sign ruled by Pluto. Scorpios are known for their intensity and depth.

Cancer (June 21 – July 22) is a Water sign ruled by the Moon. Cancers are highly empathetic, although they can be initially perceived as cold and distant. They're often caregivers and nurturing.

ELEMENT: Water rules emotions and is a symbol of healing, peace, dreams, and compassion. It is associated with Winter, the Suit of Cups, and the West cardinal direction.

HERMETIC QABALAH Associated Hebrew Letter: Heh – Window (Vision, Reasoning)

QABALISTIC SEPHIROT: Binah (Understanding)

TIMING: July 2 – July 11

FOUR OF CUPS

MINOR ARCANA

Tree:
Meditation

Cup:
Gifts, Creativity,
Second Chances

Person:
Contemplation

Yes/No Reading:

○ ☑
Yes No **Maybe**

Names in Other Tarot Systems:
Golden Dawn: Lord of Luxury
Tarot of Marseilles: Four of Cups
Thoth: Luxury

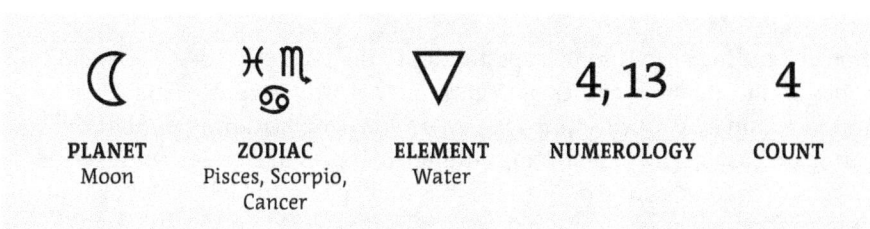

☾	♓ ♏ ♋	▽	4, 13	4
PLANET	**ZODIAC**	**ELEMENT**	**NUMEROLOGY**	**COUNT**
Moon	Pisces, Scorpio, Cancer	Water		

Upright: *Apathy, Boredom, Missed Opportunities, Remorse, Regret, Stagnant*
The upright Four of Cups denotes a time of looking within oneself, pondering, and occasionally experiencing dissatisfaction with one's current state. Despite the universe offering opportunities and emotional adventures, a person may feel disconnected or uninterested, possibly due to a previous disappointment or an internal moment of reflection. The card portrays a feeling of emotional stagnation, where the present moment or available offers may not seem appealing or fulfilling.

Alternatively, the Four of Cups may warn against becoming too self-absorbed or disengaged from the world. It serves as a reminder that, while introspection is beneficial, it is equally important not to disregard the blessings and possibilities available. At times, this card implies that a person is so absorbed in their discontent or past regrets that they overlook valuable offers, lessons, or gestures of kindness right before them. It emphasizes the importance of finding a balance between introspection and external awareness.

Reversed: *Sudden Awareness, Focus, Gratitude, Motivation, Acceptance*
The Four of Cups in reverse suggests a shift in one's perspective, which can lead to a realization or awakening to previously missed opportunities or overlooked blessings. While the upright position of this card may indicate introspection, apathy, or discontentment with one's current situation, its reversed counterpart can prompt a renewed sense of clarity and a desire to re-engage with the world. This renewed awareness can lead to a greater appreciation of opportunities that were once dismissed and a willingness to embrace new experiences.

Moreover, the reversed Four of Cups can signify the end of a period of introspection. For those feeling stuck or in a rut, this card can herald a period of motivation and forward movement. It's a reminder to break free from stagnation, embrace change, and actively seek out positive experiences. This card reminds us to focus on our blessings and be open to the many possibilities life offers.

Upright Interpretations

General Reading: The Four of Cups alludes to the possibility of experiencing a sense of unfulfillment or lack of inspiration towards current events. This may stem from an overwhelming apathy towards circumstances, either from fixating on past letdowns or getting entangled in personal emotions. It serves as a reminder to take note of one's feelings and be mindful of the opportunities available for one's grasp.

Love Reading: The presence of emotional distance or lack of interest may lead to tension and difficulties. Those not currently in a relationship may be experiencing a sense of disconnection from the dating world or finding it challenging to move on from previous romantic experiences, making it difficult to pursue new connections.

Health Reading: You're in a phase of emotional disinterest or lack of concern towards your physical and mental health. To address this, it is vital to reconnect with your body and emotions. Seeking professional help can also prove beneficial. Avoid overlooking any signs and symptoms that may arise and ensure to prioritize your mental well-being.

Career Reading: This signals a lack of satisfaction or challenge in one's professional role. Though possibilities for progress or transformation may exist, one could be missing them due to either complacency or fear.

Reversed Interpretations

General Reading: There's a shift in perspective, indicating a growing consciousness and eagerness to re-engage with the world. No longer feeling stagnant, the card pushes for a movement away from self-reflection towards action.

Love Reading: Having previously kept a distance or been closed off, you may be inclined to repair relationships or pursue new romantic opportunities. This suggests that your emotions are beginning to awaken.

Health Reading: There are signs of a favorable change in one's outlook on health. The individual displays heightened eagerness to tackle and enhance physical and mental wellness. This could imply a recognition of certain behaviors or ways of thinking negatively impacting their health.

Career Reading: Your perspective on your career may shift as you begin to recognize previously overlooked opportunities. You may feel a renewed drive to pursue growth, embrace challenges, or alter your course if you feel stagnant.

The Four of Cups is a Tarot card that often depicts a figure sitting beneath a tree, in deep contemplation or perhaps even disillusionment. In front of the individual are three cups, typically filled and standing upright, symbolizing life's emotional offers or experiences. Floating above or to the person's side is a fourth cup, presented by a hand emerging from a cloud, indicating an additional offer or opportunity from the universe.

The scene encapsulates a feeling of introspection, indifference, or dissatisfaction. The figure's demeanor suggests they are engrossed in their thoughts and possibly missing out on the present moment or the opportunities that life presents.

Depending on one's perspective, the lone floating cup symbolizes a new opportunity or a missed one. Overall, the card brings forth themes of contemplation, missed chances, disinterest in current circumstances, and the need for emotional re-evaluation. It reminds us to be aware of our surroundings and not to get too lost in introspection, lest we miss out on what life has to offer.

♓ **ZODIAC:** Pisces (February 19 – March 20) is a Water sign ruled by Neptune. Pisceans are known for their emotional depth and keen intuition.

♏ Scorpio (October 23 – November 21) is a Water sign ruled by Pluto. Scorpios are known for their intensity and depth.

♋ Cancer (June 21 – July 22) is a Water sign ruled by the Moon. Cancers are highly empathetic, although they can be initially perceived as cold and distant. They're often caregivers and nurturing.

▽ **ELEMENT:** Water rules emotions and is a symbol of healing, peace, dreams, and compassion. It is associated with Winter, the Suit of Cups, and the West cardinal direction.

ה **HERMETIC QABALAH** Associated Hebrew Letter: Heh – Window (Vision, Reasoning)

QABALISTIC SEPHIROT: Chesed (Mercy)

TIMING: July 12 – July 21

FIVE OF CUPS
M I N O R   A R C A N A

River:
Challenges

Fallen Cups:
Failure

Person:
Melancholy

Upright Cups:
Future Gifts and
Opportunities

Yes/No Reading:

Yes   No   Maybe

Names in Other Tarot Systems:
Golden Dawn: Lord of Loss in Pleasure
Tarot of Marseilles: Five of Cups
Thoth: Disappointment

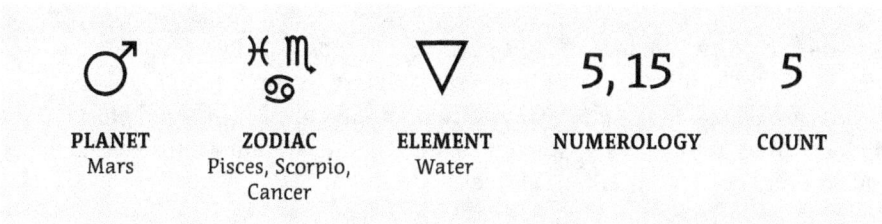

PLANET	ZODIAC	ELEMENT	NUMEROLOGY	COUNT
Mars	Pisces, Scorpio, Cancer	Water	5, 15	5

Upright: *Tragedy, Loss, Grief, Remorse, Lost Opportunity, Heartbreak, Misery*
The upright Five of Cups encompasses emotions of regret, disappointment, and loss. Its illustration often portrays a cloaked figure standing before three cups spilled over while two remain behind them. This visual representation evokes a feeling of sadness for what was lost or opportunities that were missed. The cups that have spilled signify sorrow, previous mistakes, or events that have caused emotional distress, emphasizing the concept of dwelling on past sorrows.

Despite its negative connotations, the Five of Cups conveys a subtle but significant message of optimism and outlook. The two cups behind the figure symbolize the good that remains or the new possibilities yet to be recognized. While the past pain is authentic and reasonable, this card urges the reader to shift their attention from what has been lost to what can still be achieved or appreciated. It serves as a reminder that although we cannot alter the past, we can impact our present and future by selecting where we direct our attention.

Reversed: *Moving On, Forgiveness, Recovering, Healing, Acceptance*
The reversed Five of Cups indicates a transition from sorrow and regret to acceptance and optimism. This shift in perspective implies that the period of intense grieving or disappointment is fading or has fulfilled its purpose. Dwelling solely on past losses or errors is now seen as unproductive. Instead, there is a growing desire to move forward with newfound knowledge and a heart open to healing.

Additionally, the reversed Five of Cups represents resilience and renewal. It marks the start of emotional healing and a renewed spirit. This card urges the querent to practice forgiveness, whether towards oneself or others, and to look for the positives or opportunities in their situation. By accepting and integrating past pain, one can make way for new beginnings and a brighter outlook for the future.

Upright Interpretations

General Reading: The Five of Cups in its upright position denotes a sense of loss, grief, and disappointment in general readings. It could stem from past events or mistakes leading to regret. Although the spilled cups signify lost opportunities or pain, it's important to note the two standing cups behind the figure as evidence that not all is lost.

Love Reading: In love readings, this card could indicate a rough patch, a breakup, or lingering regret in a relationship. It serves as a reminder to focus on what can still be salvaged or the lessons that can be learned. For singles, it might represent dwelling on past relationships and overlooking potential new ones.

Health Reading: For health readings, the card represents feelings of despair or depression, with emotional pain taking a toll on physical well-being. Seeking help is essential, and one must remember that healing and recovery are possible.

Career Reading: Regarding career matters, this card highlights potential challenges, disappointments, or even job losses. Regret over past decisions may be weighing heavily. Nevertheless, there are still options to explore and paths to consider, even if they are not immediately apparent.

Reversed Interpretations

General Reading: When the Five of Cups is reversed, it serves as a sign of acceptance, progress, and newfound hope following a time of disappointment or sorrow. While the lingering pain of the past may still exist, there is a stronger focus on moving forward and recognizing the positive aspects of life.

Love Reading: In matters of love, this card's reversal can signify the process of healing, forgiveness, and the possibility of reconciliation after a disagreement for those in relationships. For singles, it can indicate the start of a journey to move on from past hurt and be open to new romantic possibilities.

Health Reading: Regarding health, the reversed Five of Cups denotes a period of renewal and recovery. Emotional wounds are starting to heal, leading to a restored sense of well-being and hope. It reminds us of the resilience of our minds and bodies.

Career Reading: This card's reversal prompts reflection, learning from previous mistakes, and a positive outlook on future professional endeavors. New job opportunities or a change in perspective about one's career path may arise.

The somber scene depicted on the Five of Cups captures feelings of regret and loss, often showcasing a figure draped in black or dark clothing to symbolize grief. Positioned before them are three cups that have been overturned, spilling their contents onto the ground, representing missed opportunities, past errors, or disappointments. This sorrowful image encourages dwelling on past sorrows or missed chances, emphasizing the primary theme of the card.

Despite the grief that consumes the central figure, two cups remain upright, often overlooked and serving as symbols of hope, new possibilities, or things worth cherishing amidst disappointment. The card's background might feature a river, bridge, or castle in the distance, hinting at the journey of life and the need to keep moving forward. Altogether, the Five of Cups powerfully reminds us that pain and hope coexist in life, urging us to shift our focus from what's lost to what remains and the potential of the future.

♓ **ZODIAC:** Pisces (February 19 – March 20) is a Water sign ruled by Neptune. Pisceans are known for their emotional depth and keen intuition.

♏ Scorpio (October 23 – November 21) is a Water sign ruled by Pluto. Scorpios are known for their intensity and depth.

♋ Cancer (June 21 – July 22) is a Water sign ruled by the Moon. Cancers are highly empathetic, although they can be initially perceived as cold and distant. They're often caregivers and nurturing.

▽ **ELEMENT:** Water rules emotions and is a symbol of healing, peace, dreams, and compassion. It is associated with Winter, the Suit of Cups, and the West cardinal direction.

ה **HERMETIC QABALAH** Associated Hebrew Letter: Heh – Window (Vision, Reasoning)

QABALISTIC SEPHIROT: Geburah (Severity)

🕐 **TIMING:** October 23 – November 1

SIX OF CUPS

MINOR ARCANA

Person:
Offering Help,
Giving

Person:
Accepting Help

Flowers:
Growth,
Blossoming

Yes/No Reading:

☑ ○ ○

Yes *No* *Maybe*

Names in Other Tarot Systems:
Golden Dawn: Lord of Pleasure
Tarot of Marseilles: Six of Cups
Thoth: Pleasure

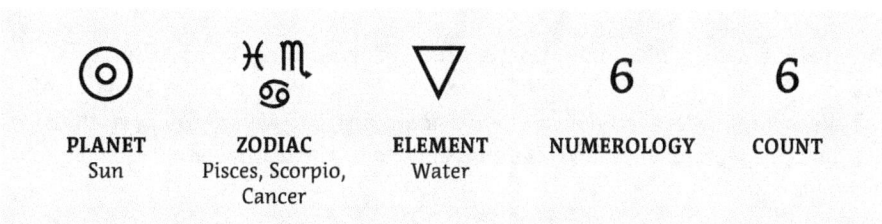

PLANET	ZODIAC	ELEMENT	NUMEROLOGY	COUNT
Sun	Pisces, Scorpio, Cancer	Water	6	6

Upright: *Nostalgia, Memories, Innocence, Family, Kindness, Creativity*

The upright Six of Cups symbolizes deep sentimentality and evokes memories of the past, particularly those from childhood or early years. This prompts introspection, encouraging us to reconnect with our inner child, reflect on past experiences, and understand how they have shaped our present.

Moreover, the card suggests the possibility of reunions or reconciliations, be it with a former flame, childhood friend, or someone with whom we share a history. Its warm aura connotes comfort, wisdom, and insight, highlighting the value of human connections.

The Six of Cups also embodies kindness and generosity, promoting respect, understanding, and compassion. It inspires us to approach situations with an open heart, offer service without any expectations, and cherish life's simple moments and gestures of goodwill. Ultimately, this card reminds us of the beauty of human connection and the joy it can bring our lives.

Reversed: *Boredom, Immobility, Child Abuse, Stagnation, Leaving Home*

Memories of the past can be overwhelming, and there may be a distorted perception of past events. This could indicate an excessive attachment to the past that prevents one from moving forward. The reversed Six of Cups can bring up past traumas or negative experiences that may impact one's emotional state or decision-making. It could signify unaddressed childhood issues or unresolved past hurts that need healing. It is crucial to learn from our past but not let it control our present or future. Seeking introspection or therapy may help to address and heal these wounds.

This reversal also advises caution when revisiting past relationships or situations. Not all connections from the past align with our current goals and well-being, and there is a risk of repeating old patterns or mistakes. It is essential to carefully evaluate the reasons for wanting to reconnect or revisit.

Upright Interpretations

General Reading: This can represent a time of reflection and nostalgia, where you may find yourself reminiscing about your past and cherishing your childhood memories. You may also experience a strong sense of déjà vu that reminds you of simpler times. This card exudes warmth and comfort in those memories.

Love Reading: In love readings, this card could signify a rekindling of an old flame or the resurgence of feelings from a past relationship. For those in a relationship, it suggests a period of deeper connection by revisiting shared memories or returning to significant places. If single, you might find solace in past memories or reconnect with someone from your past.

Health Reading: This suggests a period of healing and rejuvenation. You can find therapeutic ways to manage stress and emotional challenges by connecting with your roots or childhood practices. It may also be an opportunity to revisit old health habits or treatments that once brought you comfort.

Career Reading: Past experiences and efforts might come into play. You may receive an opportunity from an old colleague or revisit past projects. It's also an excellent opportunity to learn from past professional experiences and ensure you don't repeat the same mistakes.

Reversed Interpretations

General Reading: You're feeling trapped in the past. This can result in difficulty moving forward due to unresolved problems or excessive sentimentality. It encourages releasing the past and embracing the present moment.

Love Reading: Unresolved emotions or past traumas can impact your present relationships and hinder your ability to form new romantic connections. Carefully consider why past relationships ended before attempting to reignite them.

Health Reading: Your mental or emotional wellbeing may be impacted by past traumas or negative experiences that are resurfacing. You may be neglecting your current health by dwelling too much on past habits.

Career Reading: Your career trajectory could be hindered by past mistakes or unresolved professional issues that have the potential to create patterns of repetition. To move forward with clarity and purpose, it is essential to address these issues.

The essence of nostalgia, memories, and childhood innocence is imbued in the Six of Cups, which often depicts tranquil and heartwarming scenes that transport one back to simpler times. It speaks to the human desire to reconnect with our roots, reflecting on simpler times, and the yearning to return to moments when life was uncomplicated and full of wonder. The card encourages kindness, understanding, and recognizing the bonds formed early in life.

Two people are shown in an old courtyard or garden setting, one offering a cup of flowers to the other, symbolizing acts of kindness, generosity, and pure-hearted exchanges of sharing.

The six cups on the card are arranged in a specific pattern and are overflowing with flowers, particularly the white five-petaled flower, representing purity, innocence, and spiritual insight. The lush and well-tended garden or courtyard signifies a safe and nurturing environment, evoking feelings of security, harmony, and joy when reminiscing about fond memories.

♓ **ZODIAC:** Pisces (February 19 – March 20) is a Water sign ruled by Neptune. Pisceans are known for their emotional depth and keen intuition.

♏ Scorpio (October 23 – November 21) is a Water sign ruled by Pluto. Scorpios are known for their intensity and depth.

♋ Cancer (June 21 – July 22) is a Water sign ruled by the Moon. Cancers are highly empathetic, although they can be initially perceived as cold and distant. They're often caregivers and nurturing.

▽ **ELEMENT:** Water rules emotions and is a symbol of healing, peace, dreams, and compassion. It is associated with Winter, the Suit of Cups, and the West cardinal direction.

ה **HERMETIC QABALAH** Associated Hebrew Letter: Heh – Window (Vision, Reasoning)

🍇 **QABALISTIC SEPHIROT:** Tiphareth (Beauty)

🕐 **TIMING:** November 2 – November 12

SEVEN OF CUPS

MINOR ARCANA

Bust: Beauty, Love, Wisdom

Shrouded Figure: Potential

Castle: Security

Treasure: Wealth

Snake: Passion, Desire

Cups: Chalices of Vision

Dragon: Anger, Envy

Laurel: Success, Status, Honor

Clouds: Imagination

Yes/No Reading:

○ Yes   ○ No   ☑ *Maybe*

Names in Other Tarot Systems:
Golden Dawn: Lord of Illusory Success
Tarot of Marseilles: Seven of Cups
Thoth: Debauch

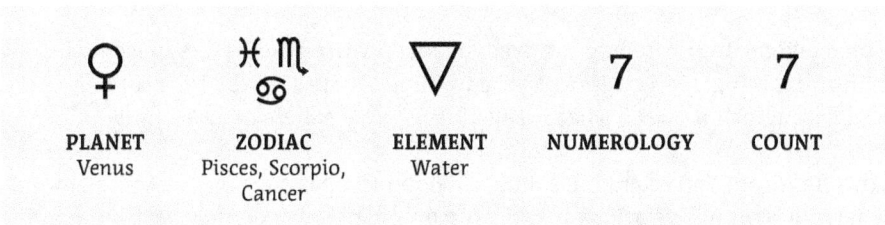

PLANET	ZODIAC	ELEMENT	NUMEROLOGY	COUNT
Venus	Pisces, Scorpio, Cancer	Water	7	7

Upright: *Options, Dreaming, Fantasy, Illusion, Meditation, Decisions*
The upright Seven of Cups represents dreams, imagination, and choices, offering many possibilities to those who draw them. The individual is presented with several enticing options, which may evoke a sense of wonderment and confusion. This card symbolizes a phase in life where opportunities or potentials are available, requiring careful contemplation.

While imagining various paths and outcomes is natural, one may need to be more engrossed in these visions, ultimately losing touch with reality. This card warns against being overwhelmed by choices or chasing unrealistic dreams, which could result in missed opportunities. It's a reminder to distinguish between mere fantasies and actual possibilities.

This card encourages introspection and self-awareness, urging individuals to carefully ground themselves and assess each option's pros and cons. Doing so lets one discern which cup or path aligns most closely with their genuine desires and long-term goals. This is a call to harness the power of imagination and use it as a tool for clarity rather than allowing it to become a source of confusion or escapism.

Reversed: *Lack of Purpose, Sobriety, Confusion, Overwhelmed by Choice*
This indicates a transition from confusion and delusion to clarity and decision-making. After being indecisive or feeling overwhelmed by too many options, there is a drive to ground oneself and make a concrete choice. The fog of fantasy dissipates, providing a clearer understanding of what is achievable and worth pursuing.

However, gaining this newfound clarity can be a challenging process. A decision is being forced due to external circumstances or an internal realization. There may be feelings of regret or missed opportunities from not taking action sooner or getting lost in fanciful daydreams for too long. It serves as a wake-up call, urging individuals to confront the realities of their situation, even if they are challenging to face, and to take responsibility for their past indecisiveness.

Upright Interpretations

General Reading: You may feel overwhelmed by the possibilities presented. While dreaming and imagination are valuable, there's a need to ground oneself and distinguish between what's realistic and what's mere daydreaming.

Love Reading: You might have multiple potential partners or be unsure of what you truly want in a relationship. If in a relationship, you or your partner might be idealizing the relationship or avoiding confronting its realities. It's crucial to understand the difference between love and illusion.

Health Reading: You might be considering various paths to wellness or feeling unsure about a diagnosis or treatment. Ensure that any health decisions are based on well-researched information rather than jumping to conclusions.

Career Reading: Many paths or opportunities might be presenting themselves. While it's an exciting time, it's also easy to become paralyzed by choice. Prioritize your long-term goals, and be wary of pursuits that seem too good to be true.

Reversed Interpretations

General Reading: The Seven of Cups reversed suggests that clarity is emerging from previous confusion. You're starting to see through the illusions and discern what truly matters. This might also indicate missed opportunities due to indecision.

Love Reading: Past illusions about a relationship might become clear, leading to decisions about moving forward. If single, you might realize that your ideal partner's image doesn't match the reality of what you truly want or need.

Health Reading: You're becoming more clear-headed about a health issue or the steps you need to take for wellbeing. There's a move towards action and tangible solutions rather than getting lost in anxiety or possible outcomes.

Career Reading: After a period of uncertainty or too many options, you're now focused on a clear career path or goal. You're becoming more decisive and recognizing which opportunities align best with your aspirations.

The Seven of Cups showcases seven cups or chalices, each resting on a cloud and filled with distinct symbols or treasures. The imagery of the cups can vary across different decks but typically includes various items such as a castle, a dragon, jewels, a snake, a shrouded figure, and more. The cups' arrangement evokes a sense of mystery and wonder, lending to the dreamlike state that the card conveys.

This dreamlike state portrays a world of numerous possibilities, fantasies, and potentials. However, the cups' cloud-bound nature highlights the fleeting and intangible quality of these visions, suggesting they might be mere illusions or wishful thinking. While the many options can be advantageous, it can also result in confusion, indecision, and detachment from reality.

The Seven of Cups underscores the power of imagination, the importance of choices, and the potential for delusion. It prompts introspection, encouraging individuals to distinguish between reality and wishful thinking. The card warns of being seduced by unrealistic or unattainable desires, urging individuals to remain grounded and make informed choices.

♓ **ZODIAC:** Pisces (February 19 – March 20) is a Water sign ruled by Neptune. Pisceans are known for their emotional depth and keen intuition.

♏ Scorpio (October 23 – November 21) is a Water sign ruled by Pluto. Scorpios are known for their intensity and depth.

♋ Cancer (June 21 – July 22) is a Water sign ruled by the Moon. Cancers are highly empathetic, although they can be initially perceived as cold and distant. They're often caregivers and nurturing.

▽ **ELEMENT:** Water rules emotions and is a symbol of healing, peace, dreams, and compassion. It is associated with Winter, the Suit of Cups, and the West cardinal direction.

ה **HERMETIC QABALAH** Associated Hebrew Letter: Heh – Window (Vision, Reasoning)

QABALISTIC SEPHIROT: Netsach (Victory)

🕐 **TIMING:** November 13 – November 22

EIGHT OF CUPS

MINOR ARCANA

Sun/Moon:
Psyche Paradox

Mountains:
Challenges

Figure: Avoidance of Choices

Yes/No Reading:

Yes   **No** ✓   Maybe

Names in Other Tarot Systems:

Golden Dawn: Lord of Abandoned Success
Tarot of Marseilles: Eight of Cups
Thoth: Indolence

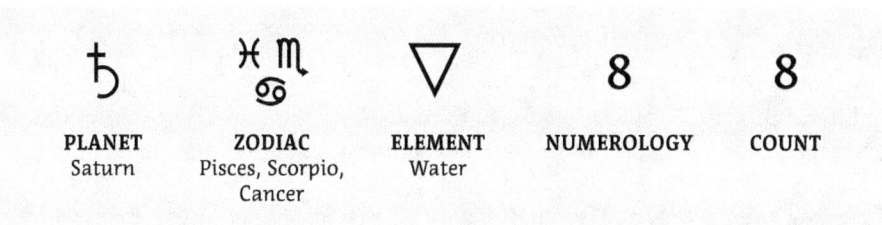

PLANET	ZODIAC	ELEMENT	NUMEROLOGY	COUNT
Saturn	Pisces, Scorpio, Cancer	Water	8	8

Upright: *Disillusionment, Abandonment, Fatigue, Withdrawal, Escapism*
This positioning indicates a moment in life when, due to self-reflection or external events, one realizes that what used to bring joy, satisfaction, or emotional fulfillment is no longer fulfilling. Things, relationships, or situations that once provided happiness may now feel hollow or unsatisfying.

This card symbolizes bravery and the challenging decision to escape what is familiar. Leaving behind what is comfortable is never easy, but the Eight of Cups indicates that this departure is essential for growth and self-discovery.

The Eight of Cups is about something other than aimlessly wandering or escaping problems. It's a deliberate and thoughtful journey towards a higher purpose or state of being. While a sense of loss or sadness may be associated with leaving the past behind, there is also an underlying sense of optimism. The card encourages trust in one's intuition and the belief that, though the path ahead may be uncertain, it will ultimately lead to a more fulfilling and meaningful existence.

Reversed: *Avoidance, Doubt, Fear of Change, Aimless Drifting, Stagnation*
The reversed Eight of Cups alludes to hesitation and reluctance. The upright position concentrates on the brave choice of abandoning what no longer serves to pursue a more significant goal. One may be avoiding the profound introspective work needed to move forward. This can lead to a vicious cycle in which one finds themselves in the same unfulfilling circumstances repeatedly, seeking escape but not addressing the underlying cause of their dissatisfaction.

The reversed Eight of Cups also indicates a realization that something once discarded still has value. In such cases, the card encourages a thoughtful return, reconciliation, or reintegration, but with a clearer understanding of its worth and significance in one's life.

Upright Interpretations

General Reading: It's possible that you're sensing a desire to move away from circumstances or connections that no longer nourish your greater self. The guidance this card offers is to have faith in your instincts and venture towards what feels best, regardless of the fact that it may require leaving what's familiar.

Love Reading: You're not feeling fulfilled. It's essential to evaluate if this can be addressed or if it's time to move on for personal growth. For singles, it can signify the need to leave behind old wounds or past relationships to invite new love.

Health Reading: You need to leave behind unhealthy routines or mindsets to seek better health and mental peace. It could also point towards seeking alternative treatments or therapies.

Career Reading: It might be time to evaluate if your current job or profession aligns with your deeper passion or purpose. If you're feeling unfulfilled, the Eight of Cups encourages considering a change, even if it means venturing into the unknown.

Reversed Interpretations

General Reading: You're having a hard time letting go due to unresolved emotions. It can also suggest returning to old situations or relationships, not necessarily because they offer fulfillment but because of fear or familiarity.

Love Reading: There might be a reluctance to address underlying issues. There's a possibility of clinging to a relationship due to fear of being alone, even if it isn't emotionally satisfying. For singles, it can signify being stuck in the past, hindering the potential for new relationships.

Health Reading: You may be struggling to let go of unhealthy habits or in denial about aspects of your health. The reversed Eight of Cups is a call to confront these issues directly and make necessary changes. Alternatively, you might be reconsidering a health choice or returning to a previous therapy or treatment.

Career Reading: There might be a reluctance to leave a secure job, even if it doesn't resonate with your true calling. On the flip side, it could also mean revisiting a previous job or profession that still has lessons to offer.

In the Eight of Cups, a solitary figure is captured striding away from a pile of eight cups. Traditionally regarded as representative of past experiences and emotional ties, the cups appear lopsided, with one cup needing to be put in the right place. The backdrop is usually rugged terrain, indicating an arduous journey or spiritual pilgrimage ahead. The moon, typically full or crescent, symbolizes the subconscious and the domain of intuition and dreams.

The card imagery evokes a sense of abandonment, but not a result of a capricious or heedless act. Instead, it indicates a more profound, introspective rationale for departure. The formerly treasured cups are now regarded as insufficient or no longer gratifying. The protagonist's quest embodies a personal voyage seeking purpose, a higher truth, or a spiritual awakening.

The Eight of Cups epitomizes personal transformation, forsaking the familiar or comfortable to pursue more profound significance and contentment. It resonates with disenchantment but also underscores the courage to follow one's true calling, even traversing unfamiliar terrain.

ZODIAC: Pisces (February 19 – March 20) is a Water sign ruled by Neptune. Pisceans are known for their emotional depth and keen intuition.

Scorpio (October 23 – November 21) is a Water sign ruled by Pluto. Scorpios are known for their intensity and depth.

Cancer (June 21 – July 22) is a Water sign ruled by the Moon. Cancers are highly empathetic, although they can be initially perceived as cold and distant. They're often caregivers and nurturing.

ELEMENT: Water rules emotions and is a symbol of healing, peace, dreams, and compassion. It is associated with Winter, the Suit of Cups, and the West cardinal direction.

HERMETIC QABALAH Associated Hebrew Letter: Heh – Window (Vision, Reasoning)

QABALISTIC SEPHIROT: Hod (Splendor)

TIMING: February 19 – February 28

NINE OF CUPS

MINOR ARCANA

Cups:
Fulfillment

Red Hat:
Passion

Figure:
Confidence

Yes/No Reading:

☑   ○   ○
Yes   *No*   *Maybe*

Names in Other Tarot Systems:
Golden Dawn: Lord of Material Happiness
Tarot of Marseilles: Nine of Cups
Thoth: Happiness

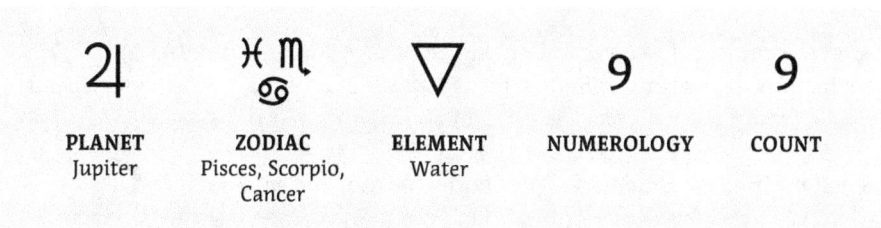

♃	♓♏♋	▽	9	9
PLANET	**ZODIAC**	**ELEMENT**	**NUMEROLOGY**	**COUNT**
Jupiter	Pisces, Scorpio, Cancer	Water		

Upright: *Wish Fulfillment, Rewards, Luxury, Satisfaction, Success, Gratitude*
When the Nine of Cups appears, it affirms an individual's personal achievement and inner joy. It signifies the hard work and emotional efforts invested in achieving happiness, allowing the individual to enjoy the rewards. However, this card is not just about momentary pleasures but also represents a sustained sense of satisfaction where one can reflect on their emotional journey and take pride in their well-being.

Despite the celebration, the Nine of Cups reminds us not to become complacent and encourages us to appreciate the present blessings while acknowledging the journey that led us here. It is crucial to maintain a balanced perspective, understanding that personal growth continues and new aspirations will emerge over time. Contentment is a beautiful state, but it is essential to remain mindful of the ongoing journey.

Reversed: *Smugness, Pessimism, Dissatisfaction, Materialism, Nightmares*
The appearance of the reversed Nine of Cups in a reading signifies a potential for unfulfilled desires, inner emptiness despite external achievements, and disappointment. It suggests that emotional or material rewards may have yet to materialize as hoped or may not bring expected satisfaction. This card represents disillusionment, implying that material success does not always satisfy inner emotional needs.

Additionally, the reversed Nine of Cups warns against complacency and overindulgence, which can lead to taking blessings for granted. It may indicate a tendency to excessively indulge in luxuries or pleasures to the point of neglecting health, relationships, or responsibilities. This card calls for introspection and reflection on what truly brings contentment, ensuring that pursuing desires aligns with personal values and long-term well-being.

Upright Interpretations

General Reading: The Nine of Cups suggests a period of contentment, satisfaction, and wishes coming true. It's a sign of abundance in many aspects of your life. You're enjoying the fruits of your efforts.

Love Reading: For singles, the card indicates that you may soon find a relationship that brings emotional fulfillment. For those in relationships, it speaks of a time of joy, mutual understanding, and satisfaction. Your emotional bond is deepening, and you are in a period where love and understanding flow effortlessly.

Health Reading: You're likely feeling good both mentally and physically. This card is a positive omen for health, suggesting that you're in a harmonious state or are on the road to recovery if you've been ill. It might also indicate a time where emotional healing is taking place.

Career Reading: Your efforts are paying off, and you're enjoying what you do. It could also hint at a long-desired job opportunity coming your way.

Reversed Interpretations

General Reading: There might be a realization that what you thought would bring happiness isn't fulfilling you as anticipated.

Love Reading: For singles, this card suggests that there might be unrealistic expectations in love or a tendency to seek perfection, leading to potential disappointments. For those in relationships, it can indicate taking a partner for granted or not appreciating the love present in the relationship.

Health Reading: While there may not be severe health problems, there's a sense of not feeling your best. It could be due to overindulgence or neglecting some aspects of your well-being. Emotional or mental health may need some attention.

Career Reading: The the reversed Nine of Cups suggests missed opportunities or a feeling of underachievement. There might be a gap between your aspirations and the current state of your career. This card can also warn against resting on laurels and encourages a proactive approach to professional growth.

Often dubbed the "Wish Card," the Nine of Cups holds a reputation as one of the most encouraging and positive cards in the deck. Typically depicted as a comfortable figure surrounded by an arc of nine golden cups, this card exudes contentment, prosperity, and a profound sense of satisfaction.

The confident posture of the individual suggests they have attained their heart's desires and are relishing the rewards of their success. The setting evokes a state of emotional well-being and fulfillment, with the cups symbolizing abundance in the realm of feelings, relationships, and personal experiences.

Overall, the Nine of Cups emanates a feeling of gratitude, joy, and the realization of one's wishes. Not only has the seeker achieved their objectives, but they also enjoy the contentment and satisfaction accompanying such achievements. This card serves as a reminder that inner fulfillment and emotional satisfaction bring true happiness rather than just material gain.

♓ **ZODIAC:** Pisces (February 19 – March 20) is a Water sign ruled by Neptune. Pisceans are known for their emotional depth and keen intuition.

♏ Scorpio (October 23 – November 21) is a Water sign ruled by Pluto. Scorpios are known for their intensity and depth.

♋ Cancer (June 21 – July 22) is a Water sign ruled by the Moon. Cancers are highly empathetic, although they can be initially perceived as cold and distant. They're often caregivers and nurturing.

▽ **ELEMENT:** Water rules emotions and is a symbol of healing, peace, dreams, and compassion. It is associated with Winter, the Suit of Cups, and the West cardinal direction.

ה **HERMETIC QABALAH** Associated Hebrew Letter: Heh – Window (Vision, Reasoning)

QABALISTIC SEPHIROT: Yesod (Foundation)

TIMING: March 1 – March 10

TEN OF CUPS
M I N O R   A R C A N A

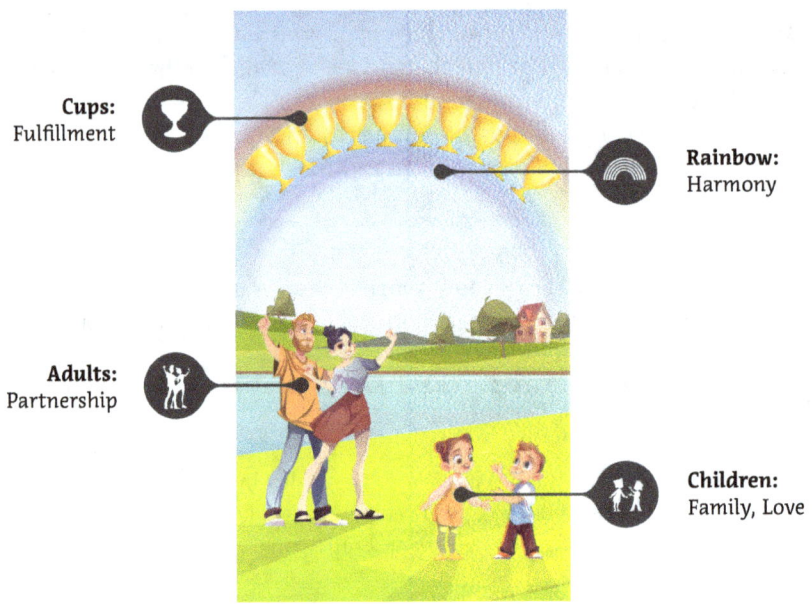

Cups:
Fulfillment

Rainbow:
Harmony

Adults:
Partnership

Children:
Family, Love

Yes/No Reading:

Yes ✓   No ○   Maybe ○

Names in Other Tarot Systems:
Golden Dawn: Lord of Perfected Success
Tarot of Marseilles: Ten of Cups
Thoth: Satiety

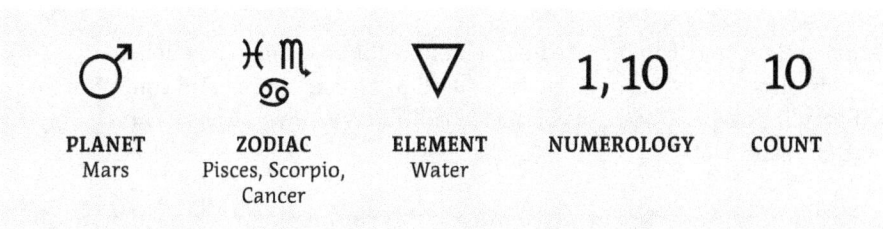

♂	⚥	▽	1, 10	10
PLANET	**ZODIAC**	**ELEMENT**	**NUMEROLOGY**	**COUNT**
Mars	Pisces, Scorpio, Cancer	Water		

Upright: *Blessings, Stability, Divine Love, Family, Harmony, Alignment, Bliss*
The Ten of Cups upright symbolizes emotional fulfillment, happiness, and harmonious relationships. It embodies the ideal of a life full of joy, peace, and strong familial ties. When drawn in a reading, it acts as a beacon of hope, indicating that you are in a place where love and mutual respect flourish or where such a time is soon to come. This card often represents deep and meaningful connections in family, friendships, or romantic partnerships. It signifies long-lasting and shared contentment built on trust, understanding, and shared experiences.

In addition to relationships, this card also indicates a personal sense of fulfillment and alignment. It suggests that you are in harmony with your emotions and values, living a life that resonates with your highest self. The challenges and tribulations have led to this moment of serenity and gratitude. You feel rich, blessed, and complete emotionally, mentally, and spiritually.

Reversed: *Domestic Strife, Separation, Broken Home, Shattered Dreams*
The reversed Ten of Cups points to potential disturbances in the emotional realm, such as unfulfilled dreams, broken relationships, or familial strife. This card suggests that you or someone close is struggling to maintain a perfect facade, unwilling to address underlying issues or disappointments.

There may be a disconnect within family or close relationships, possibly caused by unaddressed conflicts, lack of communication, or external stresses that strain the bonds of trust and mutual respect. It's essential to confront these issues head-on to prevent them from eroding the foundation of your relationships.

The reversed Ten of Cups may indicate a misalignment with your true emotional needs or feelings of isolation, even in the company of others. It's a reminder to reevaluate personal values, desires, and dreams.

Upright Interpretations

General Reading: The Ten of Cups in an upright position in a general reading suggests a time of emotional fulfillment, happiness, and contentment. This could be a period where you feel surrounded by love, support, and mutual respect.

Love Reading: For those in relationships, this card represents a deepening of bonds and a time of harmony and joy. Commitments might be made or renewed, indicating lasting love and happiness. For singles, it signifies the potential for a fulfilling and harmonious relationship on the horizon.

Health Reading: The Ten of Cups suggests emotional and physical well-being. You may be feeling particularly in tune with your body and emotions. It's a good time for healing and recovery, surrounded by the love and support of family and friends.

Career Reading: Your work environment is likely to be harmonious and fulfilling. There's a strong sense of camaraderie among colleagues or a feeling of achievement in your chosen field. It can also indicate a job or project that not only brings financial rewards but also emotional satisfaction.

Reversed Interpretations

General Reading: The reversed Ten of Cups may indicate disruptions in personal harmony or feelings of disconnection from those you hold dear. There might be a sense of disillusionment or a realization that not everything is as perfect as it seemed.

Love Reading: Tensions or unresolved issues might be surfacing in a relationship. For couples, it may be a period of miscommunication or feeling out of sync with each other. Singles might be feeling a sense of loneliness or a longing for a deeper connection.

Health Reading: Emotionally, you might be feeling drained or out of balance. It's essential to address any underlying emotional issues or stressors. There might be family issues affecting your mental well-being, so seeking support and open communication is crucial.

Career Reading: There could be tensions or disagreements in the workplace. The reversed Ten of Cups might suggest that while things might look good on the surface, there are underlying issues that need addressing. It's a call to ensure emotional fulfillment in your career and not just superficial achievements.

The Ten of Cups brings immense joy, happiness, and emotional satisfaction. Typically, the imagery portrays a cheerful family with their arms raised towards the sky in jubilation, surrounded by children playing nearby, standing under a rainbow filled with ten cups. The idyllic setting is usually a serene and picturesque landscape with a cozy home or cottage in green fields, symbolizing peace, stability, and comfort.

This card is deeply reminiscent of the concept of a "happy ever after" from fairy tales. The rainbow, with its cups, represents the manifestation of dreams and the presence of blessings in one's life. The family symbolizes harmonious relationships, and the idyllic setting underlines contentment and finding happiness in life's simple pleasures. The Ten of Cups embodies the ideal of a loving family, a secure home, and the joy that arises from deep emotional connections. It is a powerful affirmation of positive energy, emotional abundance, and a loving environment. The card exudes gratitude and celebrates the beauty of love, unity, and the unbreakable bonds that connect us all.

ZODIAC: Pisces (February 19 – March 20) is a Water sign ruled by Neptune. Pisceans are known for their emotional depth and keen intuition.

Scorpio (October 23 – November 21) is a Water sign ruled by Pluto. Scorpios are known for their intensity and depth.

Cancer (June 21 – July 22) is a Water sign ruled by the Moon. Cancers are highly empathetic, although they can be initially perceived as cold and distant. They're often caregivers and nurturing.

ELEMENT: Water rules emotions and is a symbol of healing, peace, dreams, and compassion. It is associated with Winter, the Suit of Cups, and the West cardinal direction.

HERMETIC QABALAH Associated Hebrew Letter: Heh – Window (Vision, Reasoning)

QABALISTIC SEPHIROT: Malkuth (Kingdom)

TIMING: March 11 – March 20

PAGE OF CUPS

MINOR ARCANA

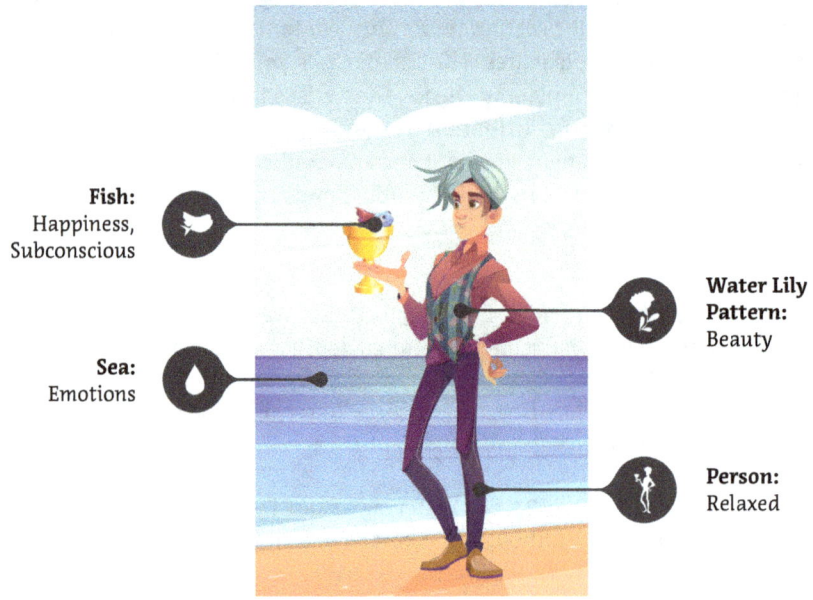

Fish: Happiness, Subconscious

Sea: Emotions

Water Lily Pattern: Beauty

Person: Relaxed

Yes/No Reading:

✓ Yes ◯ No ◯ Maybe

Names in Other Tarot Systems:

Golden Dawn: Princess of Cups
Tarot of Marseilles: Valet of Cups
Thoth: Princess of Cups

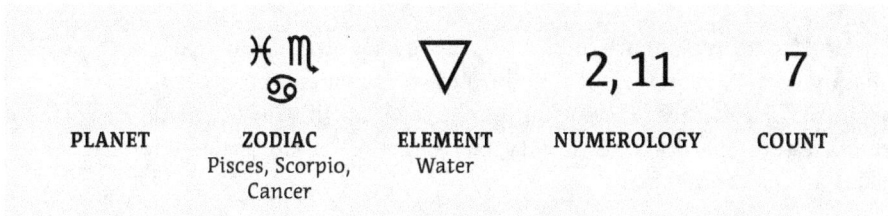

PLANET	ZODIAC	ELEMENT	NUMEROLOGY	COUNT
	Pisces, Scorpio, Cancer	Water		

Upright: *Happy Surprise, Youth, Dreamer, Sensitivity, Intuitive Messages*
The Page of Cups symbolizes the initial stages of exploring one's emotions and intuition, promoting introspection and a willingness to embrace emotional sensitivity. It indicates a heightened awareness of emotions, dreams, and spiritual journeys. With an innocent and pure approach, this card often leads to heartwarming surprises and unexpected discoveries. It also represents a strong connection with one's intuition, often receiving messages through dreams, symbols, or intuitive feelings that provide deeper insights into oneself or one's circumstances.

The Page of Cups can signal a new emotional beginning, whether it's blossoming a romantic relationship, rekindling a friendship, or initiating a creative endeavor fueled by passion. It encourages a childlike curiosity towards emotions and an urge to listen to one's heart while trusting one's intuition. This isn't a time for overthinking but for experiencing emotions authentically and with depth.

Reversed: *Emotional Immaturity, Obsession, Envy, Creative Blocks, Insecurity*
The reversed Page may represent individuals who exhibit emotional impulsivity, frequent mood swings, or a tendency to daydream and avoid reality. Such emotional fluctuations can result from a lack of grounding and unrealistic expectations or fantasies. This absence of emotional grounding may also make it challenging to interpret intuitive messages, leaving individuals unable to differentiate between authentic insights and mere whims or fears.

Furthermore, the reversed Page of Cups can signify a period of creative stagnation or strained personal relationships due to emotional insensitivity or miscommunication. It is a time for introspection and reconnection with one's emotional core, clearing any internal turbulence, and striving for clarity and sincerity in emotional expression. Acknowledging and addressing these challenges can pave the way for emotional growth and deeper intuitive understanding.

Upright Interpretations

General Reading: Embark on a voyage led by your intuition, heart, and imagination. Remain receptive to unforeseen developments, pursue your aspirations, and have faith in your instincts. Allow this card to inspire you to embrace your emotional sensitivity, pay attention to your inner emotions, and chase after your dreams.

Love Reading: This could indicate a new relationship, a deepening of an existing bond, or a period of emotional exploration within the relationship. If single, you might receive a gesture from a potential romantic interest.

Health Reading: The Page of Cups in a health reading can signify a time of emotional healing and rejuvenation. Listening to your body and intuition can lead to insights about your well-being. It can also point to a positive message or news related to health.

Career Reading: In terms of career, the Page of Cups may indicate new creative opportunities or projects coming your way. It suggests trusting your intuition in professional matters and being open to unexpected opportunities. This is a good time to embrace your creative ideas and share them.

Reversed Interpretations

General Reading: You're feeling emotional immaturity, disillusionment, or a disconnect from your intuition. It might suggest you are letting your emotions control your actions without considering the consequences or you're failing to listen to your intuitive insights.

Love Reading: When reversed in a love reading, the Page of Cups suggests emotional misunderstandings, miscommunication, or unexpressed feelings. There might be unrealistic expectations or daydreams about a relationship that don't align with reality.

Health Reading: In its reversed position, this card might indicate neglecting emotional well-being or suppressing feelings, leading to stress or anxiety. It's a call to pay attention to emotional and mental health and to seek support if needed.

Career Reading: There may be missed opportunities due to emotional uncertainty or creative blocks. It can also suggest miscommunication or misunderstandings at the workplace. It's essential to ground oneself and approach situations with clarity.

The Page, a youthful figure, is typically portrayed in the card standing by the water's edge and holding a golden cup that contains a fish or other sea creature, seemingly communicating with him. Unlike other cups in the suit that carry heavy emotional symbolism, this cup brings a surprise element. The fish within symbolizes the card's connection to emotions, intuition, and the subconscious.

The Page's clothing is adorned with images of waves or clouds, highlighting a link to emotions' fluidity and the realm of dreams. The card's background often displays water and land, suggesting a balance between emotion and reality, or perhaps the edge where conscious and unconscious meet.

The overall aura of the card is one of dreaminess, introspection, and curiosity. The Page's youthful appearance represents emotional exploration, vulnerability, and innocence. The fish's unexpected conversation indicates sudden intuitive insights or surprising emotional truths that can arise when least expected, necessitating an approach with openness and curiosity.

ZODIAC: Pisces (February 19 – March 20) is a Water sign ruled by Neptune. Pisceans are known for their emotional depth and keen intuition.

Scorpio (October 23 – November 21) is a Water sign ruled by Pluto. Scorpios are known for their intensity and depth.

Cancer (June 21 – July 22) is a Water sign ruled by the Moon. Cancers are highly empathetic, although they can be initially perceived as cold and distant. They're often caregivers and nurturing.

ELEMENT: Water rules emotions and is a symbol of healing, peace, dreams, and compassion. It is associated with Winter, the Suit of Cups, and the West cardinal direction.

HERMETIC QABALAH Associated Hebrew Letter: Heh – Window (Vision, Reasoning)

QABALISTIC SEPHIROT: Malkuth (Kingdom)

TIMING: September 21 – December 20

KNIGHT OF CUPS

M I N O R A R C A N A

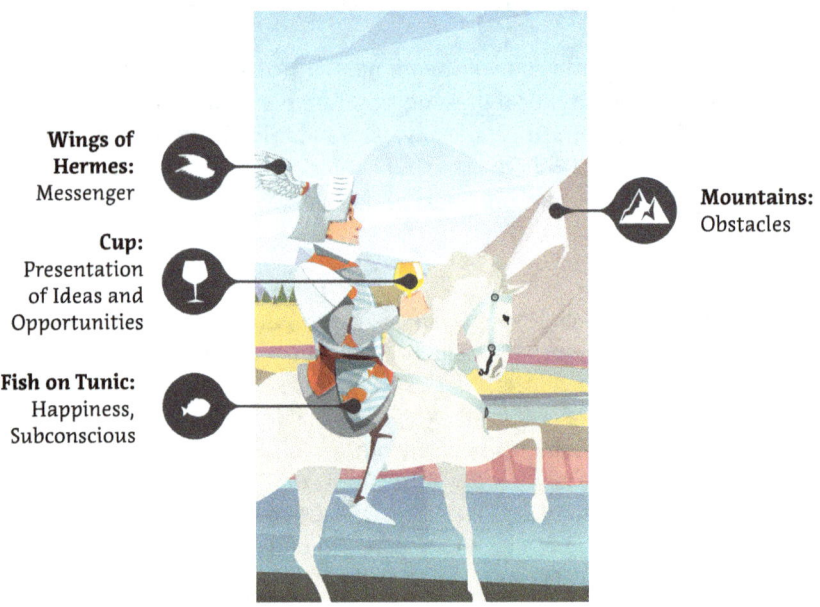

Wings of Hermes: Messenger

Cup: Presentation of Ideas and Opportunities

Fish on Tunic: Happiness, Subconscious

Mountains: Obstacles

Yes/No Reading:

☑ ◯ ◯
Yes *No* *Maybe*

Names in Other Tarot Systems:
Golden Dawn: Prince of Cups
Tarot of Marseilles: Cavalier of Cups
Thoth: Prince of Cups

PLANET	ZODIAC	ELEMENT	NUMEROLOGY	COUNT
♓ ♏ ♋	Pisces, Scorpio, Cancer	▽ Water	3, 12	4

Upright: *Idealist, Romantic, Chivalry, Grace, Imaginative, Sensitive*
This knight embodies the qualities of a romantic and poetic soul, approaching situations with compassion and understanding. They often bring messages of love and emotional proposals, such as romantic invitations, new friendships, or heartfelt offerings of emotion. The knight is a dreamer deeply in tune with their feelings and those of others, making them highly empathetic and considerate.

The upright Knight of Cups also represents creativity and artistic flair. This card can signify when one feels inspired to embark on a new creative project, explore their imagination, or delve into their subconscious through dreams and meditative experiences. The knight encourages introspection and encourages individuals to trust their inner voice and intuitive pulls and to express these emotions through art or spiritual practices. The Knight of Cups also cautions against becoming too lost in emotions and dreams. One should be mindful of the temptation to be overly idealistic, ignoring the practical aspects of a situation.

Reversed: *Moodiness, Deception, Vanity, Disappointment, Heartbreak*
When introspecting, the reversed Knight of Cups suggests a period of emotional confusion, disillusionment, or creative block. It represents feelings of artistic stagnation or when emotional expression feels challenging or inauthentic. Becoming trapped in a world of unrealistic expectations or emotional escapism can prevent one from facing daily life's real challenges and responsibilities.

Even in its reversed state, the Knight of Cups card calls for individuals to better understand their emotional landscape. It highlights the need to find balance by harnessing the depth and richness of emotions and intuition without becoming overwhelmed. It's a reminder to ground oneself, seek clarity, and ensure that emotions, while a valuable guide, don't cloud judgment to the point of inaction or self-deception. Taking a step back, reflecting, and seeking a balanced approach to emotions can help steer the ship back in the right direction and bring a sense of stability and peace.

Upright Interpretations

General Reading: It may represent an invitation or proposal, or the arrival of something new and emotionally fulfilling in your life. The energy is dreamy, artistic, and introspective, signaling a time to trust your intuition and emotions.

Love Reading: This could indicate a new romantic proposal, invitation, or someone entering your life who embodies these traits. For those in a relationship, it suggests a deepening emotional bond and understanding.

Health Reading: This card is a gentle reminder to take care of your emotional and mental well-being. There might be a need for emotional healing or taking time to nurture oneself. Listening to your intuition and understanding your feelings will play a key role in maintaining or restoring health.

Career Reading: Expect proposals, new creative projects, or opportunities that align with your passions. The Knight of Cups in a career reading indicates pursuing what you love and possibly collaborating with someone who shares your vision and passion.

Reversed Interpretations

General Reading: The Knight of Cups reversed suggests emotional turmoil, unrealistic daydreaming, or moodiness. It can indicate a person who is overly emotional, potentially manipulative, or not trustworthy. Alternatively, you might be feeling out of touch with your own emotions or facing creative blocks.

Love Reading: In the realm of romance, this card reversed might signify a relationship that's based more on fantasy than reality, or a lover who's elusive, moody, or insincere. It can also point towards infatuations that are short-lived or a warning against wearing rose-colored glasses.

Health Reading: You might be neglecting your emotional health or internalizing stress and feelings. There could be mood swings or a feeling of being overwhelmed by emotions. It's crucial to seek balance and possibly professional help if these feelings become too much to handle on your own.

Career Reading: There might be a lack of inspiration or motivation in your current job or project. The reversed Knight of Cups can also point to missed opportunities, feeling unfulfilled, or dealing with colleagues or clients who are unreliable or emotionally draining.

Depicted as a knight riding a white horse, the Knight of Cups is often viewed as the most romantic of the court cards. While the knight's armor serves as protection, it's lighter than other knights', suggesting a balance between guardedness and openness. Unlike the Knight of Swords' steed, the horse moves gracefully, reflecting a calm approach.

Holding a single cup, the knight signifies emotional offerings or messages. The cup is often ornate, showcasing the depth and beauty of emotional experience and the arts. The background typically includes flowing streams or a calm river, reinforcing the theme of emotions and intuition. The knight's helmet or heels might have wings decorated on them, symbolizing their connection with the fluid and dreamy realm of emotions and imagination.

The card's overall feeling is dreaminess, creativity, and romance. The Knight of Cups leads with their heart instead of their head, navigating the world with intuition, empathy, and emotional understanding.

♓ **ZODIAC:** Pisces (February 19 – March 20) is a Water sign ruled by Neptune. Pisceans are known for their emotional depth and keen intuition.

♏ Scorpio (October 23 – November 21) is a Water sign ruled by Pluto. Scorpios are known for their intensity and depth.

♋ Cancer (June 21 – July 22) is a Water sign ruled by the Moon. Cancers are highly empathetic, although they can be initially perceived as cold and distant. They're often caregivers and nurturing.

▽ **ELEMENT:** Water rules emotions and is a symbol of healing, peace, dreams, and compassion. It is associated with Winter, the Suit of Cups, and the West cardinal direction.

ה **HERMETIC QABALAH** Associated Hebrew Letter: Heh – Window (Vision, Reasoning)

QABALISTIC SEPHIROT: Tiphareth (Beauty)

🕐 **TIMING:** October 13 – November 22

QUEEN OF CUPS

M I N O R   A R C A N A

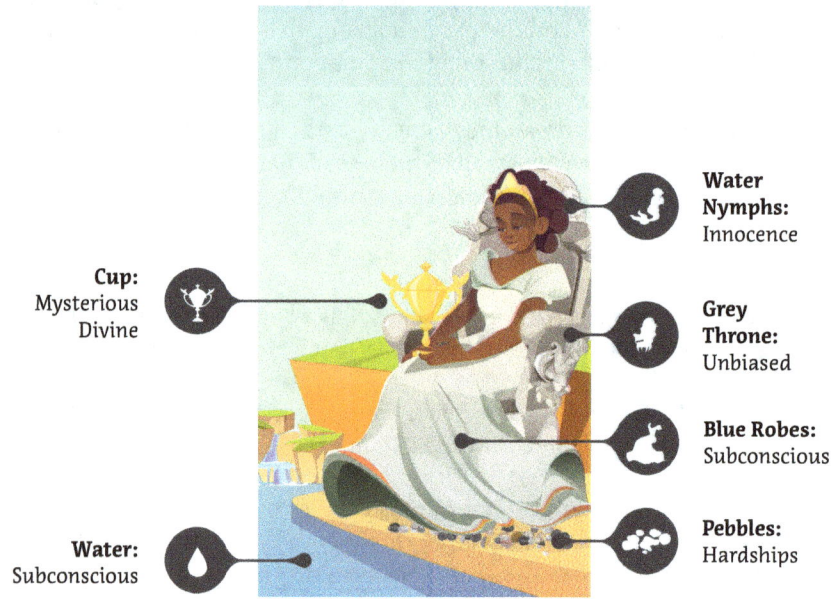

Cup:
Mysterious
Divine

Water:
Subconscious

Water Nymphs:
Innocence

Grey Throne:
Unbiased

Blue Robes:
Subconscious

Pebbles:
Hardships

Yes/No Reading:

Yes   *No*   *Maybe*

Names in Other Tarot Systems:
Golden Dawn: Queen of Cups
Tarot of Marseilles: Dame of Cups
Thoth: Queen of Cups

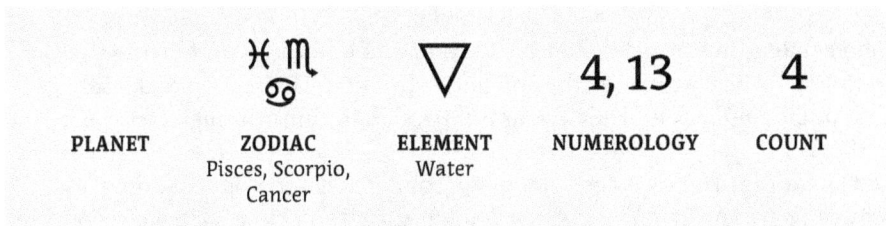

PLANET	ZODIAC	ELEMENT	NUMEROLOGY	COUNT
	Pisces, Scorpio, Cancer	Water		

Upright: *Loving, Intuitive, Empath, Beauty, Psychic, Calm, Spiritual, Faithful*
The Queen of Cups epitomizes emotional intelligence, intuition, and compassion. In a reading, the card often indicates an individual deeply attuned to their emotions and those of others. This person leads with their heart, offering a listening ear and a shoulder to cry on. Their insights are not solely cerebral but arise from a profound understanding and empathy.

The Queen of Cups prompts introspection and the exploration of intuition, dreams, and unconscious feelings. It emphasizes the importance of emotional responses that stem from understanding and wisdom rather than mere reactions. This encourages the nurturing of psychic abilities and the development of an innate sense of knowing that often defies logical explanation. Like water flows and ripples, the Queen of Cups suggests that creative energy is overflowing and waiting to be harnessed and shared with the world through writing, music, art, or any other form of expression.

Reversed: *Self-Care, Sensitive, Shallow, Martyrdom, Insecurity, Dependence*
The reversed Queen of Cups may point to an individual who relies heavily on others for emotional support or smothers those around them with excessive care and attention. This behavior can become overbearing and even manipulative, using emotional sensitivity as a weapon to play the victim or guilt others into getting their way. The genuine compassion and empathy typically associated with this card may be replaced by emotional insecurity and neediness.

Furthermore, the appearance of this card may suggest a disconnect from intuition and inner knowing, prompting the individual to reconnect with their intuitive self and trust their gut feelings. Just because something cannot be logically explained does not mean it is invalid. Taking time for self-reflection and meditation can help ground and regain the emotional and intuitive balance the Queen of Cups represents in its upright position. It is a reminder to prioritize emotional well-being and to find healthy ways to express and manage one's feelings.

Upright Interpretations

General Reading: You're in touch with your emotions and can tap into the feelings of others with empathy and understanding. This is a time to trust your inner guidance and allow your compassion to shine through.

Love Reading: There's a deep emotional connection and understanding between partners. If single, this card might suggest meeting someone who resonates with you on an emotional and spiritual level or the need to love oneself deeply before entering into a relationship.

Health Reading: Your emotional and mental well-being is just as important as your physical health. The Queen of Cups suggests that you're in a period where emotional healing can lead to physical healing. Listen to your body and your emotions. Seeking therapies that address both mind and body, like meditation or counseling, might be beneficial.

Career Reading: Your intuition is your strongest asset in your professional life right now. You might be in a role where understanding and catering to people's feelings is crucial, like HR or counseling. Trust your gut feelings about decisions and people.

Reversed Interpretations

General Reading: You may be feeling out of touch with your emotions or overwhelmed by them. There's a need to recenter and find balance. Be cautious about being too emotionally dependent on others.

Love Reading: In relationships, there might be emotional distance or misunderstandings. One partner may be overly clingy or emotionally manipulative. For singles, there could be a tendency to dream of an ideal partner without taking action or to enter relationships without genuine emotional connection.

Health Reading: Repressed emotions might be affecting your health. It's essential to address any feelings you're holding onto, as they might manifest as physical symptoms. Consider seeking emotional therapy or counseling.

Career Reading: You might be taking things too personally at work or letting emotions cloud your judgment. Ensure you're not letting your feelings lead you to make unwise choices or create unnecessary conflicts in the workplace.

Depicted as a majestic, otherworldly figure seated on a throne by the sea, the Sovereign of Cups is often illustrated with an exquisite, elaborate cup in their delicate grasp. This vessel, frequently sealed or capped, symbolizes the profound depths of their emotions and subconscious. The waters around them and the cup in their possession signify their deep bond with the emotional realm and their intuitive gifts.

Seashells commonly adorn their throne, underscoring their reign over the domain of feelings and their connection to the unconscious mind's unfathomable depths. The calm sea and cloudless sky behind them convey tranquility, indicating their control over their emotions, utilizing them as a source of strength rather than becoming overwhelmed.

Their serene and compassionate demeanor is apparent as they intently gaze at their cup, signifying their awareness and respect for their internal world and others' emotional needs. Their presence in a reading often points to characteristics such as empathy, intuition, emotional depth, and a sympathetic nature.

♓ **ZODIAC:** Pisces (February 19 – March 20) is a Water sign ruled by Neptune. Pisceans are known for their emotional depth and keen intuition.

♏ Scorpio (October 23 – November 21) is a Water sign ruled by Pluto. Scorpios are known for their intensity and depth.

♋ Cancer (June 21 – July 22) is a Water sign ruled by the Moon. Cancers are highly empathetic, although they can be initially perceived as cold and distant. They're often caregivers and nurturing.

▽ **ELEMENT:** Water rules emotions and is a symbol of healing, peace, dreams, and compassion. It is associated with Winter, the Suit of Cups, and the West cardinal direction.

ה **HERMETIC QABALAH** Associated Hebrew Letter: Heh – Window (Vision, Reasoning)

QABALISTIC SEPHIROT: Binah (Understanding)

🕐 **TIMING:** November 13 – December 12

KING OF CUPS

M I N O R   A R C A N A

Cup: Humility

Jumping Fish: Creativity, Ideas

Water: Subconscious

Scepter: Authority

Ship: Quest for Enlightenment

Floating Throne: Levity, Virtue

Yes/No Reading:

☑ ○ ○

Yes   *No*   *Maybe*

Names in Other Tarot Systems:
Golden Dawn: King of Cups
Tarot of Marseilles: Roi of Cups
Thoth: Knight of Cups

♓ ♏ ♋	▽	5, 14	4
PLANET	**ZODIAC**	**ELEMENT**	**NUMEROLOGY**	**COUNT**
	Pisces, Scorpio, Cancer	Water		

Upright: *Wisdom, Dedication, Understanding, Focus, Balance, Peacefulness*
The King of Cups embodies the highest emotional intelligence, wisdom, and maturity level. When upright, this card signifies a deep understanding of one's emotions and the emotions of others, which suggests a nurturing and empathetic personality. The King of Cups is known to lend an ear and offer sound advice, displaying a unique ability to navigate complex emotional landscapes without becoming overwhelmed. In turn, they bring a sense of calm and understanding to those around them.

When the King of Cups appears in a personal reading, it could encourage the querent to enhance their emotional intelligence, approach situations with empathy, or seek counsel from someone who embodies these qualities. It's a reminder that strength is not always about physical might, as understanding, patience, and kindness can display profound power.

Reversed: *Cold, Indifferent, Moody, Immature, Overreaction, Manipulative*
Encountering the reversed King of Cups can prompt introspection in a personal context. It invites reflection on how one manages emotions, needs for better emotional self-control, and whether suppressed feelings disrupt decision-making and interactions. It serves as a reminder of the significance of emotional clarity and the risks of unchecked emotions guiding one's path.

This inverted card can point to someone who is emotionally unstable, prone to mood swings, or not displaying the maturity and calm that the upright King of Cups embodies. They may conceal or suppress their emotions or resort to unhealthy coping mechanisms such as excessive drinking or escapism. Instead of being an empathetic counselor, this King can become deceptive and let their emotional disturbances cloud their judgment or lead them down unreliable paths.

Upright Interpretations

General Reading: You may be interacting with or embodying someone who provides emotional support, offers wise counsel, or exudes a calming presence in tumultuous times. This card encourages a balanced approach to situations, relying on both intellect and emotion to navigate challenges.

Love Reading: For singles, this might indicate the arrival of a mature, emotionally available partner. For those in a relationship, it represents a phase of emotional stability and compassionate communication.

Health Reading: When considering health, the King of Cups encourages finding emotional balance. It suggests that emotional well-being plays a significant role in physical health. Seeking counseling or finding supportive individuals can aid in healing and wellness.

Career Reading: You or someone in a position of authority may be using emotional intelligence to guide and mentor others. It's a good time for negotiations, partnerships, and team collaborations.

Reversed Interpretations

General Reading: The King of Cups reversed might indicate emotional manipulation, moodiness, or someone who's out of touch with their feelings. It could suggest a need for better emotional self-control or indicate the presence of suppressed or unresolved emotional issues.

Love Reading: There might be issues of emotional unavailability, lack of trust, or an unwillingness to open up and be vulnerable.

Health Reading: The reversed King of Cups in a health context might point to suppressed emotional issues affecting physical health. It's a reminder that emotional and mental health shouldn't be neglected. It might also indicate unhealthy coping mechanisms like excessive drinking or escapism.

Career Reading: Emotions are running high, or there's a lack of emotional intelligence from leadership. It can also point to a situation where personal feelings are interfering with professional decisions or someone in authority is not as emotionally mature or supportive as they should be.

The King of Cups embodies emotional intelligence, balance, and diplomacy. It depicts a regal figure who has mastered their emotions, exuding a composed demeanor even when faced with tumultuous waters. The King is often shown seated on a throne, with a cup representing emotions in one hand and a scepter symbolizing authority in the other. Despite the choppy waters surrounding them, the King remains steadfast, a testament to their ability to stay balanced in times of emotional upheaval. In the distance, a ship can be seen, highlighting mastery over their emotions in all situations, calm or turbulent.

The fish jumping out of the water and the ship sailing smoothly in the background signify the King's mastery over the unconscious mind and their ability to navigate deep emotions without getting overwhelmed. The throne, adorned with sea creatures, emphasizes control over the emotional and intuitive realms, offering a compassionate and empathetic approach to wise counsel. The king's emotional stability is a model for all, showing us how to constructively manage and express our feelings. The King of Cups is a beacon of hope and understanding, offering guidance to those who need it and reminding us all to master our emotions and maintain balance in all aspects of life.

♓ **ZODIAC:** Pisces (February 19 – March 20) is a Water sign ruled by Neptune. Pisceans are known for their emotional depth and keen intuition.

♏ Scorpio (October 23 – November 21) is a Water sign ruled by Pluto. Scorpios are known for their intensity and depth.

♋ Cancer (June 21 – July 22) is a Water sign ruled by the Moon. Cancers are highly empathetic, although they can be initially perceived as cold and distant. They're often caregivers and nurturing.

▽ **ELEMENT:** Water rules emotions and is a symbol of healing, peace, dreams, and compassion. It is associated with Winter, the Suit of Cups, and the West cardinal direction.

ה **HERMETIC QABALAH** Associated Hebrew Letter: Heh – Window (Vision, Reasoning)

QABALISTIC SEPHIROT: Chokmah (Wisdom)

TIMING: February 9 – March 10

ACE OF PENTACLES

M I N O R   A R C A N A

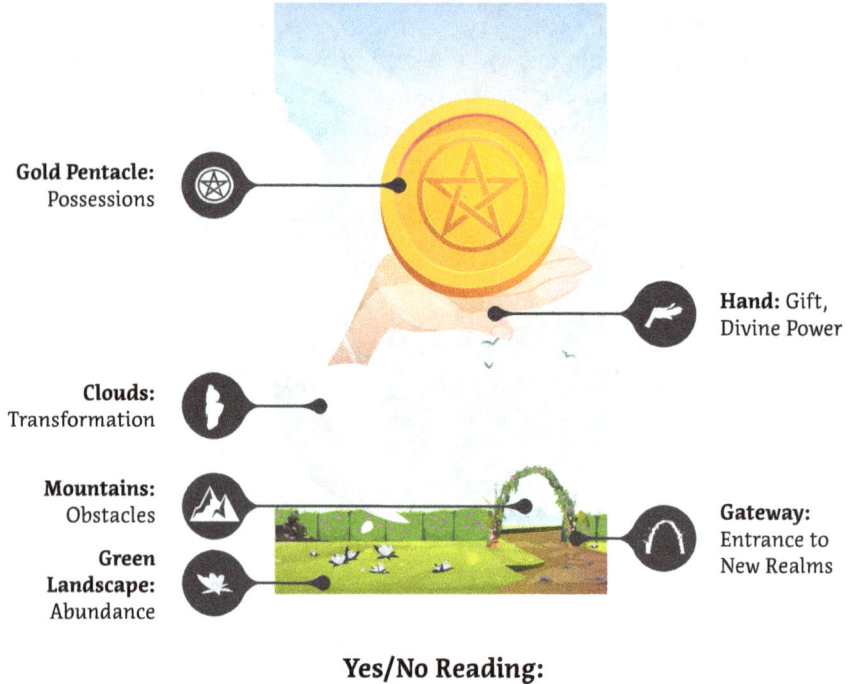

Gold Pentacle: Possessions

Hand: Gift, Divine Power

Clouds: Transformation

Mountains: Obstacles

Green Landscape: Abundance

Gateway: Entrance to New Realms

Yes/No Reading:

☑ Yes   ○ No   ○ Maybe

Names in Other Tarot Systems:

Golden Dawn: The Radix of the Powers of the Earth
Tarot of Marseilles: Ace of Coins
Thoth: The Root of the Powers of Earth

☿ ♍ ♑	▽	1, 10	5, 11
PLANET	**ELEMENT**	**NUMEROLOGY**	**COUNT**
ZODIAC Taurus, Virgo, Capricorn	Earth		

Upright: *Manifestation, Opportunity, Abundance, Prosperity, New Venture*
The Ace of Pentacles is a powerful symbol of new beginnings and potential in the tangible aspects of life. Its upright position signals the readiness to sow the seeds of prosperity, abundance, and material success. Whether you are starting a new business venture, exploring an investment opportunity, or any project with potential financial or physical rewards, this card indicates fertile ground for those endeavors.

Beyond the material gains, the Ace of Pentacles embodies the essence of manifestation, a cosmic nod from the universe that aligns energies for turning visions, dreams, and plans into concrete realities. This card encourages taking action, seizing opportunities, and grounding ambitions in the physical world, reminding us that dreams can take shape, flourish, and yield rewarding outcomes with the right intentions and efforts. This card brings a message of hope, assuring that the universe presents a golden opportunity. Embrace it, nurture it, and watch as your efforts bear fruit in the material world.

Reversed: *Bad Investment, Instability, Lost Opportunity, Lack of Foresight*
The appearance of the reversed Ace of Pentacles warns of potential obstacles that could impede progress toward goals, such as disappointing investment returns or unforeseen challenges in promising ventures. This card advises caution and encourages careful evaluation of opportunities to avoid rushing into decisions without proper due diligence.

Moreover, the reversed Ace of Pentacles can signify an imbalance in the pursuit of worldly desires, suggesting an excessive emphasis on wealth at the expense of other crucial aspects of life, such as relationships, health, or personal growth. It is a reminder to reassess priorities and ensure that material goals do not overshadow emotional or spiritual fulfillment. This card may indicate feelings of insecurity or inadequacy about one's ability to provide or achieve financial stability. These feelings could arise from past failures or societal pressures, causing hesitation to take risks or embrace new opportunities.

Upright Interpretations

General Reading: Exciting prospects lie ahead, as you stand on the cusp of a new venture that offers tangible gains. The present is pregnant with opportunities for progress, expansion, and eventual affluence, implying a divine endorsement of your pursuits and aspirations.

Love Reading: This card may suggest the beginning of a new chapter in a romantic life. It is possible that this new chapter will involve someone who brings stability and financial security. If you are currently in a relationship, this card implies that you may experience a heightened sense of security and stability. This may manifest in a variety of ways, such as moving in together, getting engaged, or making other significant financial commitments together.

Health Reading: Your health is entering a phase of rejuvenation and strength. This card could indicate the start of a beneficial health regimen, a positive medical diagnosis, or the beginning of a period of robust health and well-being.

Career Reading: New job opportunities, promotions, or the start of fruitful business ventures are on the horizon. This is a fantastic time to invest in your career or take risks, as the potential for material and financial rewards is high.

Reversed Interpretations

General Reading: Signs of missed opportunities, setbacks, or potential delays have emerged, possibly indicating obstacles to achieving your goals or the presence of crucial oversights. This is a time for reflection and reassessment, encouraging careful consideration of material decisions.

Love Reading: Material or financial issues might be causing a strain in a relationship. For singles, it could indicate missed connections or opportunities in love due to being overly focused on material goals or seeking stability at the cost of genuine connection.

Health Reading: There might be some health setbacks or missed opportunities to enhance well-being. It's a reminder to not neglect your physical health for material pursuits or to re-evaluate if your current health routines are genuinely beneficial.

Career Reading: Be wary of too-good-to-be-true career opportunities or potential setbacks in business ventures. Now is the time to thoroughly vet business partnerships and be cautious about where you invest your time and resources.

The Ace of Pentacles depicts a golden pentacle or coin held up by a divine hand. This symbolizes material wealth, tangible outcomes, and earthly possessions, with the golden hue indicating prosperity and value. The hand emerging from a cloud suggests that this opportunity or gain comes from a higher source or through divine intervention.

The lush garden in the background symbolizes fertility, growth, and abundance. With proper care, attention, and effort, the potential represented by the pentacle can flourish. The pathway represents a journey or progression leading from the garden through an archway and onto a mountain.

The mountains are symbolic of challenges or spiritual ascent. In the Ace of Pentacles context, they can indicate that the material journey or endeavor might also lead to personal growth or that there are obstacles to overcome to achieve tangible rewards. The archway between the garden and the mountain path represents a gateway or transition from one phase to another. The flowers, such as lilies and roses, are symbolic in the Tarot. Lilies are usually associated with purity, and roses with desire or passion.

ZODIAC: Taurus (April 20 – May 20) is an Earth sign ruled by Venus. This sign embodies those that are grounded, practical, and stable.

Virgo (August 23 – September 22) is an Earth sign ruled by Mercury. Virgos are selfless and dedicated, often putting others' needs above their own.

Capricorn (December 22 – January 19) is an Earth sign ruled by Saturn. Capricorns are known for their grounded, pragmatic approach, and are often focused on tangible outcomes.

ELEMENT: Earth represents death and rebirth. It is the realm of abundance, prosperity, and wealth. It is associated with Autumn, the Suit of Pentacles, and the North cardinal direction.

HERMETIC QABALAH Associated Hebrew Letter: Heh – Window (Vision, Reasoning)

QABALISTIC SEPHIROT: Kether (Crown)

TIMING: March 21 – June 20

TWO OF PENTACLES

MINOR ARCANA

Hat: Fun, Playfulness

Gold Pentacles: Possessions

Lemniscate: Life's Highs and Lows

Ship: Transformation

Person: Lighthearted

Rough Sea: Life's Highs and Lows

Yes/No Reading:

○   ○   ✅

Yes   No   **Maybe**

Names in Other Tarot Systems:

Golden Dawn: Lord of Change
Tarot of Marseilles: Two of Coins
Thoth: Change

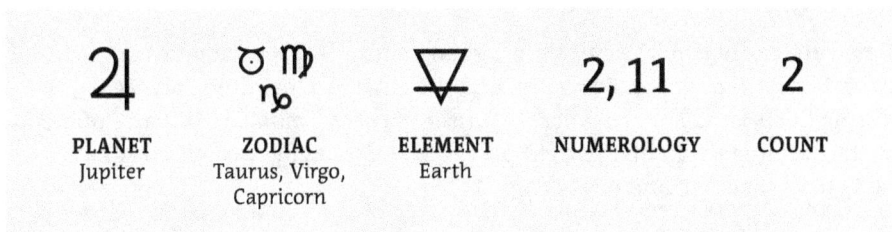

2	♉ ♍ ♑	▽	2, 11	2
PLANET	**ZODIAC**	**ELEMENT**	**NUMEROLOGY**	**COUNT**
Jupiter	Taurus, Virgo, Capricorn	Earth		

Upright: *Priorities, Balance, Time Management, Adapting to Change*

Despite the swirling seas of change in one's circumstances, the Two of Pentacles carries an inherently optimistic undertone. The Two of Pentacles speaks of balance and adaptability in the face of shifting responsibilities and challenges. It's a card that surfaces when juggling multiple tasks, roles, or commitments in personal, professional, or financial realms. You might find yourself managing two jobs, balancing work and personal life, or handling fluctuating finances. The card underscores the ebb and flow of life and the inherent dance we all do when navigating daily challenges and opportunities.

As circumstances change – and they invariably do – one's ability to adapt, recalibrate, and continue forward is essential. The juggling figure in the card's imagery reminds us that sometimes, maintaining equilibrium requires a certain skill or finesse, not unlike a performer keeping multiple balls in the air. The message is clear: Embrace change, be agile, and understand that life's demands, although sometimes overwhelming, can be managed with grace and agility.

Reversed: *Disorganization, Unorganized, Overwhelmed, Over-Committed*

This position of the card brings forth the themes of imbalance, overextension, and mismanagement. You might be feeling like you need to catch up on essential tasks or need help to keep up with the juggling act that your responsibilities demand. The pressures of daily life, whether financial, emotional, or practical, are getting the better of you. A lack of prioritization can lead to burnout, mistakes, and missed opportunities.

The first step towards regaining equilibrium is to recognize that you're in over your head or that your current approach to tasks and responsibilities is unsustainable. It may be time to delegate, seek assistance, or take a moment to reassess and reorganize your priorities. While challenges are evident, the reversed Two of Pentacles is a call to action, urging you to find new strategies and approaches to restore balance in your life.

Upright Interpretations

General Reading: You're currently juggling multiple responsibilities or situations. Adaptability, flexibility, and the ability to maintain balance during fluctuating circumstances are essential now. Embrace the dance of life, understanding that with the right perspective, managing various tasks can be both challenging and rewarding.

Love Reading: You might be trying to strike a balance between your romantic life and other commitments. For those dating, you might be weighing options or deciding between potential partners. For those in established relationships, this card emphasizes the need to maintain equilibrium between relationship demands and external responsibilities.

Health Reading: You're trying to balance multiple aspects of your health, possibly integrating a new fitness regime while managing other health commitments. Find a harmonious routine that caters to both physical and mental well-being.

Career Reading: Your adaptability is a strength, and you're effectively navigating the demands of your job. For those considering a career change, this card can indicate weighing multiple offers or opportunities.

Reversed Interpretations

General Reading: You're feeling overwhelmed by the number of tasks or responsibilities you're trying to manage. This could indicate overextension, a lack of prioritization, or an inability to maintain balance. It's crucial to reassess and potentially delegate or drop some obligations.

Love Reading: The pressures of juggling multiple aspects of life might be causing strain in your romantic relationship. For singles, this might mean missed romantic opportunities due to being spread too thin. In committed relationships, there might be feelings of neglect or imbalance.

Health Reading: Your health might be suffering due to neglect or trying to manage too many things at once. This card suggests that it's crucial to prioritize your well-being and not let it be overshadowed by other demands.

Career Reading: You're feeling swamped at work and struggling to keep up with the demands or dropping the ball on some tasks. Prioritize delegation, reprioritization, or seeking assistance.

The Two of Pentacles speaks of balance and adaptability in the face of shifting responsibilities and challenges. It's a card that surfaces when juggling multiple tasks, roles, or commitments in personal, professional, or financial realms. You might find yourself managing two jobs, balancing work and personal life, or handling fluctuating finances. The card underscores the ebb and flow of life and the inherent dance we all do when navigating daily challenges and opportunities.

In addition to the theme of balance, the Two of Pentacles champions flexibility. As circumstances change – and they invariably do – one's ability to adapt, recalibrate, and continue forward is essential. The juggling figure in the card's imagery reminds us that sometimes, maintaining equilibrium requires skill or finesse, not unlike a performer keeping multiple balls in the air. The message is clear: Embrace change, be agile, and understand that life's demands, although sometimes overwhelming, can be managed with grace and agility. It's a reminder that challenges, while inevitable, are surmountable, especially when approached with a dynamic and adaptable spirit.

ZODIAC: Taurus (April 20 – May 20) is an Earth sign ruled by Venus. This sign embodies those that are grounded, practical, and stable.

Virgo (August 23 – September 22) is an Earth sign ruled by Mercury. Virgos are selfless and dedicated, often putting others' needs above their own.

Capricorn (December 22 – January 19) is an Earth sign ruled by Saturn. Capricorns are known for their grounded, pragmatic approach, and are often focused on tangible outcomes.

ELEMENT: Earth represents death and rebirth. It is the realm of abundance, prosperity, and wealth. It is associated with Autumn, the Suit of Pentacles, and the North cardinal direction.

HERMETIC QABALAH Associated Hebrew Letter: Heh – Window (Vision, Reasoning)

QABALISTIC SEPHIROT: Chokmah (Wisdom)

TIMING: December 22 – December 30

THREE OF PENTACLES

M I N O R   A R C A N A

Arch:
Achievement

Artisan:
Consciousness

Bench:
Foundation

Pentacles:
Rewards,
Growth

Architect:
Planning,
Preparation

Architect:
Planning,
Preparation

Yes/No Reading:

☑   ◯   ◯

Yes   No   Maybe

Names in Other Tarot Systems:
Golden Dawn: Lord of Works
Tarot of Marseilles: Three of Coins
Thoth: Works

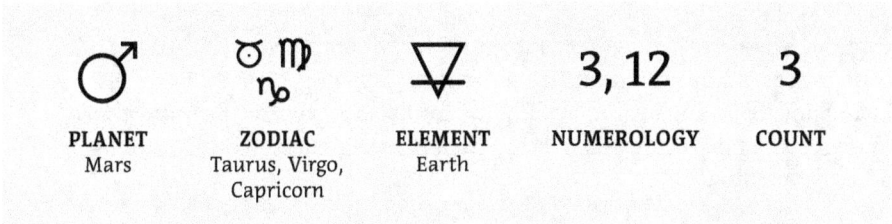

PLANET	ZODIAC	ELEMENT	NUMEROLOGY	COUNT
Mars	Taurus, Virgo, Capricorn	Earth	3, 12	3

Upright: *Teamwork, Improving Skills, Implementation, Collaboration*
Whether in a work environment, a personal project, or any endeavor that requires multiple hands and minds, this card heralds the success that arises from cooperative effort. The Three of Pentacles emphasizes that quality outcomes often require hard work and a deep understanding and proficiency in one's field. This card might pop up when recognition is due for someone's skills or when seeking an expert in a particular domain is needed. It reminds us that while many hands make light work, skilled hands make work exceptional.

This card embodies the initial stages of a project or endeavor. While the foundation is being set, it's essential to ensure that everything aligns perfectly at this juncture for the project's long-term success. The presence of planning, structure, and strategy is crucial. Thus, the Three Pentacles speaks of collective effort and skill and the importance of laying solid and precise foundations for future success.

Reversed: *Disharmony, Ego, Disorganization, Group Conflict, Working Alone*
There are potential misalignments in team dynamics, lack of cohesion, or issues related to individual contributions and skills. One of the central themes of the reversed Three of Pentacles is a lack of teamwork or collaboration. This could manifest as group conflicts, miscommunication, or even a feeling of not being valued or recognized for one's contributions. Disjointed efforts can lead to projects stalling or goals needing to be met.

The reversed card might also hint at needing more expertise or preparation. Perhaps there's a rush to complete a project without paying attention to the details, or there might be a need for more planning and foresight. The craftsmanship and skill associated with the upright card may need to be utilized, leading to subpar results. It's a warning to ensure that the right skills are being applied to tasks and to pay heed to the foundational stages of any endeavor for long-term success.

Upright Interpretations

General Reading: It suggests that your efforts, combined with those of others, are leading to success. It's a period of learning, growth, and the laying down of a solid foundation. This card also speaks to the importance of recognizing expertise and valuing each person's unique contribution to a project or situation.

Love Reading: The Three of Pentacles suggests a relationship where both partners are willing to work together to build a solid foundation. It may indicate that seeking external advice or counseling could be beneficial. For singles, it's a sign that collaborating on mutual interests or projects could lead to romantic connections.

Health Reading: This is a good time to consider consulting specialists or getting a second opinion. Collaborating with various health professionals to create a comprehensive health plan could be beneficial.

Career Reading: This is a time where your skills are recognized, and you're encouraged to work in tandem with others. Projects undertaken now have a strong foundation. It also could indicate mentoring opportunities or learning phases that will contribute positively to your career growth.

Reversed Interpretations

General Reading: When this card is reversed in a general reading, it may indicate miscommunication, lack of cooperation, or conflicts within a team. It can also suggest that your work or contributions are going unnoticed or undervalued.

Love Reading: There might be struggles in finding common goals or working together. For singles, it might suggest that potential partnerships are not developing due to a lack of shared efforts or mutual understanding.

Health Reading: In a reversed position, this card warns against neglecting professional advice or not actively participating in one's own health and wellness journey. It may also suggest complications due to miscommunication or misunderstanding medical advice.

Career Reading: When reversed in a career context, the Three of Pentacles might suggest conflicts at work or projects that are stalling due to a lack of collaboration. It can also indicate feeling undervalued or overlooked in your professional contributions. The card advises reassessing team dynamics and ensuring clear communication to overcome challenges.

At the forefront of the card, an eye-catching triad of pentacles, which signify the fruits of one's labor and the rewards of their efforts. The central figure, often depicted as a skilled artisan or craftsman. This representation embodies the unwavering commitment and focus necessary to produce quality work that is valued by all. The tools held by the craftsman symbolize the practical aspect of the work, highlighting the skills in action and the means through which ideas come to life.

Working alongside the artisan are typically one or two additional figures, shown holding blueprints or architectural plans. These figures emphasize the importance of planning, collaboration, and foresight, highlighting that exceptional work requires practical skills and visionary planning.

The structure on which the craftsman stands or works is an emblem of progress and the creation process, representing the foundation of the project and its early stages. Meanwhile, the background showcases the beginnings of a grand structure, often a cathedral or other spiritual edifice, underscoring the themes of construction, progress, and collective achievement.

ZODIAC: Taurus (April 20 – May 20) is an Earth sign ruled by Venus. This sign embodies those that are grounded, practical, and stable.

Virgo (August 23 – September 22) is an Earth sign ruled by Mercury. Virgos are selfless and dedicated, often putting others' needs above their own.

Capricorn (December 22 – January 19) is an Earth sign ruled by Saturn. Capricorns are known for their grounded, pragmatic approach, and are often focused on tangible outcomes.

ELEMENT: Earth represents death and rebirth. It is the realm of abundance, prosperity, and wealth. It is associated with Autumn, the Suit of Pentacles, and the North cardinal direction.

HERMETIC QABALAH Associated Hebrew Letter: Heh – Window (Vision, Reasoning)

QABALISTIC SEPHIROT: Binah (Understanding)

TIMING: December 31 – January 9

FOUR OF PENTACLES

M I N O R A R C A N A

Person:
Loneliness,
Greed, Defensive

Pentacles:
Materialism,
Greed, Control

**Pentacles
Under Feet:**
Grounded

Yes/No Reading:

○   ✓   ○

Yes   *No*   *Maybe*

Names in Other Tarot Systems:
Golden Dawn: Lord of Earthly Power
Tarot of Marseilles: Four of Coins
Thoth: Power

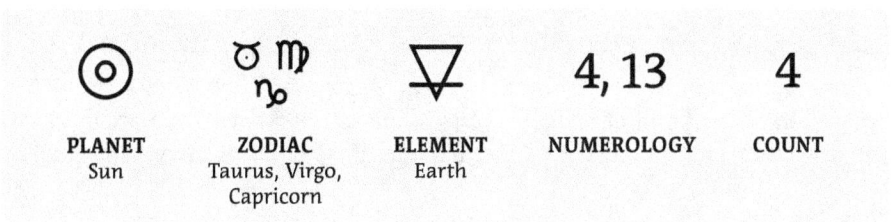

PLANET	ZODIAC	ELEMENT	NUMEROLOGY	COUNT
Sun	Taurus, Virgo, Capricorn	Earth	4, 13	4

Upright: *Security, Frugality, Conservatism, Scarcity, Control, Restraint*
The Four of Pentacles speaks to the fundamental human need for stability and security, especially in finance and material possessions. This card's upright position highlights control, attachment, and the desire for stability. However, this card is more than just prudence and protecting one's possessions. The Four of Pentacles warns against holding on too tightly, being overly possessive or miserly, or becoming too focused on accumulating wealth at the expense of other experiences in life. It suggests a fine line between being careful and becoming overly controlling or fearful of loss or scarcity.

It can also indicate a guarded heart, a reluctance to open up and be vulnerable due to past hurts, or fears of future pain. This card challenges us to find a balance between maintaining security without letting it stifle growth, protecting ourselves without becoming isolated, and recognizing that true security lies in adaptability and openness, not rigid control.

Reversed: *Over-Spending, Generosity, Greed, Possessiveness, Stinginess*
The Four of Pentacles reveals a loosening grip on material possessions, control, and emotional barriers when reversed. This represents a shift from the card's upright themes of holding on tightly and being overly guarded to an indication of letting go, releasing control, and embracing change or vulnerability. In contrast to the upright position's fear of loss or extremely conservative stance, the reversed card hints at spending, donating, or investing money. This can signify a change in financial circumstances that leads to a less restrictive attitude toward resources.

Emotionally, the reversed card often serves as a beacon of personal growth, signifying a willingness to be vulnerable, trust again after betrayal, or share personal thoughts and feelings more openly. It represents breaking down walls, dispelling fears, and embracing the world with a more open heart.

Upright Interpretations

General Reading: You have a strong desire for security and control, especially concerning material assets. This card indicates safeguarding resources, potentially to the point of being overly cautious or possessive. Evaluate if you're holding on too tightly to something out of fear or insecurity.

Love Reading: This card suggests guarding one's heart or being protective of one's feelings. It can mean that someone is not willing to open up fully due to past hurts or fear of vulnerability. For singles, it might imply being stuck on past relationships, preventing new love from entering.

Health Reading: You may be holding onto stress or tension, particularly in the physical body. It might indicate a need to relax and release control, potentially pointing towards issues caused by stress, such as tight muscles or tension headaches.

Career Reading: There's a strong focus on financial security. It can indicate someone who's reluctant to invest or take risks, preferring to safeguard what they have. It might also hint at feeling possessive about one's job role or responsibilities.

Reversed Interpretations

General Reading: In its reversed position, the Four of Pentacles might point to a release or letting go of control. It can also suggest recklessness with finances or being overly generous to a fault. On the other hand, it might indicate a breaking free from material constraints or obsessive thinking related to security.

Love Reading: Reversed, this card in a love context indicates a possible release of past emotional baggage or an opening up to new romantic experiences. For those in a relationship, it could mean letting go of old wounds or barriers that have prevented deeper intimacy.

Health Reading: In its reversed form in a health context, the card suggests a possible release of tension or the need to let go of unhealthy habits or rigid routines. It's a reminder to loosen up and allow for more flexibility in health practices.

Career Reading: Reversed, this card could suggest either a reckless approach to finances or business decisions. Or more positively, a willingness to take calculated risks. It might also indicate letting go of certain job roles, responsibilities, or even changing careers for personal fulfillment over monetary gains.

At the center is a figure clutching a pentacle tightly against their chest, symbolizing the need for control and the fear of losing what one has accumulated. Typically, the figure is shown standing on two pentacles, representing the desire to be in complete control or on top of one's finances and material possessions. It can also indicate the importance of being grounded in material or worldly matters at the cost of emotional or spiritual growth. Another pentacle is often placed above the figure's head or as a crown. This placement can signify a preoccupation with a sense of worth; identity is linked to possessions or financial status.

The figure's posture is often closed off, implying defensiveness, insecurity, or an unwillingness to share or open up. This is usually reflective of individuals who are emotionally closed off due to placing too much emphasis on material security.

In some decks, a town or other structures are visible in the far background, which can signify societal values or external pressures. It could also imply that the figure's focus on their possessions is causing them to miss out on the broader world or community.

♉ **ZODIAC:** Taurus (April 20 – May 20) is an Earth sign ruled by Venus. This sign embodies those that are grounded, practical, and stable.

♍ Virgo (August 23 – September 22) is an Earth sign ruled by Mercury. Virgos are selfless and dedicated, often putting others' needs above their own.

♑ Capricorn (December 22 – January 19) is an Earth sign ruled by Saturn. Capricorns are known for their grounded, pragmatic approach, and are often focused on tangible outcomes.

♁ **ELEMENT:** Earth represents death and rebirth. It is the realm of abundance, prosperity, and wealth. It is associated with Autumn, the Suit of Pentacles, and the North cardinal direction.

ה **HERMETIC QABALAH** Associated Hebrew Letter: Heh – Window (Vision, Reasoning)

🍇 **QABALISTIC SEPHIROT:** Chesed (Mercy)

🕐 **TIMING:** January 10 – January 19

FIVE OF PENTACLES

M I N O R   A R C A N A

Stained Glass:
Hope, Sanctuary, Solace, Aid

Snow:
Challenges, Harshness

People:
Lonliness, Isolation

Worn Clothing:
Poverty, Hardships

Yes/No Reading:

○   ☑   ○
Yes   *No*   *Maybe*

Names in Other Tarot Systems:
Golden Dawn: Lord of Material Trouble
Tarot of Marseilles: Five of Coins
Thoth: Worry

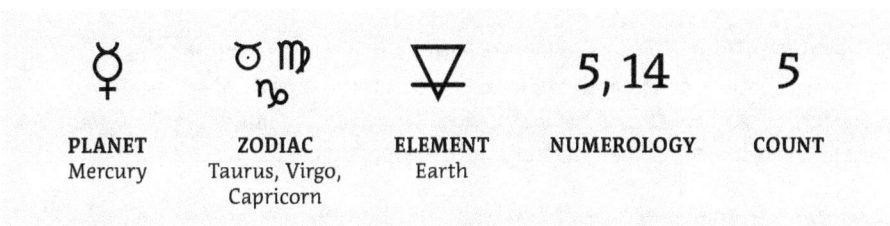

PLANET	ZODIAC	ELEMENT	NUMEROLOGY	COUNT
Mercury	Taurus, Virgo, Capricorn	Earth	5, 14	5

Upright: *Insecurity, Hardship, Poverty, Financial Strife, Isolation, Worry*
When upright, the Five of Pentacles highlights financial, health, and emotional hardships, leaving one feeling isolated and excluded. It serves as a reminder that everyone faces difficulties in life, whether it's losing a job, financial troubles, health issues, or rejection. The figures in the card trudging through the snow signify being marginalized, indicating external circumstances or choices might be responsible for this challenging phase.

Despite this, a subtle yet powerful message of hope is embedded in this card. The church window, which is illuminated in traditional depictions, serves as a beacon of spiritual guidance and comfort. It indicates that help is within reach, whether from spiritual sources or others and encourages introspection to identify these resources. The Five of Pentacles reminds us that adversities are often short-lived and that opportunities for comfort and recovery may be closer than we initially thought.

Reversed: *Recovery from Financial Loss, Luck, Spiritual Poverty, Charity*
When the Five of Pentacles appears in a reversed position during a reading, it can often signify a change in one's circumstances or perspective, usually for the better after a period of hardship or adversity. The reversed card indicates a recovery, be it financial, physical, or emotional. It may represent overcoming financial stress or finding new opportunities after losing a job. The sense of isolation or rejection from the upright position fades, making room for new connections, support, or avenues of assistance. A renewed sense of hope and positivity indicates that the worst is behind and brighter days are ahead.

Moreover, the reversed Five of Pentacles can also indicate a transformation in one's internal mindset. It may point to a shift in how one views challenges or adversity, recognizing the lessons and growth from such experiences. Instead of feeling marginalized or discouraged, there is a sense of empowerment and resilience, understanding that setbacks are a natural part of life's ebbs and flows and recovery and progress are always possible.

Upright Interpretations

General Reading: The card of Five of Pentacles symbolizes difficulties, adversities, and a sense of detachment. It can imply financial setbacks, isolation, or confronting external hurdles. However, it's important to remember that such trying times are transient, and support or relief may be within reach.

Love Reading: This may signify feelings of emotional isolation, even if in a relationship. It can indicate feeling distanced from your partner or a phase where external pressures affect the relationship. For singles, it might represent feelings of loneliness or the belief that love is elusive.

Health Reading: Regarding health, the Five of Pentacles can signify physical ailments or a period where mental and emotional well-being feels challenged. It might be a reminder to seek support to address these issues.

Career Reading: This card can signify financial challenges, job loss, or feeling undervalued in your work environment. It might point to external pressures affecting job performance or a period of professional uncertainty.

Reversed Interpretations

General Reading: Recovery and hope dominate the reversed Five of Pentacles. A change in circumstances or mindset is on the horizon, suggesting you're moving out of a challenging period. This card indicates growth from adversity and the potential for a brighter future.

Love Reading: Reversed, this card signals a potential return of warmth and connection. Past wounds or misunderstandings might start to heal. For singles, this could mean opening oneself up to the possibility of new romantic encounters or a shift in perspective about one's love life.

Health Reading: Recovery and rejuvenation are suggested by the reversed Five of Pentacles. Whether you've been addressing a specific health issue or general well-being, there's an indication of improvement and a positive shift in health circumstances.

Career Reading: The reversed position in a career context indicates potential new opportunities. It might suggest job offers, financial improvement, or a renewed sense of purpose in your profession. The card embodies the idea of overcoming professional hurdles and moving toward a more promising phase in your career.

The Five of Pentacles aligns with the numerical symbolism of the number five in Tarot, representing change, conflict, and adversity. The card signifies material struggles and challenges. It depicts people traversing through harsh weather conditions. The figures are often shown in ragged or tattered clothing, emphasizing their state of poverty or hardship. One of the figures may also be shown as physically impaired, highlighting their health struggles.

A bright stained glass window featuring five pentacles shines behind them. Despite the current circumstances, this symbolizes the possibility of sanctuary, comfort, and spiritual support. The snowy or cold background of the card represents challenging conditions in both the physical and emotional sense, implying isolation from assistance or relief. The people are often shown barefoot, emphasizing their vulnerability and the severity of their situation.

☉ **ZODIAC:** Taurus (April 20 – May 20) is an Earth sign ruled by Venus. This sign embodies those that are grounded, practical, and stable.

♍ Virgo (August 23 – September 22) is an Earth sign ruled by Mercury. Virgos are selfless and dedicated, often putting others' needs above their own.

♑ Capricorn (December 22 – January 19) is an Earth sign ruled by Saturn. Capricorns are known for their grounded, pragmatic approach, and are often focused on tangible outcomes.

▽ **ELEMENT:** Earth represents death and rebirth. It is the realm of abundance, prosperity, and wealth. It is associated with Autumn, the Suit of Pentacles, and the North cardinal direction.

ה **HERMETIC QABALAH** Associated Hebrew Letter: Heh – Window (Vision, Reasoning)

QABALISTIC SEPHIROT: Geburah (Severity)

TIMING: April 21 – April 30

SIX OF PENTACLES

M I N O R A R C A N A

Six Pentacles: Material Wealth

Scales: Balance

Less Fortunate: Need, Humility

Wealthy Person: Giving, Charity

Yes/No Reading:

Yes   No   Maybe

Names in Other Tarot Systems:
Golden Dawn: Lord of Material Success
Tarot of Marseilles: Six of Coins
Thoth: Success

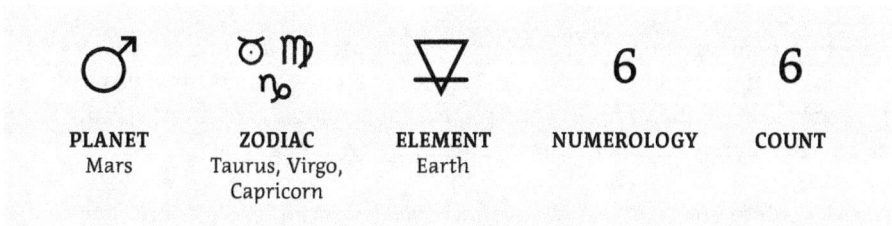

PLANET	ZODIAC	ELEMENT	NUMEROLOGY	COUNT
Mars	Taurus, Virgo, Capricorn	Earth		

Upright: *Charity, Sharing, Giving, Sharing Wealth, Generosity, Receiving*
When the Six of Pentacles is upright, it represents generosity, charity, and balance in material matters. This card is associated with exchanging resources, including time, money, knowledge, and other forms of assistance. Its main message is that giving and receiving should be in harmony. This card serves as a reminder that life is cyclical, and we may find ourselves in a position to give or receive help at any time. It also stresses the importance of giving gracefully and receiving gratitude without expecting anything in return. The universe has a way of rewarding those who practice selflessness.

The scales on the card symbolize fairness and balance. They urge us to treat people and situations equitably regarding material possessions and with our time and effort. The Six of Pentacles suggests that we approach life with a generous spirit and strive to be fair in our dealings with others. We should also remember that our positive or negative actions have karmic consequences.

Reversed: *Power and Domination, Strings Attached, Stinginess, Self-Care*
The reversed Six of Pentacles moves away from the concept of equal give-and-take, shifting its focus to themes of unfairness, manipulation, and hidden agendas. It could also imply that acts of kindness come with strings attached or are merely performed for show. This could manifest as deceitful business practices, unhealthy relationships, or charitable actions performed for ulterior motives.

Furthermore, the reversed Six of Pentacles may indicate feelings of reliance or inadequacy, pointing to instances where someone might be excessively dependent on external validation or assistance. It encourages an evaluation of one's relationship with material possessions and the outside world, questioning if patterns need breaking or if a fear of scarcity is driving certain behaviors. Ultimately, this card urges balance, mutual respect, and a straightforward and discerning approach to all situations.

Upright Interpretations

General Reading: The Six of Pentacles encapsulates the act of both giving and receiving in a harmonious exchange. Whether you find yourself in a position to offer assistance or accept it, this card serves as a reminder of life's cyclical nature and the significance of generosity and gratitude.

Love Reading: The Six of Pentacles suggests a balanced relationship where both partners contribute equitably to the partnership. Acts of generosity and kindness strengthen the bond. For singles, it could point to meeting someone who is generous in spirit or to the importance of ensuring balance in any budding relationship.

Health Reading: You're either in a position to offer support to someone in their health journey or that it's a good time to seek out assistance for your own well-being. This card points to the beneficial exchange of health advice, support, or care.

Career Reading: The Six of Pentacles suggests a fair exchange of work. You might be recognized for your efforts, receive a bonus, or be in a position to help colleagues. It's a positive card for collaborations and mutual support in professional settings.

Reversed Interpretations

General Reading: When the Six of Pentacles is reversed, its core concepts of imbalance and inequity are brought to the forefront. It's essential to be cautious of any concealed agendas, whether from others or within oneself and to ensure that generosity is not taken advantage of.

Love Reading: There's an imbalance in the relationship, where one partner is giving more than the other. There might be feelings of being taken for granted. Singles should be wary of potential partners with ulterior motives or of giving too much in a new relationship without reciprocity.

Health Reading: Reversed, this card might suggest imbalances in your well-being. Perhaps you need to pay more attention to certain aspects of your health, or there's an over-dependency on remedies without addressing root causes.

Career Reading: The reversed Six of Pentacles cautions against the possibility of being exploited or feeling unappreciated in one's profession. This serves as a reminder to maintain a sense of equity in professional dealings and to assert one's own value.

The card portrays a well-dressed individual distributing coins to two less fortunate individuals. Often, the figure holding the coins has a pair of scales in the other hand. The scales symbolize balance, justice, and fairness. They highlight the importance of distributing resources in a balanced manner, and they can also hint at the karmic implications of our actions, suggesting that what we give (or take) will eventually come back to us. The individuals receiving the coins can symbolize those in need or those experiencing lack. Their presence highlights the theme of dependency, humility, or asking for help when needed.

The background and environment in the Six of Pentacles can vary across decks, but it's typically neutral, emphasizing the central action of giving and receiving. However, in some depictions, the ground might be barren or the setting may be urban, underscoring the contrast between abundance and poverty.

ZODIAC: Taurus (April 20 – May 20) is an Earth sign ruled by Venus. This sign embodies those that are grounded, practical, and stable.

Virgo (August 23 – September 22) is an Earth sign ruled by Mercury. Virgos are selfless and dedicated, often putting others' needs above their own.

Capricorn (December 22 – January 19) is an Earth sign ruled by Saturn. Capricorns are known for their grounded, pragmatic approach, and are often focused on tangible outcomes.

ELEMENT: Earth represents death and rebirth. It is the realm of abundance, prosperity, and wealth. It is associated with Autumn, the Suit of Pentacles, and the North cardinal direction.

HERMETIC QABALAH Associated Hebrew Letter: Heh – Window (Vision, Reasoning)

QABALISTIC SEPHIROT: Tiphareth (Beauty)

TIMING: May 1 – May 10

SEVEN OF PENTACLES

MINOR ARCANA

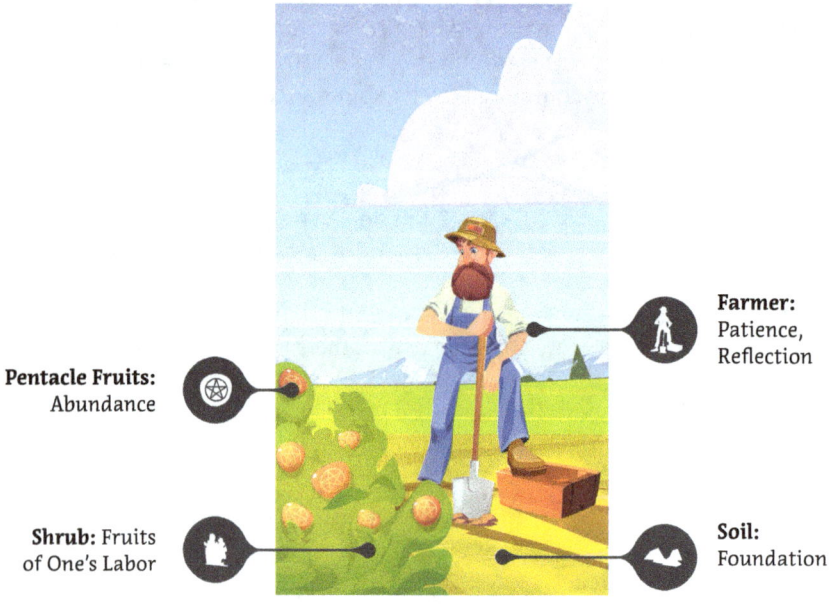

Pentacle Fruits:
Abundance

Shrub: Fruits
of One's Labor

Farmer:
Patience,
Reflection

Soil:
Foundation

Yes/No Reading:

○ Yes ○ No ☑ *Maybe*

Names in Other Tarot Systems:

Golden Dawn: Lord of Success Unfulfilled
Tarot of Marseilles: Seven of Coins
Thoth: Failure

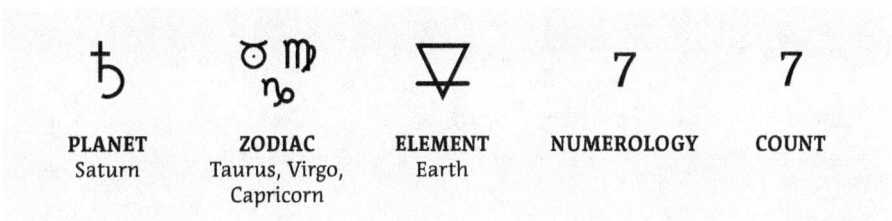

PLANET	ZODIAC	ELEMENT	NUMEROLOGY	COUNT
Saturn	Taurus, Virgo, Capricorn	Earth	7	7

Upright: *Perseverance, Patience, Growth, Diligence, Investment, Hard Work*
The upright Seven of Pentacles symbolizes patience, contemplation, and the hopeful expectation of outcomes. As you wonder whether your efforts are worthwhile, the Seven of Pentacles encourages you to step back and reflect on the value and potential of your actions. This card acknowledges that great things take time, and while immediate gratification is satisfying, some of the most rewarding outcomes require persistent effort and patience.

Moreover, the Seven of Pentacles may suggest that you are on the right track, but some modifications could be beneficial. It's a time for thoughtful contemplation and assessment to determine if continuing on the same path or changing strategies would be more advantageous. This card advocates for mindful evaluation rather than blindly persevering or giving up. By reflecting on your goals and efforts, the Seven of Pentacles helps you understand whether your actions align with your aspirations and whether the rewards are worth the wait.

Reversed: *Distractions, Lack of Rewards, Waste, Questioned Investments*
The reversed Seven of Pentacles can elicit frustration, doubt, and impatience regarding time, effort, or resource investments. It highlights the challenges and inner conflicts that arise when desired results are delayed or fall short of expectations. This card's appearance in the reversed position can trigger self-doubt about the value of one's endeavors. Despite the significant effort and time invested, little or no return seems forthcoming, leading to disillusionment and impatience. It may provoke the sense that one's actions were futile or unworthy.

The card does not imply defeat but signals a pivotal moment for decision-making. It's an occasion to gain insight from the current situation, refine one's approach, and choose a course that aligns better with the desired results.

Upright Interpretations

General Reading: You're in a phase of evaluation. After investing time and energy into something important, you're now reflecting on your progress and considering the next steps. It's a time for patience, understanding that worthwhile results may take time, and ensuring that you're on the right path.

Love Reading: In terms of romance, the Seven of Pentacles suggests a period of reflection on the relationship. Perhaps it's a time to evaluate where the relationship is heading and whether both partners are investing equitably. For singles, it may indicate a phase of introspection about what they truly want in a partner.

Health Reading: Your health journey is under review. Perhaps you've adopted new habits or treatments and are now evaluating their effectiveness. It's a time for patience and persistence, understanding that health improvements often take time.

Career Reading: You're in a phase of assessing your career progress. After dedicating considerable effort to projects or tasks, you're taking a step back to review outcomes and plot future strategies. This is a key moment to ensure you're aligned with your professional goals.

Reversed Interpretations

General Reading: Feelings of doubt and frustration loom large. The efforts you've invested seem to be yielding little or not aligning with your expectations. It's a moment to reconsider if you're on the right path or if a change of strategy or direction is needed.

Love Reading: Doubts about the relationship might emerge. Are both partners putting in the effort? For some, it could mean questioning if the relationship is truly worth the invested time and energy. Singles might be feeling disillusioned with the dating scene.

Health Reading: Frustration might be felt regarding health issues or routines. Perhaps a treatment isn't working as anticipated or efforts to improve wellness aren't showing results. It may be time to consider a different approach or consult a specialist.

Career Reading: You might feel like you're not getting the returns for your hard work or that you're stuck in a dead-end role. Consider if it's time to change direction, seek new opportunities, or reevaluate your career goals.

In the Seven of Pentacles, a person gazes at a shrub heavy with pentacle fruits, representing the results of one's efforts. The plant's growth from previously planted seeds symbolizes the previous endeavors, now yielding outcomes.

They're often shown leaning on a shovel or hoe, embodying the hard work and effort invested, pausing momentarily to reflect and evaluate the progress. This image conveys qualities such as patience, contemplation, and the act of assessment. The figure's reflective posture illustrates the importance of taking a moment to pause, contemplate and anticipate, emphasizing the necessity of patience while awaiting the fruits of one's labor.

The pentacles present on the plant denote potential rewards or outcomes of the efforts invested. The card suggests that while some results may already be visible, the complete harvest or outcomes might still be in the future. The soil or ground below the plant serves as a reminder that the quality and consistency of one's efforts determine the growth and results of a project or endeavor. When tools such as a shovel or hoe appear, they symbolize the dedication required to achieve the desired outcomes.

♉ **ZODIAC:** Taurus (April 20 – May 20) is an Earth sign ruled by Venus. This sign embodies those that are grounded, practical, and stable.

♍ Virgo (August 23 – September 22) is an Earth sign ruled by Mercury. Virgos are selfless and dedicated, often putting others' needs above their own.

♑ Capricorn (December 22 – January 19) is an Earth sign ruled by Saturn. Capricorns are known for their grounded, pragmatic approach, and are often focused on tangible outcomes.

▽ **ELEMENT:** Earth represents death and rebirth. It is the realm of abundance, prosperity, and wealth. It is associated with Autumn, the Suit of Pentacles, and the North cardinal direction.

ה **HERMETIC QABALAH** Associated Hebrew Letter: Heh – Window (Vision, Reasoning)

QABALISTIC SEPHIROT: Netsach (Victory)

🕐 **TIMING:** May 11 – May 20

EIGHT OF PENTACLES

M I N O R   A R C A N A

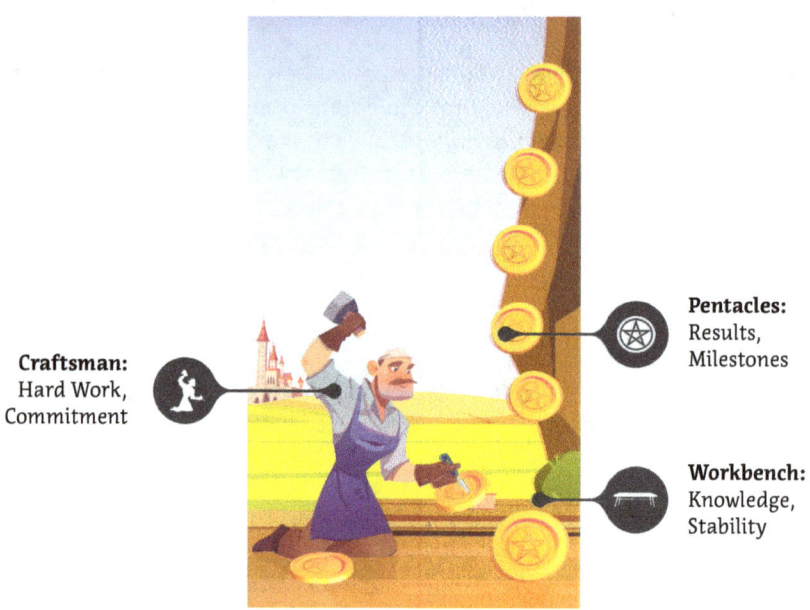

Craftsman:
Hard Work,
Commitment

Pentacles:
Results,
Milestones

Workbench:
Knowledge,
Stability

Yes/No Reading:

○ Yes   ○ No   ☑ *Maybe*

Names in Other Tarot Systems:

Golden Dawn: Lord of Prudence
Tarot of Marseilles: Eight of Coins
Thoth: Prudence

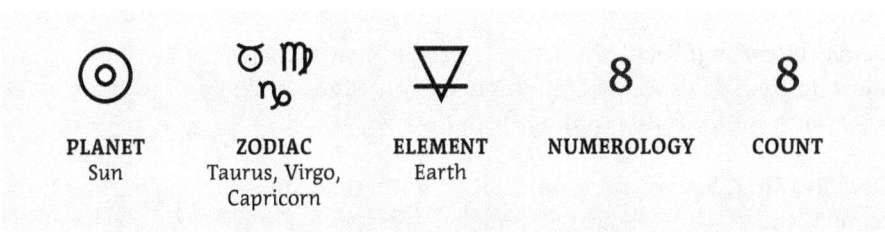

PLANET	ZODIAC	ELEMENT	NUMEROLOGY	COUNT
Sun	Taurus, Virgo, Capricorn	Earth	8	8

Upright: *Mastery, Skill Building, Diligence, Passion, Standards, Craftsmanship*
The upright Eight of Pentacles card encompasses themes of diligence, mastery, and consistent effort. This card represents a celebration of one's dedication to a craft or skill, emphasizing the journey of becoming, continuous learning, refining, and perfecting one's abilities. It conveys that one can achieve mastery in their chosen field with focused and consistent effort.

In addition, the Eight of Pentacles signifies the value of hard work and its eventual rewards. It indicates that someone is laying the groundwork for future success, dedicating themselves to their pursuit and putting in the necessary hours. While immediate rewards may not be apparent, the card assures that the fruits of this labor will manifest over time. The message is clear: perseverance, dedication, and continuous self-improvement pave the way for recognition and achievement.

Reversed: *Lack of Passion or Quality, Uninspired, No Motivation, Laziness*
When the Eight of Pentacles is reversed, it can signal disruptions, distractions, and potential misalignment with one's craft or purpose. The reversed card may suggest a lack of focus or dedication to the task, with distractions or a loss of passion hindering progress. Meticulous effort and attention to detail, associated with the upright position, might be lacking or misdirected. As a result, one may rush jobs, neglect duties, or produce subpar work.

Additionally, feelings of inadequacy or imposter syndrome could be present, causing doubt and leading to potential procrastination or avoidance. Alternatively, overworking without genuine passion could lead to burnout. Regardless, the reversed Eight of Pentacles calls to realign with one's purpose, rekindle passion, and address the factors causing disruptions or feelings of uncertainty.

Upright Interpretations

General Reading: You're dedicated to mastering a particular skill or task, showing great diligence and commitment. Your efforts will pay off if you maintain your focus and continue your hard work.

Love Reading: In a relationship, it might mean that you're putting in the effort to make things work, dedicating time to understand your partner, or working towards common goals. For singles, you might be working on self-improvement or understanding what you truly want in a partner.

Health Reading: You might be dedicating time and energy to improve your health, perhaps through a consistent exercise regimen, diet, or therapeutic practice. The effort you invest in your well-being now will yield positive results.

Career Reading: Your dedication and hard work are shining in your profession. You're putting in the time, learning, and perfecting your skills, which will lead to recognition and advancement. It's a favorable card for students or those in apprenticeships.

Reversed Interpretations

General Reading: There may be a lack of focus or attention to detail in your current endeavors. This could be a time of distractions, procrastination, or feeling disconnected from your tasks.

Love Reading: You or your partner may be taking things for granted, neglecting the needs of the relationship, or not investing the required effort. For singles, it may suggest not putting in the necessary work to foster a healthy relationship or feeling disillusioned with dating.

Health Reading: Potential neglect of health or well-being is indicated. You might be skipping routines, neglecting recommended treatments, or not being diligent about health practices. It's a call to refocus on self-care.

Career Reading: You might be feeling disconnected from your job or studies, producing subpar work, or perhaps feeling like you're in a rut. This card suggests that it's essential to find passion in what you do or consider if you're in the right professional path. It's also a warning against cutting corners.

The theme of the Eight of Pentacles centers on dedication, precision, and the journey towards mastering a skill or craft. It emphasizes the importance of persistence and the rewards from consistent effort and attention to detail.

The card typically features a craftsman diligently at work, chiseling, carving, or hammering away at a pentacle. This figure embodies the virtues of hard work, commitment, and dedication necessary to perfect a craft or skill.

These crafted items may be displayed as finished products or in the process of being prepared, representing the tangible results of hard work and the various steps or milestones in a project or learning process. The imagery suggests a stable environment for work, study, or crafting and highlights the foundational knowledge or tools needed for success.

Some depictions include a distant town or city in the background, representing the broader community or market for the craftsman's work and indicating that their skills and craftsmanship have a place in the wider world. The craftsman's posture, often hunched over in concentration, underscores their focus, attention to detail, and dedication to the task.

♉ **ZODIAC:** Taurus (April 20 – May 20) is an Earth sign ruled by Venus. This sign embodies those that are grounded, practical, and stable.

♍ Virgo (August 23 – September 22) is an Earth sign ruled by Mercury. Virgos are selfless and dedicated, often putting others' needs above their own.

♑ Capricorn (December 22 – January 19) is an Earth sign ruled by Saturn. Capricorns are known for their grounded, pragmatic approach, and are often focused on tangible outcomes.

🜃 **ELEMENT:** Earth represents death and rebirth. It is the realm of abundance, prosperity, and wealth. It is associated with Autumn, the Suit of Pentacles, and the North cardinal direction.

ㄇ **HERMETIC QABALAH** Associated Hebrew Letter: Heh – Window (Vision, Reasoning)

🍇 **QABALISTIC SEPHIROT:** Hod (Splendor)

☉ **TIMING:** August 23 – September 1

NINE OF PENTACLES

M I N O R   A R C A N A

Garden:
Abundance,
Results

Person:
Independence

Snail:
Patience

Falcon:
Focus, Strategy

Grapes:
Fertility,
Abundance

Pentacles:
Financial Gain,
Stability

Yes/No Reading:

✓   ○   ○
Yes   No   Maybe

Names in Other Tarot Systems:
Golden Dawn: Lord of Material Gain
Tarot of Marseilles: Nine of Coins
Thoth: Gain

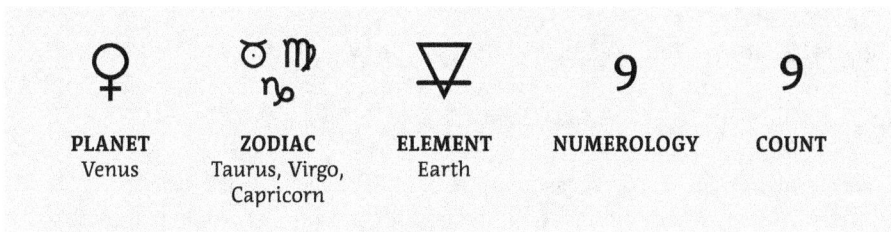

PLANET	ZODIAC	ELEMENT	NUMEROLOGY	COUNT
Venus	Taurus, Virgo, Capricorn	Earth	9	9

Upright: *Abundance, Luxury, Success, Independence, Security, Prosperity*
The Nine of Pentacles represents a time of financial stability and independence, where one is reaping the rewards of their hard work. This card celebrates the idea that one can create abundance and luxury externally and internally through diligence, patience, and personal discipline. It emphasizes the importance of relying on one's resources and enjoying one's own company. This independence can manifest in various aspects of life and lead to personal growth, emotional stability, and spiritual fulfillment.

This card serves as a reminder that after all the hard work, it's essential to savor achievements and allow oneself moments of leisure and pleasure. Whether indulging in personal hobbies or relaxing in a personal sanctuary, this card celebrates the benefits of taking a moment to enjoy life.

Reversed: *Dishonesty, Recklessness, Deceit, Termination, Wild Spending*
When the Nine of Pentacles appears in a reversed position, it can imply various obstacles, including the risk of financial instability or dependence on others. The feeling of security and abundance previously experienced might falter, calling for a reassessment of one's financial strategies and the need to avoid complacency. On a personal level, this card's reversed position can indicate a lack of self-worth and confidence, leading to dependence on external validation.

It's a call to focus on nurturing self-confidence and inner contentment. Neglecting oneself can also be a potential issue, leading to burnout and decreased self-esteem. Thus, the reversed Nine of Pentacles emphasizes balancing hard work, responsibility, self-care, and acknowledging one's accomplishments.

Upright Interpretations

General Reading: You're enjoying the results of your hard work, demonstrating self-sufficiency and financial stability. It's a time of contentment, luxury, and taking a moment to savor life's rewards.

Love Reading: This card suggests a time of stability and contentment. Both partners feel self-sufficient, which leads to a balanced and harmonious relationship. For singles, it might indicate a period of enjoying one's own company and relishing personal independence.

Health Reading: You're likely in a good place health-wise, reaping the benefits of previous efforts to look after yourself. This might also indicate a period of mental peace and well-being.

Career Reading: Your hard work and dedication in your profession or business are paying off. You might be enjoying the fruits of your labor, feeling financially stable, and being recognized for your efforts. It's a time of achievement and satisfaction in your career.

Reversed Interpretations

General Reading: There might be issues with financial stability or an over-reliance on others. You could be neglecting self-care or feeling a lack of independence and self-worth.

Love Reading: There could be issues of dependency in a relationship or feelings of insecurity. Singles might feel a lack of confidence in their dating life or be longing for external validation.

Health Reading: There could be some neglect regarding health and well-being. It's a reminder to not take good health for granted and to prioritize self-care.

Career Reading: There might be some setbacks in your professional life. Perhaps you're not feeling as rewarded or acknowledged for your efforts, or there could be financial challenges at play. It's a cue to reassess and realign your career strategies.

The Nine of Pentacles card embodies personal prosperity and growth, encompassing more than just material wealth. It highlights the significance of self-discipline, self-reliance, and diligence in achieving inner and outer abundance. This card often features a lavish garden, symbolizing consistent effort and abundance. It represents financial success, a more prosperous inner life, and personal growth. A person is often depicted amidst the garden, dressed opulently and denoting independence and confidence, enjoying the fruits of their labor on their terms.

The presence of a trained bird of prey, usually a falcon, highlights focus, strategy, and higher vision. The falcon symbolizes discipline, mastery, and well-directed power. The arrangement of the pentacles, often structured, can signify financial gain, material comfort, and the rewards of hard work. It also signifies order and a structured approach to one's finances or resources.

Some versions show a snail, symbolizing a slow and steady pace leading to success. It serves as a reminder that outstanding achievements often come with patience and consistent effort. Overall, the Nine of Pentacles card encourages one to focus on personal growth, discipline, and self-reliance to achieve abundance in all aspects of life.

ZODIAC: Taurus (April 20 – May 20) is an Earth sign ruled by Venus. This sign embodies those that are grounded, practical, and stable.

Virgo (August 23 – September 22) is an Earth sign ruled by Mercury. Virgos are selfless and dedicated, often putting others' needs above their own.

Capricorn (December 22 – January 19) is an Earth sign ruled by Saturn. Capricorns are known for their grounded, pragmatic approach, and are often focused on tangible outcomes.

ELEMENT: Earth represents death and rebirth. It is the realm of abundance, prosperity, and wealth. It is associated with Autumn, the Suit of Pentacles, and the North cardinal direction.

HERMETIC QABALAH Associated Hebrew Letter: Heh – Window (Vision, Reasoning)

QABALISTIC SEPHIROT: Yesod (Foundation)

TIMING: September 2 – September 11

TEN OF PENTACLES

MINOR ARCANA

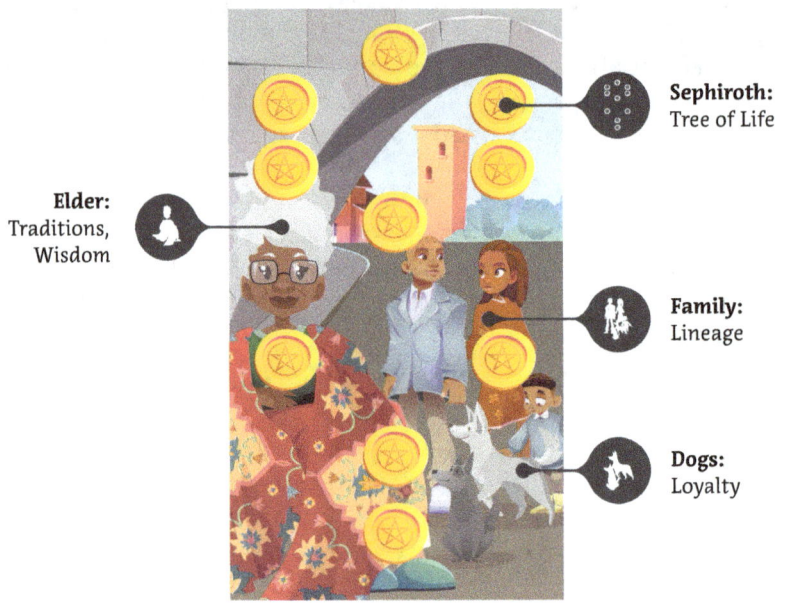

Sephiroth: Tree of Life

Elder: Traditions, Wisdom

Family: Lineage

Dogs: Loyalty

Yes/No Reading:

☑ Yes   ◯ No   ◯ Maybe

Names in Other Tarot Systems:

Golden Dawn: Lord of Wealth
Tarot of Marseilles: Ten of Coins
Thoth: Wealth

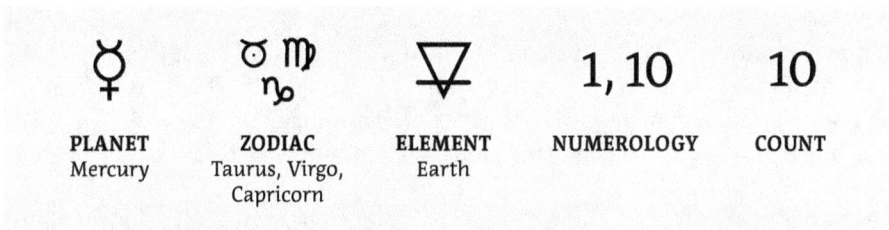

PLANET	ZODIAC	ELEMENT	NUMEROLOGY	COUNT
Mercury	Taurus, Virgo, Capricorn	Earth	1, 10	10

Upright: *Family, Wealth, Contribution, Ancestors, Financial Security, Legacy*
The Ten of Pentacles represents a culmination of various themes, all centered around legacy, prosperity, and familial bonds. It serves as a beacon of financial and material success, highlighting the attainment of personal wealth and the prosperity that can be passed down from one generation to the next.

The Ten of Pentacles underscores the importance of family and tradition. It represents the strength of lineage and deep-rooted connections, highlighting the value and support that can be found within a family. Whether it is the family one is born into or the one that is chosen, this card signals a time of unity, celebration, and shared values. The Ten of Pentacles also represents a period of integration, where various aspects of life—such as career, family, and personal pursuits—unite in harmony. There is a profound sense of completion and fulfillment as past efforts pave the way for a present marked by security, contentment, and a solid foundation for the future.

Reversed: *Fleeting Success, Financial Failure, Lack of Resources, Family Strife*
The reversed Ten of Pentacles indicates legacy, family harmony, and financial security disturbances. The foremost implication is a period of financial instability or apprehension about long-term security. It may also be a time to assess financial strategies and ensure wealth is protected for future generations.

In terms of family dynamics, conflicts, disagreements, or estrangements within the family unit are suggested by the reversed card. Old disputes may reemerge, or new issues could strain family bonds. The cohesive unit and shared values signified by the upright position might feel fragmented or disjointed. This can also hint at neglecting family traditions or legacies, indicating a possible disconnection from one's roots or heritage. What was once integrated and harmonious may now feel disjointed. There may be a conflict between career ambitions and family responsibilities or personal pursuits that are at odds with one's established life.

Upright Interpretations

General Reading: Your life is currently filled with a sense of completeness and satisfaction. Whether it's through family unity, financial stability, or both, you're experiencing the rewards of long-term planning and hard work. There's a strong emphasis on legacies, traditions, and enduring success.

Love Reading: For those in a relationship, it may indicate reaching a significant milestone, such as engagement, marriage, or starting a family. Singles might be considering what they want in a long-term partner or are moving towards a phase where they find such stability in love.

Health Reading: Your health is likely in a stable and secure place. The efforts you've made towards maintaining or improving your health are paying off, leading to a sense of overall well-being. There's also a possibility of beneficial health practices or remedies passed down through generations.

Career Reading: You're in a phase where your career efforts are coming to fruition. Whether it's a family business or individual enterprise, there's a sense of accomplishment and security. It may also signify the solidification of a lasting business legacy or establishing foundations for long-term projects.

Reversed Interpretations

General Reading: You may be facing disruptions in family harmony or financial stability. It can signify setbacks in long-term financial plans or issues related to inheritance. Additionally, there may be a feeling of disconnection from family or one's heritage.

Love Reading: There might be disagreements about financial planning, or family members might disapprove of a partner. Singles may feel disconnected from the idea of a stable, long-term relationship.

Health Reading: You might be neglecting long-term health considerations, or there could be inherited health issues. It's a reminder to be proactive in managing your health and being cautious of potential problems that might emerge in the long run.

Career Reading: Challenges might emerge in your professional life, particularly related to long-term plans or projects. There might be disruptions in a family business or concerns regarding financial stability in your career.

The Ten of Pentacles features a multi-generational family, highlighting the importance of lineage, inheritance, and family traditions. This can represent the transmission of knowledge, values, or wealth from one generation to the next. The ten pentacles are arranged in the shape of the sephiroth, symbolizing stability, wealth, and material success and framing the family to represent protection and the complete integration of material success into their lives.

An arch or gateway is often depicted, indicating protection, prosperity, or entering a new phase of life that promises security and abundance. The presence of an older person close by but separate from the family signifies wisdom, the passage of time, and leaving a legacy. Dogs are present, symbolizing loyalty, trust, and protection and creating an environment of comfort and security.

The background might feature a grand home or castle, emphasizing wealth, stability, and the idea of assets or property being passed down. Vines and grapes may also represent growth, fertility, and abundance and suggest that wealth has grown over time or through the generations.

ZODIAC: Taurus (April 20 – May 20) is an Earth sign ruled by Venus. This sign embodies those that are grounded, practical, and stable.

Virgo (August 23 – September 22) is an Earth sign ruled by Mercury. Virgos are selfless and dedicated, often putting others' needs above their own.

Capricorn (December 22 – January 19) is an Earth sign ruled by Saturn. Capricorns are known for their grounded, pragmatic approach, and are often focused on tangible outcomes.

ELEMENT: Earth represents death and rebirth. It is the realm of abundance, prosperity, and wealth. It is associated with Autumn, the Suit of Pentacles, and the North cardinal direction.

HERMETIC QABALAH Associated Hebrew Letter: Heh – Window (Vision, Reasoning)

QABALISTIC SEPHIROT: Malkuth (Kingdom)

TIMING: September 12 – September 22

PAGE OF PENTACLES
M I N O R   A R C A N A

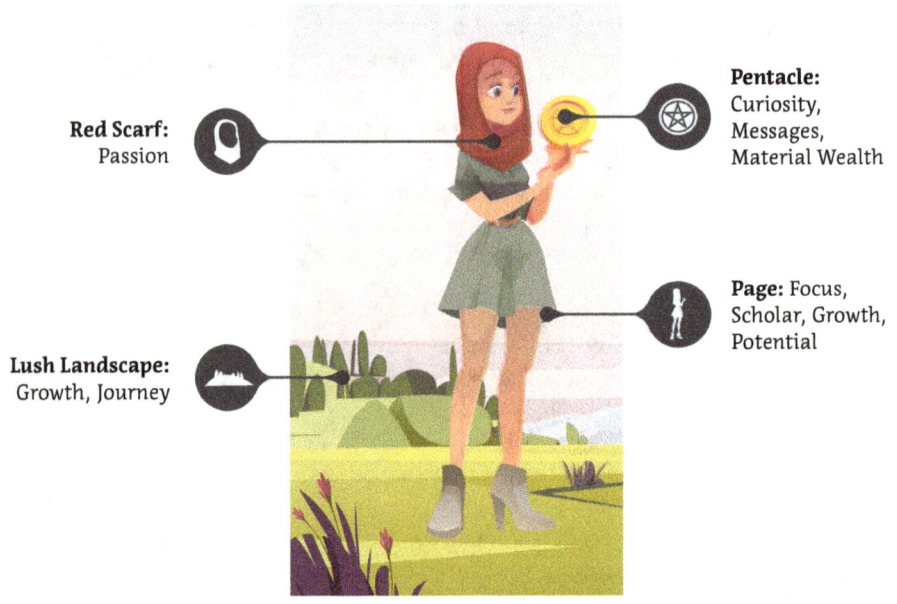

Red Scarf: Passion

Pentacle: Curiosity, Messages, Material Wealth

Page: Focus, Scholar, Growth, Potential

Lush Landscape: Growth, Journey

Yes/No Reading:

Yes   No   Maybe

Names in Other Tarot Systems:
Golden Dawn: Princess of Pentacles
Tarot of Marseilles: Valet of Coins
Thoth: Princess of Pentacles

♉ ♍ ♑	▽	2, 11	7
PLANET	**ELEMENT**	**NUMEROLOGY**	**COUNT**
ZODIAC Taurus, Virgo, Capricorn	Earth		

Upright: *Ambition, Desire, Manifest, Goals, Loyalty, Financial Opportunity*
The Page of Pentacles is commonly linked to the beginning of a new endeavor, mainly those relating to work, finances, or the material world. However, this does not imply taking a rash leap into unknown territory; instead, it's about prudent preparation, unwavering dedication, and the willingness to exert oneself. Whether exploring new educational opportunities, following a career path, or devoting time to a skill or pastime, this card represents a time where meticulousness, tenacity, and attention to detail will bear positive outcomes.

Furthermore, the Page of Pentacles represents a mindset not solely confined to financial or professional aspirations. It reminds us to remain inquisitive, respect the learning process, and embrace life with awe and respect. It inspires us to recognize the value in every experience, adopt a systematic approach, and remain receptive to learning and exploring. Whether reflecting a stage in life or an actual young individual, this card embodies an attitude of bright possibilities firmly grounded in reality.

Reversed: *Procrastination, Irresponsible, Lack of Progress, Greediness, Laziness*
When the Page of Pentacles appears in reverse during a Tarot reading, it can indicate a lack of focus, impracticality, or disconnection from material goals. This can be due to distractions, procrastination, or even laziness. Although one may still hold onto their dreams and ambitions, a lack of drive or practical approach may hinder one's success.

Financial dealings may be overlooked, leading to potential losses. An educational opportunity may be missed due to a lack of commitment. Success and growth are still attainable, but it requires renewed focus and a commitment to taking practical steps toward one's goals. This could involve reigniting a passion for learning, reorganizing finances, or simply reassessing one's path. This card is a call to align one's actions with their aspirations and serves as a reminder to stay grounded and disciplined in pursuing one's material goals.

Upright Interpretations

General Reading: This is a period of learning and growth, and you're embracing new ventures, especially those related to the physical and material realm. This is a time of inspiration, where laying a solid foundation for the future is possible.

Love Reading: Someone is taking a relationship seriously and thinking about the long-term. For singles, it might mean that a potential suitor with genuine intentions is on the horizon. This card represents a relationship that grows gradually but has a lot of potentials.

Health Reading: You may be at the beginning of a new health regimen or trying to educate yourself more about a particular health concern. Stick with it, and the results will show.

Career Reading: You're starting a new job, business, or project that requires attention to detail and steady progress. You might be in a learning phase professionally or considering further studies to enhance your career.

Reversed Interpretations

General Reading: You're feeling ungrounded or being distracted from your goals. There may be a lack of commitment or direction, leading to missed opportunities. This is a time to reevaluate and realign your priorities.

Love Reading: This reversal could mean that someone isn't ready for a serious commitment or there's a lack of maturity in the relationship. There may be unrealistic expectations or a tendency to be too caught up in the fantasy without considering the practical aspects of a relationship.

Health Reading: When it comes to health, the reversed Page suggests neglecting one's well-being or overlooking signs that the body needs attention. It could be a reminder to not take health for granted and to seek information or treatment if something has been bothering you.

Career Reading: In a professional context, the reversed Page of Pentacles may indicate a lack of focus or preparation. There might be a tendency to cut corners, miss details, or neglect important tasks. It's a prompt to be more grounded in your approach and to recommit to your work with diligence and care.

The Page of Pentacles embodies the spirit of youthful energy and curiosity, with a deep interest in tangible aspects of life. As a symbol of the pursuit of knowledge and progress, the Page represents a pupil or apprentice seeking to establish a solid foundation for the future. Their pragmatic and down-to-earth attitude is combined with a sense of potential and hope.

With a delicate grip on a singular pentacle, the Page is fascinated with the material world and the fruits of one's labor. This interest extends to financial matters and may signal the arrival of news or a message. Many decks place the Page in a lush landscape with cultivated fields in the distance, emphasizing the potential for growth and the early stages of a fruitful endeavor. The fertile ground reminds us that the Page's ideas have the potential to flourish with proper care and attention.

Despite the potential for obstacles, the Page's focused demeanor indicates a willingness to confront challenges head-on in pursuit of knowledge and growth. The card's bright sky reflects an optimistic outlook on future endeavors while blooming flowers and sturdy trees underscore growth, potential, and the rewards of hard work and dedication. The Page's decorative attire nods to material wealth and abundance.

♉ **ZODIAC:** Taurus (April 20 – May 20) is an Earth sign ruled by Venus. This sign embodies those that are grounded, practical, and stable.

♍ Virgo (August 23 – September 22) is an Earth sign ruled by Mercury. Virgos are selfless and dedicated, often putting others' needs above their own.

♑ Capricorn (December 22 – January 19) is an Earth sign ruled by Saturn. Capricorns are known for their grounded, pragmatic approach, and are often focused on tangible outcomes.

▽ **ELEMENT:** Earth represents death and rebirth. It is the realm of abundance, prosperity, and wealth. It is associated with Autumn, the Suit of Pentacles, and the North cardinal direction.

ה **HERMETIC QABALAH** Associated Hebrew Letter: Heh – Window (Vision, Reasoning)

❈ **QABALISTIC SEPHIROT:** Malkuth (Kingdom)

◐ **TIMING:** March 21 – June 20

KNIGHT OF PENTACLES

MINOR ARCANA

Red Cloak: Passion

Armor: Protection

Horse: Patience, Strength

Yes/No Reading:

Yes   *No*   *Maybe*

Names in Other Tarot Systems:

Golden Dawn: Prince of Pentacles
Tarot of Marseilles: Cavalier of Coins
Thoth: Prince of Pentacles

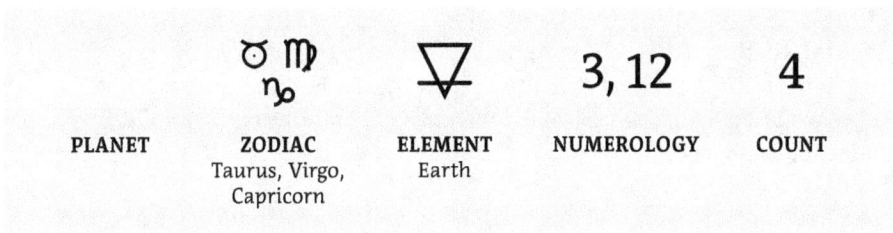

PLANET	ZODIAC	ELEMENT	NUMEROLOGY	COUNT
	Taurus, Virgo, Capricorn	Earth		

Upright: *Efficiency, Responsibility, Reliable, Hard Work, Productivity, Routine*
The Knight of Pentacles personifies qualities such as dedication, responsibility, and steady progress when appearing upright in a Tarot reading. This knight is an emblem of reliability and unwavering commitment, distinct from other Tarot knights who might be more inclined to act impulsively or emotionally. Being practical and grounded, the Knight of Pentacles approaches any task after considering all possible aspects.

Drawing this card suggests that the person might be going through a phase in their life where they must put in diligence, routine, and attention to detail. Slow and steady progress will be more fruitful than haste. While the pace might feel tedious, the efforts will pay off and have a long-lasting impact. The Knight of Pentacles also symbolizes someone trustworthy who offers sound advice. This person could be financially savvy, dependable at work, or just a reliable friend or partner.

Reversed: *Boredom, Perfectionism, Laziness, Obsessiveness, Possessive, Risky*
The reversed Knight of Pentacles suggests a need for more progress due to an unwillingness to change or being preoccupied with small details. This could lead to missed deadlines, unfulfilled duties, and broken promises due to overconfidence or a simple lack of effort. While the Knight values methodical routines, this trait can become counterproductive in its reversed position, leading to rigidity and an inability to adapt to new situations or ideas.

Moreover, the reversed Knight of Pentacles might reveal a fear of change or an unwillingness to step out of one's comfort zone. Despite the potential for growth, travel, or new experiences, some individuals may need to be more patient and cautious, causing them to miss out on such opportunities. Therefore, it is crucial to reassess priorities, recognize when routines or habits become obstacles, and be open to necessary changes in mindset and approach.

Upright Interpretations

General Reading: This card is a positive omen for anyone working towards long-term goals or seeking stability in their lives. You're taking a methodical approach to challenges and you're on a path of commitment, reliability, and responsibility.

Love Reading: If you're in a relationship, it could mean that things are stable and both partners are willing to put in the consistent effort required to make the relationship work. For singles, it might indicate that someone with these loyal qualities is on the horizon or that it's a good time to approach dating with a slow and steady mindset.

Health Reading: Your health journey requires patience and consistent effort. The Knight of Pentacles advises a methodical approach to health and wellness. This could be sticking to routines, maintaining regular check-ups, or being disciplined in diet and exercise. It's not about quick fixes, but rather a long-term commitment.

Career Reading: This is a time to be thorough and pay attention to details. It might not be the most glamorous or fast-paced period, but the diligent effort you put in now will lead to long-term rewards. You might also be recognized for your reliability and consistent performance.

Reversed Interpretations

General Reading: You might be feeling stuck or too rigid in your ways. It's a reminder not to get so engrossed in routine that you miss out on new opportunities or fail to see the bigger picture.

Love Reading: This could suggest a partner who is being overly cautious or hesitant to commit, or perhaps one that is bored or feeling unappreciated. For singles, it could indicate a period of inertia or hesitancy in the dating scene.

Health Reading: The reversed Knight of Pentacles warns against being complacent or neglecting routine check-ups. It might also indicate a lack of motivation to maintain healthy habits or a tendency to look for quick fixes rather than sustainable solutions.

Career Reading: There may be potential delays, procrastination, or a lack of progress. Projects may be stalled or you might feel trapped in a tedious role. It's a reminder to reassess your approach, seek innovative solutions, and not allow yourself to become too complacent or resistant to change.

The Knight of Pentacles epitomizes responsibility, duty, and unwavering dedication. Unlike other Knights in the deck, this Knight appears focused and diligent rather than in motion. Their methodical and cautious nature is emphasized by their stillness. Their horse reflects their steadfast character with its sturdy, reliable, and unruffled demeanor. The horse stands motionless, representing a consistent, unhurried pace.

The background usually features a field with freshly tilled soil or crops ready for harvest, conveying the notions of hard work, patience, and the rewards of dedication. The Knight frequently holds a shield with the pentacle emblem, indicating their association with the material world, practical endeavors, and commitment to tangible outcomes.

The Knight's armor symbolizes their preparedness and protection. They are poised to face challenges in a strategic and calculated manner, rather than with impulsive bravery. The earthy tones dominating the card ground it in the realm of the tangible and material. These colors emphasize the Knight's connection to the Earth element and their pragmatic approach to life.

ZODIAC: Taurus (April 20 – May 20) is an Earth sign ruled by Venus. This sign embodies those that are grounded, practical, and stable.

Virgo (August 23 – September 22) is an Earth sign ruled by Mercury. Virgos are selfless and dedicated, often putting others' needs above their own.

Capricorn (December 22 – January 19) is an Earth sign ruled by Saturn. Capricorns are known for their grounded, pragmatic approach, and are often focused on tangible outcomes.

ELEMENT: Earth represents death and rebirth. It is the realm of abundance, prosperity, and wealth. It is associated with Autumn, the Suit of Pentacles, and the North cardinal direction.

HERMETIC QABALAH Associated Hebrew Letter: Heh – Window (Vision, Reasoning)

QABALISTIC SEPHIROT: Tiphareth (Beauty)

TIMING: April 11 – May 10

QUEEN OF PENTACLES

MINOR ARCANA

Plants: Growth, Nurturing

Pentacle:
Material Wealth

Water:
Emotions,
Intuition

Goats:
Grounding,
Capricorn

Rabbit:
Fertility,
Reproduction

Yes/No Reading:

☑ ○ ○
Yes *No* *Maybe*

Names in Other Tarot Systems:
Golden Dawn: Queen of Pentacles
Tarot of Marseilles: Dame of Coins
Thoth: Queen of Pentacles

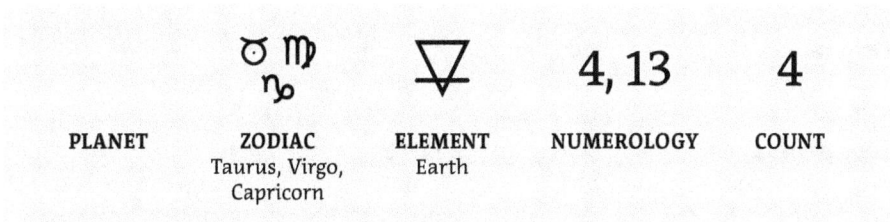

PLANET	ZODIAC	ELEMENT	NUMEROLOGY	COUNT
	Taurus, Virgo, Capricorn	Earth		

Upright: *Creature Comforts, Practical, Generous, Nuturing, Success, Security*
When the Queen of Pentacles appears upright during a reading, they symbolize warmth, abundance, and nurturing. Their presence indicates a time of stability, prosperity, and an acute understanding of the tangible world. In addition to their successful nature, they exude the essence of a nurturing mother figure or a wise confidante, making them a generous and deeply rooted individual who utilizes their resources to support their loved ones and create a harmonious environment. With their innate ability to make any space feel like home and combine practicality with intuition, the Queen of Pentacles is a valuable adviser for domestic projects or gardening.

Beyond their maternal characteristics, this card is a beacon of financial stability and good health, especially when your inquiries are career or finance-oriented. The Queen of Pentacles' grounded nature also serves as a reminder to stay connected to the physical world, appreciate the beauty of everyday life, and remain present to find joy in the present moment while still chasing your aspirations.

Reversed: *Jealousy, Financial Independence, Self Care, Selfish, Intolerant*
The reversed Queen of Pentacles may indicate feeling overwhelmed or consumed by daily responsibilities, leading to neglect in other crucial aspects of life such as relationships, self-care, or spiritual well-being. This Queen can also represent a person who has become overly fixated on wealth and status in their quest for material success, causing damage to their emotional and spiritual health. Alternatively, they can represent someone who is usually reliable and grounded but is presently experiencing a phase of unreliability or inconsistency due to external stressors or internal turmoil.

From a financial perspective, the reversed Queen of Pentacles warns against poor financial choices or resource mismanagement. One should reassess their financial situation and be careful of overindulgence, being out of touch with one's budget, or neglecting essential financial obligations.

Upright Interpretations

General Reading: You are making your environment comfortable and welcoming. This could also be a period of prosperity and well-being.

Love Reading: If single, you may be in a place where you're learning to nurture and love yourself, setting the groundwork for a solid relationship in the future. For those in relationships, this card indicates a stable, nurturing phase where both partners support and take care of each other, fostering a sense of security.

Health Reading: Your physical well-being is at the forefront, and you might be focusing on taking care of your body through proper nutrition and exercise. It's also a time of mental and emotional balance, with a harmonious connection between body and mind.

Career Reading: The Queen of Pentacles signifies prosperity and stability in career matters. This could also suggest a mentor figure in your professional life who embodies the nurturing and grounded qualities of this card. Your dedication and practical approach at work are being recognized.

Reversed Interpretations

General Reading: The reversed Queen of Pentacles suggests that you might be feeling out of touch with your surroundings or overwhelmed by daily responsibilities. There's a possibility of neglecting essential areas of life due to an imbalance in focus.

Love Reading: Singles may feel they're neglecting their own needs or not ready for a committed relationship. Those in relationships might be experiencing a phase where one partner feels taken for granted, or there's a lack of nurturing and stability

Health Reading: You may be neglecting your health or well-being. Overindulgence, ignoring warning signs, or putting off medical appointments are possibilities. It's crucial to find balance and prioritize self-care.

Career Reading: This card reversed can signal challenges in the workplace. You may feel overlooked or not valued for your contributions. Alternatively, it could indicate poor financial decisions or a period of financial instability. It's a call to reassess and make necessary changes.

The Queen of Pentacles embodies nurturing energy, practicality, material comfort, and a strong intuitive connection with nature and the Earth. This connection is evident in the cherubs, goats, and other symbols that adorn their throne, representing the deep connection with nature and fertility. Their attire is usually opulent, further indicating material success and the comforts of the physical world. Yet, their modesty speaks to their grounded nature.

Surrounded by lush gardens and forests, their environment is one of abundance and prosperity, further emphasizing their connection to nature and the Earth. As a symbol of the earth element and material wealth, they cradle a pentacle close to their chest, signifying their ability to manifest material success while caring for their possessions.

The rabbit symbolizes fertility, reproduction, and manifesting abundance, hopping in the background. A stream or river flowing through the card portrays the undercurrent of emotions and intuition that guide them despite their primarily practical nature. The flowers further symbolize growth, nature, and the cyclical nature of life, emphasizing their role as a caretaker of the Earth.

ZODIAC: Taurus (April 20 – May 20) is an Earth sign ruled by Venus. This sign embodies those that are grounded, practical, and stable.

Virgo (August 23 – September 22) is an Earth sign ruled by Mercury. Virgos are selfless and dedicated, often putting others' needs above their own.

Capricorn (December 22 – January 19) is an Earth sign ruled by Saturn. Capricorns are known for their grounded, pragmatic approach, and are often focused on tangible outcomes.

ELEMENT: Earth represents death and rebirth. It is the realm of abundance, prosperity, and wealth. It is associated with Autumn, the Suit of Pentacles, and the North cardinal direction.

HERMETIC QABALAH Associated Hebrew Letter: Heh – Window (Vision, Reasoning)

QABALISTIC SEPHIROT: Binah (Understanding)

TIMING: December 13 – January 9

KING OF PENTACLES

MINOR ARCANA

Bulls: Taurus, Earth, Resources

Castle: Security, Success, Empire

Pentacle: Prosperity

Greenery: Fertility, Growth

Yes/No Reading:

Yes   No   Maybe

Names in Other Tarot Systems:

Golden Dawn: King of Pentacles
Tarot of Marseilles: Roi of Coins
Thoth: Knight of Pentacles

♉ ♍ ♑ ▽ 5, 14 4

PLANET	ZODIAC	ELEMENT	NUMEROLOGY	COUNT
	Taurus, Virgo, Capricorn	Earth		

Upright: *Abundance, Prosperity, Security, Reliable, Wealth, Leadership*
The upright King of Pentacles represents mastery over the material world, reflecting financial stability, business acumen, and a solid connection to tangible aspects of life. This archetype points to an individual who can be relied upon as a provider, skilled in wealth creation and management. The King of Pentacles values long-term investments, be they financial, personal, or professional, and understands the importance of protecting those in his care.

In addition to their material successes, this King takes pleasure in the simpler aspects of life, finding joy in sensory experiences such as fine dining, a comfortable home, and walks in nature. Unlike those consumed by ambition, the King of Pentacles maintains a grounded perspective, striking a balance between material achievement and inner contentment. Their approach to life is marked by patience, perseverance, and a deep loyalty to those they hold dear.

Reversed: *Financially Inept, Stubborn, Greed, Indulgence, Sensuality*
Instead of displaying mastery in wealth creation and stability, the reversed King may exhibit an excessive fixation on material wealth, leading to greed or a disregard for financial responsibilities and poor money management skills. Such individuals may utilize their wealth to flaunt their power over others, resulting in unethical behavior, taking shortcuts, or lacking concern for others' well-being. This can lead to a failure to connect with others and experience intangible joys due to an unhealthy focus on material assets and status symbols.

Furthermore, the reversed King of Pentacles may indicate a lack of confidence in managing finances, fear of losing material stability or hoarding resources out of fear or insecurity despite having ample resources. This lack of balance in one's relationship with money can manifest as missed opportunities, bad investments, or financial setbacks. Therefore, evaluating one's financial management, material pursuits, and holistic well-being is crucial to maintain a healthy balance.

Upright Interpretations

General Reading: You're likely grounded and practical, with a dependable nature that attracts others to you. This card can also suggest that you have worked hard to attain your current status and are now enjoying the fruits of your labor.

Love Reading: Your partner may be dependable, financially stable, and committed to providing for the family. For singles, it may indicate attracting a partner who possesses these traits. This card emphasizes the importance of reliability and steadiness in a relationship.

Health Reading: Your approach to health is pragmatic and disciplined. This card suggests that you're making smart choices for your well-being, be it through a balanced diet, regular exercise, or attending routine check-ups. If facing health challenges, it's a sign of harnessing resources effectively to improve or maintain your health.

Career Reading: This card signifies success, financial stability, and possibly a leadership role. You may be recognized for your work ethic, practicality, and strategic thinking. It's a sign of achieving a good reputation in your professional field.

Reversed Interpretations

General Reading: The reversed King of Pentacles warns of poor financial decisions, greed, or being overly materialistic. It might suggest a misuse of power or authority, or even being out of touch with reality. On the other hand, it can also point to insecurities related to financial stability.

Love Reading: There might be issues regarding financial control or dependency. It's a call to ensure that money or status isn't taking precedence over genuine connection and emotional support.

Health Reading: Your approach to health might be misdirected or negligent. Perhaps you're not prioritizing your well-being, or maybe you're overspending on treatments that aren't effective. It's essential to reassess your health decisions and not be swayed purely by external appearances or status symbols.

Career Reading: This card might indicate a boss or superior who is domineering, greedy, or insecure. Be wary of shortcuts and ensure that you're making career decisions aligned with your long-term goals and values.

The King of Pentacles, through their various symbols, communicates the virtues of hard work, practicality, and the ability to create material success while staying grounded. They represent someone who is successful in financial and material matters and has an understanding and respect for nature, the process of growth, and the value of steadfastness.

Depicted on an ornate throne embellished with symbols of bulls and grapes, which are commonly associated with the zodiac sign Taurus, the King embodies a connection to the Earth and its plentiful resources. The verdant scenery surrounding them emphasizes their ability to nurture growth and cultivate resources, ensuring prosperity. They confidently hold a golden coin or pentacle, showcasing their proficiency in generating wealth and navigating financial undertakings. Their green robe symbolizes their unwavering reliability, stability, and practicality. Behind them, a grand castle represents success and the empire they have built. With a confident pose and a steady gaze, the King exudes assurance and calmness, demonstrating their extensive experience in handling challenges with a level head and a focused mind.

♉ **ZODIAC:** Taurus (April 20 – May 20) is an Earth sign ruled by Venus. This sign embodies those that are grounded, practical, and stable.

♍ Virgo (August 23 – September 22) is an Earth sign ruled by Mercury. Virgos are selfless and dedicated, often putting others' needs above their own.

♑ Capricorn (December 22 – January 19) is an Earth sign ruled by Saturn. Capricorns are known for their grounded, pragmatic approach, and are often focused on tangible outcomes.

▽ **ELEMENT:** Earth represents death and rebirth. It is the realm of abundance, prosperity, and wealth. It is associated with Autumn, the Suit of Pentacles, and the North cardinal direction.

ה **HERMETIC QABALAH** Associated Hebrew Letter: Heh – Window (Vision, Reasoning)

✿ **QABALISTIC SEPHIROT:** Chokmah (Wisdom)

🕐 **TIMING:** August 12 – September 11

Bibliography

Ariel Evan Mayse, and Arthur Green. *From the Depth of the Well : An Anthology of Jewish Mysticism.* Mahwah, New Jersey, Paulist Press, 2014.

Arthur Edward Waite. *Pictorial Key to the Tarot : In Full Color.* New York (N.Y.), Causeway Books, 1973.

Arthur Edward Waite, and R A Gilbert. *Hermetic Papers of A.E. Waite : The Unknown Writings of a Modern Mystic.* Wellingborough, Northamptonshire, Aquarian Press, 1987.

Cicero, Tabitha. *Essential Golden Dawn - an Introduction to High Magic.* Llewellyn, 2003.

Decker, Ronald, et al. *A Wicked Pack of Cards : The Origins of the Occult Tarot.* London, Duckworth, 2002.

Dummett, Michael, and Sylvia Mann. *The Game of Tarot : From Ferrara to Salt Lake City.* London, Duckworth, 1980.

Farley, Helen. *A Cultural History of Tarot : From Entertainment to Esotericism.* London, I.B. Tauris, 2009.

Fiebig, Johannes, and Evelin Burger. *The Ultimate Guide to the Thoth Tarot.* Llewellyn Worldwide, 8 Nov. 2015.

Gershom Scholem, et al. *On the Kabbalah and Its Symbolism.* New York, Schocken Books, 1996.

Ginzburg, Yitshak, and Moshe Genuth. *Kabbalah and Meditation for the Nations.* GalEinai Publication Society, 2007

Gray, William G. *Qabalistic Concepts.* Weiser Books, 1 Jan. 1997.

Holtz, Barry W. *Back to the Sources.* Simon and Schuster, 30 June 2008.

Huson, Paul. *Mystical Origins of the Tarot : From Ancient Roots to Modern Usage.* Rochester, Vermont, Destiny Books, 2004.

Isabel Radow Kliegman. *Tarot and the Tree of Life.* Quest Books, 1 Nov. 2013.

Jacob Immanuel Schochet. *Mystical Concepts in Chassidism.* Kehot Publications
    Society, 1 Jan. 1979.

Kenner, Corrine. *Tarot and Astrology.* Llewellyn Worldwide, 8 Jan. 2012.

Khan, Geoffrey, and Abu al-Faraj Harun ibn al-Faraj. *The Tiberian Pronunciation
Tradition of Biblical Hebrew. Volume 1 : Including a Critical Edition and English
Translation of the Sections on Consonants and Vowels in the Masoretic
    Treatise Hidāyat Al-Qāriʼ "Guide for the Reader."* Cambridge,
    Open Book Publishers, 2020.

Louv, Jason. *John Dee and the Empire of Angels.* Simon and Schuster, 17 Apr. 2018.

Rabbi Yitshak Ginsburgh. *What You Need to Know about Kabbalah.* GalEinai
    Publication Society, 2006.

Regardie, Israel, et al. *The Golden Dawn : A Complete Course in Practical
    Ceremonial Magic : The Original Account of the Teachings, Rites, and
    Ceremonies of the Hermetic Order of the Golden Dawn (Stella Matutina).*
    St. Paul, Minn., U.S.A., Llewellyn Publications, 1989.

Regardie, Israel, and John Michael Greer. *The Golden Dawn.* Llewellyn Worldwide,
    8 Jan. 2016.

About the Author

Pamela Coe (they/she) is a Creative Director, award-winning artist, and author who champions neurodiversity and gender nonconformity in spiritual spaces. They created the Tarotorial Tarot Training Deck, a beginner-friendly resource that makes tarot more visual, intuitive, and accessible—especially for neurodivergent readers. Their work has helped thousands build confidence by breaking down complex symbolism into simple, approachable guidance.

Tarotorial was born during Pamela's recovery from an ischemic stroke at age 36. Sketching and designing the deck by hand became part of their therapy, helping them regain fine motor control and reconnect with art, intuition, and purpose.

Through their company, Raven and Rogue, Pamela advocates for inclusive, empowering spiritual education. Their tools invite readers of all backgrounds to explore tarot in a way that feels grounded, welcoming, and magical.

Keep in touch with them on the web:
Website: ravenandrogue.com
TikTok and Instagram: @ravenandrogue